NAVIGATION

IN THE AGE OF DISCOVERY

AN INTRODUCTION

NAVIGATION

IN THE AGE OF DISCOVERY

AN INTRODUCTION

by

Duane A. Cline

MONTFLEURY, INC.

© Duane A. Cline, 1990

All rights reserved. No part of this book may be used or reproduced in any manner whatsoever without written permission from the publisher.

Published by Montfleury, Inc.,
P.O. Box 697, Rogers, AR 72757-0697

Printed by Heritage Press,
P.O. Box 16148, North Little Rock, AR 72231-6148

Library of Congress Catalog Card Number 90-91870
ISBN No. 0-9627213-0-1

Cover photo courtesy of Elroy Sanford, Photographer, 2116 SOM Center Road, Willoughby Hills, OH 44094

Frontispiece based on the engraving on the cover of Lucas Janszoon Waghenaer's *Mariner's Mirror*, London, 1588.

CONTENTS

Contents v
Illustrations vii
Acknowledgements xi
Preface xiii
   1. HISTORICAL BACKGROUND 01
        Sample of Known Voyages 11
   2. INTRODUCTION TO NAVIGATION 15
   3. CHRISTOPHER JONES: MASTER OF MAYFLOWER 27
   4. THE SHIP MAYFLOWER 31
   5. THE CREW 37
   6. THE LEAD LINES 45
   7. NAVIGATION AIDS 55
   8. TIME-KEEPING 69
   9. THE NOCTURNAL 81
 10. ALMANACS & CALENDARS 89
 11. TIDE TABLES 93
 12. THE MARINER'S COMPASS 103
 13. THE LOG-LINE 111
 14. THE TRAVERSE BOARD & SLATE 119
 15. THE MARINER'S QUADRANT 125
 16. THE MARINER'S ASTROLABE 129
 17. THE CROSS-STAFF 135
 18. THE BACK-STAFF 141
 19. COMPASS VARIATION 145
 20. RUTTERS & WAGGONERS 157
 21. TYPES OF SAILINGS 161
 22. THE SEA CHARTS 165
 23. THE GLOBES 173
 24. NAUTICAL TABLES & GRAPHS 179
 25. PLOTTING INSTRUMENTS 183
 26. THE JOURNAL 191
 27. COMMUNICATION 195

28. CONCLUSIONS 201
Sources for Further Reading
    Books to Read 209
    Articles of Interest 213

ILLUSTRATIONS

1. Portuguese caravel 02
2. 16th century merchant ship...02
3. English man-of-war..03
4. Dutch flute 05
5. John Smith's map of New England..09
6. Theodore de Bry's map of the Western Hemisphere............................10
7. Wind patterns of the Atlantic Ocean..20
8. Mediterranean rhumbs of the wind 21
9. Map of America, 1534...22
10. The compass rose of Cortes 23
11. The English compass rose..23
12. Currents of the Atlantic Ocean 25
13. Sailors carrying a tun...31
14. Cut-away of Mayflower 34
15. The helmsman's view..35
16. MAYFLOWER under sail 43
17. Title page of *The Mariners Mirrour*, 1584..44
18. Cut-away of a sounding lead..46
19. Markings on a hand lead line...47
20. Leadsman using the sounding lead...49
21. Chart of the English Channel...51
22. Dipsie lead and hand lead 53
23. Chart of the Thames estuary..59
24. Navigation aids and routes in the Thames estuary..............................60
25. Reculver Castle, Kent..61
26. Chart symbols 63
27. Examples of beacons & lighthouses 65
28. The compass clock 69
29. Four sand-glasses framed together 72
30. Helmsman's sand-glass 73
31. Pocket-type sundials...76

32.	The diptych	77
33.	The equatorial sun dial	77
34.	The universal ring dial	78
35.	The equinoctial sun dial	78
36.	Various types of Nocturnals	80
37.	The 'guard'	81
38.	Movement of the constellations around Polaris	83
39.	A nocturnal	85
40.	A nocturnal for both Bears	86
41.	The nocturnal in use	87
42.	A broadsheet almanac	88
43.	Pages of a pocket-type almanac	92
44.	The rose calendar by Brouscon	98
45.	Thirty point rose calendar	99
46.	The establishment of port	100
47.	A sixteenth century tide calculator	101
48.	The mariners compass	106
49.	Exploded view of a mariner's compass	108
50.	The compass card & needle	109
51.	A lodestone case	109
52	The log line	113
53.	The log-line in use	115
54	The traverse board	121
55.	Various styles of the traverse board	122
56.	A Spanish helmsman's slate	123
57.	An astronomer's quadrant	126
58.	The mariner's quadrant	127
59.	The mariner's quadrant in use	128
60.	The mariner's astrolabe	131
61.	An astrolabe with full scale	132
62.	The astrolabe in use	133
63.	The cross-staff	136
64.	The cross-staff adjustment	138
65.	The back-staff	142
66.	The Davis back-staff or quadrant	144
67.	The geomagnetism of the earth	145

68.	The geomagnetic patterns of the Atlantic	146
69.	An azimuth compass	150
70.	A dip circle	151
71.	A compass rose	152
72.	A meridional compass	153
73.	Sample pages from a rutter	158
74.	A rhumb line course	163
75.	A great circle course	164
76.	Waghenaer's chart of the English Channel	171
77.	Molyneux's celestial globe	174
78.	Molyneux's terrestrial globe	176
79.	A declination table	180
80.	A sinical quadrant and traverse board	181
81a.	Straight leg dividers	183
81b.	Circular dividers	184
82.	A possible protractor from MARY ROSE	184
83.	A protractor from BATAVIA	185
84.	A Gunter's scale	186
85.	A sector with geometric compass	188
86.	A Gunter's sector	189
87.	Sample page of Davis' journal	192
88.	A sample of Champlain's journal	194
89.	Boatswain's pipe from MARY ROSE	196
90.	Boatswain's pipe from *Mariners Mirrour*	196
91.	Parts of a boatswain's pipe	197
92.	Some of the boatswain's piped calls	198
93.	Examples of telescopes	200

AUTHOR'S NOTE and ACKNOWLEDGMENTS

A large body of information has been brought to public attention in recent years concerning ships from the early history of navigation. This has been due, in large part, to the new and improved methods employed in underwater archaeology. Among the artifacts which have been recovered from sunken ships have been a number of navigation instruments. As a result, there has been a growing interest in those ships and the various techniques of navigation employed during the Golden Age of Discovery. A great deal of scholarly research has been published on the topic of maritime history. However, a vast amount of the published material is aimed at those who already have some basic knowledge of navigation and is, therefore, almost incomprehensible to the casual reader, who is just beginning to investigate this area of interest.

Coming from the field of theater and theater history, my own interest in early seventeenth century navigation developed in a rather round-about way. I was well grounded in the historical background and events of the Elizabethan period — especially as those events related to Shakespeare and the many other writers and dramatists of that time. In more recent years I learned that I was a descendant of James Chilton and Francis Cooke, who made that historic voyage from Southampton, England, to Cape Cod aboard MAYFLOWER in 1620. A desire to reach a deeper understanding of my ancestors eventually led to a full-time research project, which has now consumed ten years of my attention.

Many questions concerning the ship MAYFLOWER immediately sprang to my attention. Conflicting information reported by a number of writers raised many questions as to the true condition of the vessel at the time of her sailing to the New World, the knowledge and experience of the master and crew of the ship, and, consequently, the question of how such a ship would have been navigated in the first quarter of the seventeenth century.

Information gleaned from that research has now come together in this volume, which is designed primarily for the casual reader with no prior knowledge of navigation — which, of course, is the point from which I began my own investigation.

I am deeply indebted to my wife, Carolyn, and son, Alan, who have been my tower of strength through the many years of seemingly endless research required. I am especially indebted to my son, who has worked hand-in-hand with me during most of that time as a research assistant. Without his dedication this research would still be continuing — with no hope of reaching culmination in a completed volume.

As with any continuing research effort and the compilation of materials, such a great number of people have given support, encouragement and assistance that it would be impractical to list them all. However, I must make a special note of the research assistance provided by Teresa Fox of the Fort Smith, Arkansas, Public Library, who has valiantly searched out an endless amount of resource material through the OCLC Inter-Library Loan Service. A special note of appreciation must be made to several others who have so freely given of their time and abilities to bring this volume to a completion. I want to thank Michael Carter, who helped prepare the text for the printer; to Charles Deraleau, who served as liaison between me and the printer; and a special appreciation to Elroy Sanford, who graciously gave me permission to use his photograph of MAYFLOWER II on the cover of this book.

Finally, I am deeply indebted to the many writers and scholars who have recorded the important historical facts from which I could draw the details for this kind of introduction to the subject of early seventeenth-century navigation. The most used information has come from the sources which I have listed at the end of this volume under the headings of Books to Read and Articles of Interest.

> Duane A. Cline
> Rogers, Arkansas
> June, 1990

PREFACE

It is hoped that this book can serve as an introduction to the fascinating study of navigation techniques and instruments employed by the first explorers and settlers of the North American continent. Although there have been some excellent books written on early navigation, very little has been done to introduce the subject to the casual reader, or to those just beginning to learn the fundamentals of navigation.

The readers who are just beginning to explore early navigation techniques are immediately overwhelmed by a plethora of nautical terms and scientific language with no place to begin their understanding of the basic concepts involved. Such an elementary approach to the topic of navigation may not hold the interest of a reader who has a thorough grounding in the subject. However, it seems important to give the beginner an easy approach to the many complex aspects of maritime navigation.

After considering a number of approaches which could be taken in presenting the basic elements of early navigation techniques, it was decided to use the example of one historic voyage as a theoretical example. By using the sailing of MAYFLOWER in 1620, the reader will have some practical mental pegs upon which to hang the basic problems and possible solutions employed in such a voyage.

A second purpose in writing this book is an effort to clear up some vague misconceptions about the early maritime navigators, their knowledge, and their abilities. In reading about the voyages of early explorers, one can easily develop the hazy concept that nearly every important discovery of the sixteenth and seventeenth centuries was accidental, and that none of those early seamen could have had an accurate knowledge of their positions on the seas of the world — simply because their navigation instruments and nautical aids were so crude by comparison to their modern counterparts.

Contrary to the belief that a mariner must have a chart to determine the course and distance, a compass to steer by, and a means to determine the position of a ship during the course of a voyage, many great voyages in history were made without one or more of these basic aids. As an example, Pythias of Massilia, a Greek astronomer and navigator of the second century A.D., made one of the earliest recorded voyages to the northern areas of Scotland, Norway, Germany and possibly the Baltic without the aid of such basic instruments as a compass, sextant or chronometer.

The contemporary navigator tends to look at the instruments used by those early mariners and dismiss them as practically useless on the high seas. Landfall at a predetermined location without modern precision instruments is judged by many as a "fortunate fluke." In an age of advanced instrumentation and interplanetary exploration, there seems to be a vague impression that all knowledge began with the twentieth century in nearly every area of scientific investigation.

It is easy to overlook the fact that ambitious fishermen were plying the waters of the North Atlantic very early, especially after the Newfoundland cod fishery came into prominence about 1500, at which time the Portuguese fishermen were already bringing home salted fish from that area. Quickly following their lead, we find the Spanish, Breton, Norman, Dutch, Scandinavian and English fishermen plying those same northern waters.

When Humphrey Gilbert arrived at St. John's in 1583 to take formal possession of Newfoundland for Queen Elizabeth, he found an English fisherman ruling as "admiral" over a collection of fishing camps around the harbor. Adventurous fishermen were crossing and recrossing the North Atlantic, knowing their precise destinations and accurately achieving landfall. The names of these hardy men of the sea never found their way into national maritime histories, nor were they invited to relate their many experiences in the royal courts.

These admirable seamen found their way to North Atlantic fishing areas and North American shores, possibly even before Columbus, Cartier, Drake, Hudson, Champlain and all of the others who were searching for sea routes to the Orient. Overshadowed by those who found favor at court (and were consequently recorded in the pages of history), the achievements of those able and industrious fishermen remained virtually unnoticed by the merchants and mathematicians who toiled in their offices and libraries, trying to solve the scientific problems of how such navigation could be made possible.

It would seem to be an example of the doers out on the high seas plying their trade, while the theoriticians at their drawing boards were trying to figure out how it could be achieved.

1. HISTORICAL BACKGROUND

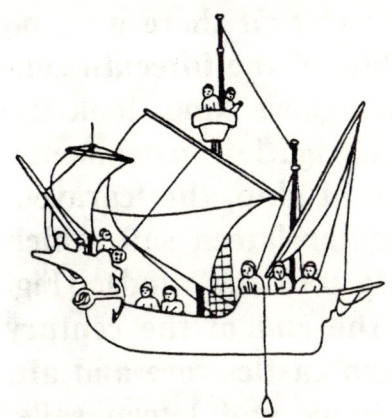

In order to better understand the forces that motivated the rapid development of navigation skills during the Golden Age of Discovery, it is necessary to understand something of the historical background and the rapid development of maritime activity during the period.

By 1450 Europe had been importing textiles, spices and numerous gems from the Far East, but the Europeans knew very little about the lands which produced these items of trade. Ptolemy's second century *Geography* was not available to the European countries until 1406. With the invention of the printing press in 1450 Ptolemy's *Geography* was published and widely read in Europe. Until that time the European knowledge of world geography had not changed much since Roman times, and European society had changed very little over the centuries. The voyages of discovery which fall generally in the period of 1450-1750 changed all this.

PORTUGAL

Portugal was a very poor country until 1450 when the invention of the printing press sparked an enthusiasm for learning. As the European nations became more aware of the geography of the world, interest in expanded trade between Europe and Asia grew. Until that time there had been very little trade between Europe and Asia. Much of the goods moving from Asia to Europe was carried overland in a very slow and costly process. A group of German cities (the Hanseatic League) provided the trading link between Russia and London by way of Bruges and Antwerp in the Low Countries.

Goods from China and India were taken to the ports of Bruges and Antwerp by Mediterranean merchants from Italy and Arabia. The Spice Islands provided the same type of link between the East and

Europe, which was one of the reasons the Portuguese began to consider the possibility of finding an all-sea route to the Spice Islands.

Portugal was ideally located to begin explorations along the coast of Africa. Realizing the profits to be made in the shipping of goods from Indonesia and the Far East, the Portuguese set out to control the main centers for the distribution of spices from Indonesia — referred to as the Spice Islands. The problem lay in the fact that there were no ships capable of long ocean voyages until the middle of the fifteenth century when Henry 'the Navigator', son of the Portuguese king, took the lead by encouraging the design of new ships and navigation instruments. As a result, the Portuguese developed a new type of ship, the 'caravel.' The caravel was a small, light ship with a triangular lateen sail, which allowed it to sail close to the wind (more directly into the wind). [Fig. 1] Henry 'the Navigator' died in 1460, but by the end of the century the Portuguese were building larger ships with high castles fore and aft. These larger ships employed the use of both square and lateen sails, which made them easier to maneuver than the ships of any other country.

Fig. 1. Portuguese caravel. Fig. 2. 16th century merchant ship.

The larger ships also meant larger holds for transporting trade goods. [Fig. 2] By 1513 the Portuguese had reached Canton; and, by 1515 they had achieved control of the ports through which the trade from Asia passed. They were then in a position to act as carriers for much of the trade between China, Japan and the Phillipines.

ENGLAND

In 1497 John Cabot sailed from Bristol, England, accompanied by his son, Sebastian. On this voyage Cabot discovered Cape Breton Island. However, the English merchants were not convinced that there was any great value in developing new types of foreign trade, since England was content to live off of its trade in wool and woolen goods which were in great demand by the commercial and industrial regions of Italy and the Low Countries. The English mariners were crossing the waters of northeast Europe as far as Iceland for fish. They were also trading the English wool, cloth, tin and hides for fine cloths and Rhenish wines in the ports of the Low Countries; for woad (used in dyeing), iron and wines in the ports of Biscay; for fruits, wax, iron and wines in the ports of Portugal and Spain. Other goods were generally carried in foreign merchant ships. The English merchant ships rarely visited the Baltic ports which were shipping naval stores such as timbers for masts and spars, hemp for rope, pitch and train oil (whale oil) for seams, bottom coating and grease.

Beginning in the late fifteenth century, England had built a large fleet of royal ships. Although the English navy was not as large as that of Venice, the quality of the English men-of-war was admired by their European competitors. They certainly gave the English a decisive edge over the Armada. The Elizabethan men-of-war were well known for their speed and maneuverability, and were recognized by their distinctive low freeboard and long, low, flush-built hull, which set them apart from the

Fig. 3. English man-of-war.

extreme height of the Mediterranean carrack. The English men-of-war were so admired that their design was copied in the 1550s by the French, and in the 1570s by the Spanish. By the end of the century ships designed on the English style were being employed by many European countries. [Fig. 3] The basic ship design from the late fifteenth century remained virtually unchanged until the age of the steam ship.

At the beginning of the sixteenth century England's major export item was still woolen cloth. However, the English fishermen were plying the waters of the North Atlantic in their cod-fishing expeditions to the coasts of Newfoundland. By the beginning of the sixteenth century the fisherman from the western counties of Devon and Cornwall were already making regular visits to the Newfoundland fishing grounds.

When the existence of the North American continent was confirmed by Verrazano's voyage of 1524 under French auspices, the English merchants began to see that new markets in gold, Oriental spices and slaves could be very profitable. However, it took a slump in the woolen trade in 1551 to convince the merchants of the full potential.

With the woolen market in difficulty the English also found themselves with a growing population, a demand for wood to fuel their industrial fires, and naval supplies needed for the building of ships. Convinced that some of the national problems could be reduced by dispatching the worst of their people abroad and bringing home much needed goods, England launched itself into a period of colonization.

By the mid-sixteenth century, exports from England were increasingly channeled through London to the great trading center at Antwerp, and the London docks were handling about 90 per cent of the English exports. In spite of England's range of maritime activities, the English commerce did not expand to anything comparable with that of the Low Countries. Unfortunately, much of the English energy was being expended in privateering, with bands of thieves way-laying commercial vessels in the Channel and elsewhere.

Over the next two hundred years other industries developed in England, including the manufacture of cannons and gunpowder, which were much in demand during the Thirty Years War, which continued from 1618 to 1648. The export of coal became an expanding market for the English as the demand for fuel increased on the Continent. England, which had exported about 200,000 tons of coal in 1550, found itself exporting three million tons in 1700. Much of the increase in English trade was due to the English colonies.

One of the major problems facing the mariner of the late fifteenth century was his inability to determine his location in terms of longitude (distance east and west on the globe). Distances in terms of latitude (north and south) could be more easily determined. There was no precise method of determining longitude until the marine chronometer was invented in 1762. It must be noted that while sailing the northern waters in 1612, William Baffin was the first navigator known to have recorded his determination of longitude on the basis of the lunar cycle. However, the inability to precisely determine longitude did not deter the mariners from crossing the open seas. Their knowledge of latitude enabled them to sail long distances out of the sight of land. The simplest method was to sail north or south to the desired latitude, then turn east or west toward their intended landfall. Sebastian Cabot's extensive voyage and return in 1530 certainly demonstrated that extended oceanic voyages did not require a specially designed vessel. In addition, it also proved that the English mariners were capable seamen at that early date.

DUTCH

The Dutch trade had begun to prosper in the fifteenth century when their fishermen found new methods of preserving and smoking the herrings which migrated from the Baltic to the North Sea. In addition to the fishing industry the Dutch brought goods from the Baltic, Lisbon and Seville, delivering them to Antwerp, where merchants from all over Europe bought them. As a result of all of the trading activities Antwerp became a rich and powerful city, eventually becoming the banking center of Europe.

Fig. 4. Dutch flute.

Feeling the growing need for improved shipping capabilities, the Dutch designed and built a type of sea-going barge to carry bulky goods such as grain and timber. The Dutch 'fly-ship', or 'flute', was inexpensive to build, which resulted in lower freight rates than could be offered by the other European trading nations. [Fig. 4]

Following Columbus's voyages to the Americas, riches began to flow into Europe through the trading efforts of the Portuguese, Dutch, English and French. Goods began to arrive from India and the Far East. When Drake returned from his plundering expedition in 1595, he brought back with him enough silver and gold to establish the East India Company and the Levant Company.

In the 1590s both the English and Dutch trading companies had reached the Spice Islands of Indonesia — each having formed its own East India Company. Finally, the Portuguese were driven out of the Indonesian trade and the Dutch were able to build an empire in that region.

NAVIGATION AIDS

Because of the immense profits to be reaped by the growing number of trading companies, governments were careful not to reveal their routes, or even their methods of navigation. Charts and journals from the ships involved in trade were jealously guarded to protect national incomes. However, printers (especially in the Netherlands) began to publish books of sailing directions, which made available to any shipmaster the notes and sailing directions for the more important ports and harbors, distances between ports, courses to be sailed, information on tides and water depths, types of sea-bed, landmarks, etc. By the latter part of the fifteenth century Martin Behaim had also produced a geographical globe. Early in the sixteenth century the Theory of the Sphere and the Table of Rules for fixing position had been introduced. It became normal procedure for a shipmaster to provision himself with pilot books, or rutters, which would cover his normal ports of call. In addition, every shipmaster worth his salt kept a personal notebook in which he recorded his own personal observations. Undoubtedly, the mariners exchanged bits of information when they gathered at the taverns in their ports of call.

By the time Magellan sailed under the flag of Spain on his voyage around the world in 1522, he carried with him sea charts, compass, instruments for determining latitude and speed, as well as solar and traverse tables.

Work in the field of mathematics was being done with the encouragement of various government officials, who were doing all in their power to encourage the improvement of navigation methods in an effort to increase their trading potential. During the fifteenth and sixteenth centuries the development of accurate navigation instruments took on added importance as the nations competed for a lion's share of the market.

By the reign of Henry VIII in England mathematicians, instrument-makers, map engravers, pilot book publishers, astronomers and geographers were beginning to make themselves known. Of great importance to pilots and shipmasters traveling the English Channel to French and English ports were the published tide tables and charts.

Sailing manuals began to appear first in Portugal about 1540. The most noteworthy examples are those produced by Pedro Medina and Martin Cortes. The Cortes manual was later translated and published in England in 1562, but it was too difficult for the ordinary sailor to understand. This led William Bourne to publish his *Almanack and Rules of Navigation* in 1567, followed by his *Regiment of the Sea*, which was published in 1574.

The Spanish and Portuguese had been leading the way in the training of mariners. Stephen Borough, who had been associated with John Cabot and Richard Chancellor, made a visit to Seville, where he saw methods used for training proficient shipmasters and pilots. On his return to England, Borough made a strong plea to Queen Elizabeth and her ministers for the establishing of a seamanship training program, which would be followed by a comprehensive testing by the Chief Pilot of England. However, no such program was implemented. Stephen Borough and his brother, William, became the chief pilots of the Muscovy Company and received instruction from John Dee, who was the leading mathematician in England. Dee, who was considered a mathematical genius, had been educated at Cambridge before going to the Continent, where he became acquainted with some of the leading mathematicians of Europe.

Stephen Borough succeeded in persuading the Muscovy Company to finance the translation and publication of Cortes' *Arte de Navegar*, which provided information for any young and ambitious sailor wanting to learn by self-study. The major problem with the book was the fact that it was long and difficult, and some of the work on solar tables and the declination of the Polar Star needed revision.

William Borough, the younger brother of Stephen, was well aware of the problems with compass variation and described two types of compasses for variation, which were made for him by Robert Norman, who was an experienced seaman. Norman had settled in Ratcliff, where he made sea-compasses, marine charts and various other nautical instruments.

By the late sixteenth century the English mathematicians and instrument-makers were making their own contributions to the development of accurate navigation instruments, and were no longer simply borrowing knowledge from the Continent. At the same time, cartographers were at work developing maps, sea charts and globes to assist the explorers and colonists of the New World. Of special interest to the Pilgrims and Christopher Jones, master of MAYFLOWER, was the map of New England constructed by Capt. John Smith in 1614. [Fig. 5]

For a better understanding of just how much of the New World had been explored by the early seventeenth century, and the number of voyages involved, compare the list of known voyages to North America with Theodore de Bry's 1596 map of the western hemisphere. [Fig. 6]

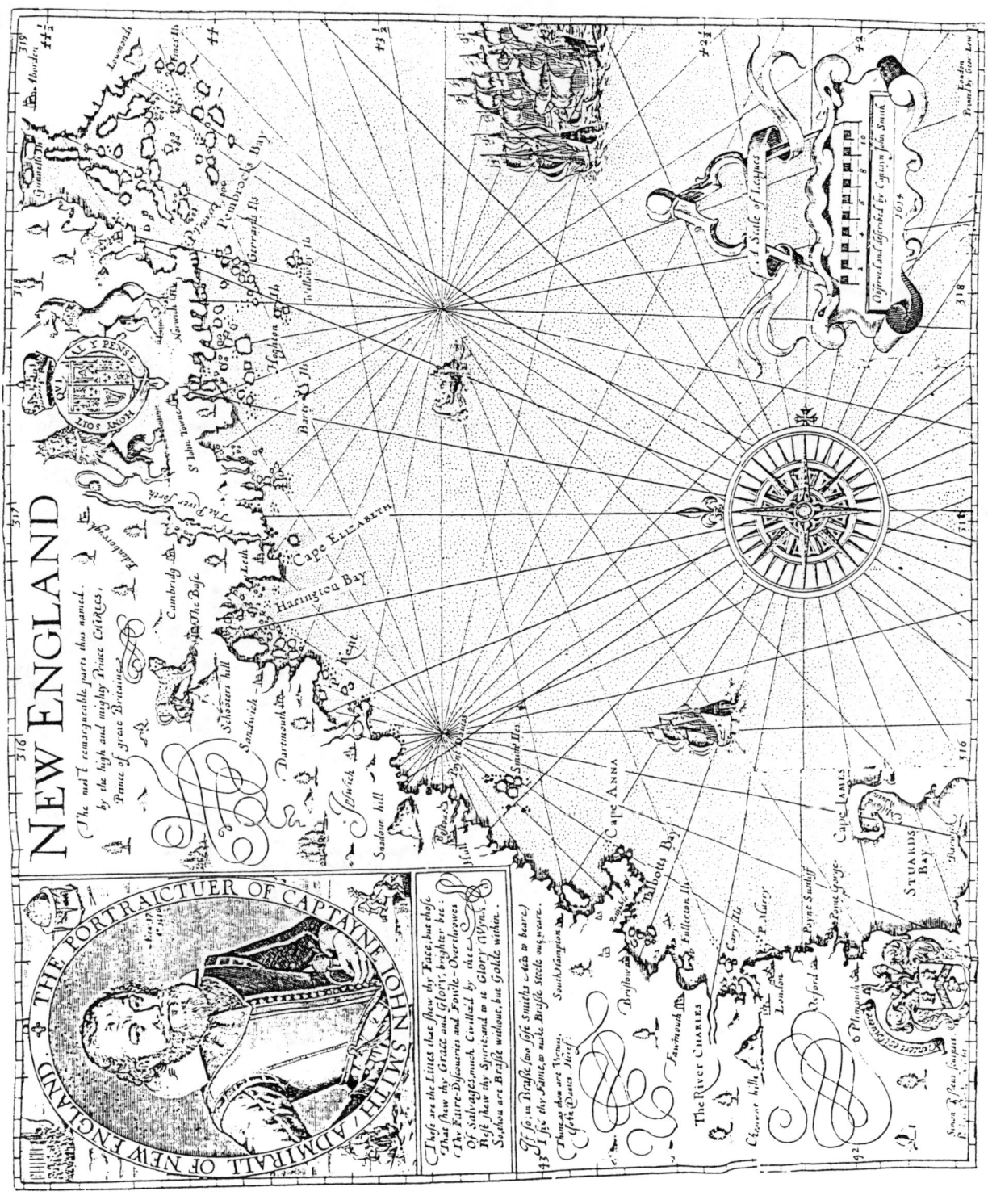

Fig. 5. John Smith's map of New England.

Fig. 6. Theodore de Bry's map of the Western Hemisphere.

A SAMPLING OF KNOWN VOYAGES TO NORTH AMERICA

1492
    Christopher Columbus, Spain, voyage to the New World.

1493
    Christopher Columbus, Spain, second voyage to the New World.

1497
    John Cabot, England, accompanied by his son, discovered Cape Breton Island, visiting Nova Scotia and Labrador or Newfoundland.

1498
    John Cabot, England, second voyage on which he followed the North American coast from 30-degrees N to the Cape of Florida.

1519-1522
    Fernando Magellan, Spain, circumnavigation of the globe.

1524
    Giovanni da Verrazano, France, to the eastern seaboard of North America from Cape Fear on the Carolina coast to Maine or Nova Scotia.

1534
    Jacques Cartier, France, to Newfoundland, seeking Northwest Passage.

1536
    Jacques Cartier, France, to the St. Lawrence region.
    Master Horem, England, to Nova Scotia.

1541
    Jacques Cartier, France, to Quebec.

1543
    Jacques Cartier, France, to Quebec.

1562
    Jean Ribault, France, with French Huguenots to South Carolina.

1564
    René Goulaine de Laudonnière, France, second French Huguenot expedition to St. John River.

1565
    Jean Ribault, France, to St. John's River.
    Pedro Memendez de Aviles, Spain, to found St. Augustine.

1567-8
    Sir John Hawkins, England, to the West Indies and on to the St. James River.
    Sir John Hawkins, England, with Francis Drake in command of one of the ships to the area of Cape Verde and the coast of Guinea, then along the Atlantic coast to Maine.

1574
    Martin Frobisher, England, reached northern regions of Labrador.

1576
    Fishermen, Spain, more than 100 ships to Newfoundland cod fishing grounds.
    Fishermen, Biscay, twenty to thirty ships to Newfoundland for whales and train oil (whale oil).
    Fishermen, France, more than one hundred ships to Newfoundland fishing grounds.
    Fishermen, England, more than one hundred ships to Newfoundland fishing grounds.
    Fishermen, Portugal, more than fifty ships to the Newfoundland fishing grounds.

1577-1580
    Sir Francis Drake, England, circumnavigation of the globe, explored the Pacific coast of North America.

1578
    Martin Frobisher, England, to area north of Labrador.

1583
: Sir Humphrey Gilbert, England, to Newfoundland with a total of 260 in his company.

1584
: Masters Philip Amadas and Arthur Barlowe, England, to Virginia for Sir Walter Raleigh.

1585-86
: Sir Richard Grenville, England, with seven vessels to Roanoke Island, North Carolina for Sir Walter Raleigh.

1586
: Governor John White, England, supply ship to the company in Virginia for Sir Walter Raleigh, but no trace of the company was found.

1587
: Governor John White, England, with three ships to Virginia.

1588
: Governor John White, England, with three ships to Virginia.

1595
: Sir Francis Drake and Sir John Hawkins, England, to the West Indies.

1602
: Bartholomew Gosnold, England, three ships bound for the West Indies also explored the northeastern shores of North America as far as southeastern New England.

1603
: Martin Pring, England, to the area of Maine and on to Whitsun's Bay (Plymouth Harbor).
Samuel de Champlain, France, to the St. Lawrence region of Quebec.

1605
: George Weymouth, England, to the area of either Nantucket or Cape Cod and on to the north of Maine.
Samuel de Champlain, France, to the New England coasts of Maine and Massachusetts.

1606
: Samuel de Champlain, France, to the New England coast from Gloucester Harbor to Cape Cod, and on to the Vineyard Sound.
Capt. Henry Challoung and Thomas Hanham, England, two ships to the coast of Maine.
Martin Pring, England, to the New England coast.
George Popham and Raleigh Gilbert, England, in two ships to Newfoundland and Sagahadoc on the coast of Maine and the entrance to the Kennebec, establishing the Popham Colony.
London Company, England, a voyage of exploration prior to the settling of Jamestown.

1607
: London Company, England, established Jamestown.

1608
: Capt. George Davies, England, with supplies to the planters at Sagahadoc.
Samuel de Champlain, France, founded Quebec.

1609
: Henry Hudson, Netherlands, to the area of Penobscot, the fishing banks, Hudson River, Manhattan and Cape Cod.
Samuel Argall, England, to Virginia.
Jesuit group, France, to Quebec.

1610
: Henry Hudson, Netherlands, to Hudson Strait, James Bay and the southern extremity of Hudson Bay.
Samuel Argall, England, to Penobscot Bay, Virginia and on to the Bermudas.

1612
: Capt. Button, England, to the west coast of Hudson Bay.
William Baffin, England, to the Arctic region. On this voyage Baffin was the first known person to calculate the longitude by the lunar cycle.

1613
- Samuel Argall, England, two voyages to New England to investigate reports that the French were making settlements at Mount Desert and at the mouth of the St. Croix River.

1614
- Capt. John Smith, England, to Virginia and New England, mapping the areas which he explored.
- Sir Francis Popham, England, to the Kennebec River.
- Adriaen Block, Dutch, to Manhattan Island, Connecticut River and along the southern side of Cape Cod.
- Thomas Hunt, England, to New England coast.

1615
- Thomas Dermer, England, to New England coast and Newfoundland.

1616
- William Baffin and Robert Bylot, England, discovered and explored the whole coastline of Baffin Bay, and visited Jones, Lancaster and Smith Sounds.

1619
- Thomas Dermer, England, to the coast of New England, and on to Virgina.

1620
- Thomas Dermer, England, to the coast of New England.
- Samuel de Champlain, France, to Quebec.
- MAYFLOWER, England, to Cape Cod.

1621
- ANNE and LITTLE JAMES, England, supplies and colonists to Plymouth, Mass.

1624
- Christopher Levett, England, landed on the Isle of Shoals and selected an island at the mouth of Portland Harbor to settle.
- Master Thomson, England, made a plantation at Pannaway (Piscataqua River).
- Master Weston, England, to the Piscataqua River.

NOTE: Colonization proceeded at a rapid pace with ships crossing the Atlantic with new colonists and supplies. By 1700 there were 12 English colonies on or near the Atlantic coast, and Georgia was added in 1713.

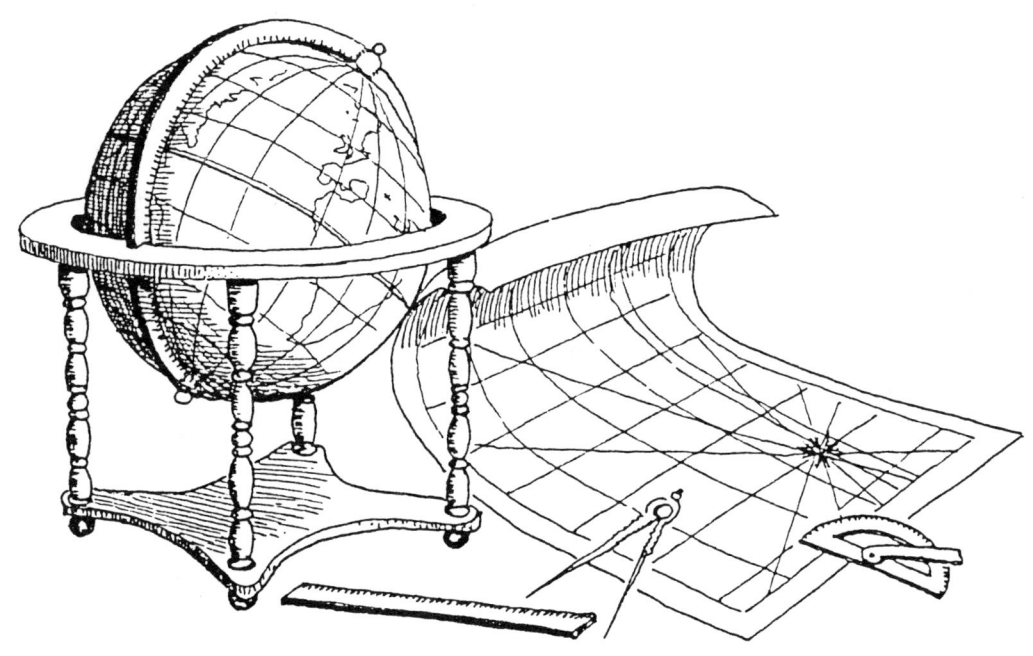

2. INTRODUCTION TO NAVIGATION

Navigation can be considered as the art or science of directing or conducting a vessel from one point to another in a safe manner. Although it has now become more of a science than an art, both elements are required in the highest form of seamanship. The word navigation comes from two Latin words: *navis*, meaning 'ship'; and *agere*, meaning 'to move or direct.' Hence, navigation is the act of directing vessels by determining position, direction, distance, estimated time of arrival, etc.

Marine navigation is different from any other type of navigation for one reason — the sea itself. On the waters of the oceans a navigator is alone in a 360-degree circle of vast sameness with nothing to indicate where he is except his compass, and some instrumentation to indicate his latitude and longitude. The scholars and scientists can discover the principles involved, develop more accurate instrumentation, and lay down the rules for safe navigation. However, the true sailor knows that no instrument yet developed can predict the approach of giant waves or sudden bursts of gale force wind which can suddenly develop on the waters of the world. Only the knowledgeable mariner has the expertise — or art — necessary to cope successfully with the many unpredictables on the high seas. Thus, even today, navigation is both a science and an art.

PILOTING or COASTAL SAILING

Man undoubtedly sailed the seas for thousands of years before instruments were available to help him plot his course. His first sailings would have been made along the coastlines and within safe sight of the landmarks on shore.

In its earliest form navigation was strictly coastal. Mariners during the first several thousand years did not have the navigation aids or instruments which would have allowed them to venture beyond the sight of land. Undoubtedly, they crept along the coastlines, keeping land within sight. From those early days of strictly coastal sailing the term 'pilot' was generally applied to those mariners who made use of landmarks on the shoreline for reference points in determining their position. Piloting became the term used for those mariners who used coastal navigation techniques. In Europe, a great deal of navigation would have been done by following the coastlines, and the term 'coaster' is sometimes used to designate those coastal pilots.

The art of pilotage consists of nothing more than knowing perfectly (by sight) the capes, ports and rivers which the mariner would meet. He would know how they appear from the sea, the distance between each landmark, and what course lay between them. In addition he would also know on what bearing of the moon to expect high and low tide, the ebb and flow of the waters, and the depth and nature of the bottom. All of these things the pilot would have learned by experience and through instruction from other pilots who had learned these things from their own experience.

The pilot's ability was measured by the skill with which he conned (directed) his ship from cape to cape in coastal waters, by his knowledge of off-shore soundings of the sea-bed, and his familiarity with landmarks, seamarks, tides, estuary shoals, etc. For his knowledge of the sea bottom, he would have been greatly dependent on the use of his mariner's compass and the lead-line as chief instruments.

Of great importance to the early coastal sailors was the development of land and sea marks which provided him with a constant check on his position. Lighthouses, beacons and buoys also provided him with a knowledge of his cross-bearings and distances by knowing the objects on shore.

Those early navigators would have made their way from headland to headland or cape to cape by dead reckoning. The term 'dead reckoning' actually developed from the term 'deduced reckoning' which was shortened to 'ded' reckoning. A misspelling of the term eventually became our present term for the art of determining the course from one known position to another.

DEAD RECKONING

Dead reckoning is a method of keeping an account of the ship's location and the course made good, which had been used by mariners since ancient times — and is still used today. The mariner using dead reckoning kept a careful record of the directions sailed, which is determined by the mariner's compass; and the speed of travel, determined in this early period by the log line. The navigator might also include notes on the direction and strength of the winds, as well as the leeway of the ship (the downwind movement of the ship caused by wind pressure on the hull and rigging). The movement of strong currents also pull a ship off course.

In sailing by dead reckoning the early navigators would have relied on their own experience of winds and currents. The mariners of that time were expert in the art of judging if the weather were going to be fair or stormy by looking at the sky as well as taking into account the color of the sea and the behavior of the dolphins and flying fish. They were also aware of how the smoke rose because it indicated wind direction and atmospheric pressure (a weather indicator). By night they could judge by the moonlight that played on the masthead and an observation of the stars.

The early pilots would have been able to judge their direction reasonably well by using the wind and currents of the sea as references to their position and direction of sailing. Early in the history of sailing the mariners knew of the prevailing winds which changed with the season. Through long and difficult experience they learned that the oceans were divided into zones where the trade winds would blow steadily in one direction during one season, but changed during another. They also discovered that there were areas where the wind was still for months at a time.

OCEANIC NAVIGATION or INSTRUMENT SAILING

It seems likely that there must have been a few courageous mariners who ventured beyond the sight of land occasionally — as when sailing from headland to headland. At such times they would have turned their eyes to the heavens and selected a course with the aid of the sun, moon and stars. What is more, they would have had to rely on their understanding of the waters which they were sailing and the various aspects of nature such as the prevailing winds, and the movement of the water currents. No one can tell how many of those mariners were lost because of fog or became hopelessly lost when the skies were overcast for days on end and the prevailing winds ceased to blow.

The chief instruments used in piloting (or coasting) were the mariner's compass for determining direction and the lead-line for sounding water depths and determining the type of seabed below. Oceanic navigation employs, in addition to the art of pilotage, several other rules and instruments derived from the art of astronomy and cosmography. Nautical science is used to determine the position of the ship at all times — both in respect to latitude and longitude — rather than simply depending upon land and sea-marks which were visible to the shipmaster.

The Elizabethan scholar, Dr. John Dee, one of the first English scholars (if not the first) to teach the art of navigation, defined it in these simple terms in 1550: 'The art of navigation demonstrateth how by the shortest good way, by the aptest direction, and in the shortest time, a sufficient ship...be conducted.'

It is as good a definition of the modern navigator's art as it was of the Elizabethan navigator's of 1570. His brief definition includes all the factors of time and space, distance, direction, speed, and seaworthiness, which govern the calculated movements of a ship. But in doing so it leaves a great deal to the imagination or knowledge of the reader.

Of what did the art of navigation consist? And how did the Elizabethan practice it? Seller in his *Practical Navigation* of 1717 states: 'Practical Navigation...consists of two general parts, First, that which may be called the 'Domestick' or more 'common Navigation' (I mean Coasting or Sailing along the shore)...Secondly, That which may properly bear the name and principally deserves to be entitled "Art of Navigation,"... that part which guides the Ship in her Course through the Immense Ocean, to any part of the Known World...'

THE FORCES OF NATURE AT WORK

The winds and currents of the earth are the result of the earth's rotation. The rotation of the earth from west to east causes the winds to move clockwise in the northern hemisphere and counterclockwise in the southern hemisphere.

The speed of the winds tends to be different at various latitudes. The circumference of the globe is about 25,000 miles at the equator, which means that a point on the equator travels about 25,000 miles in 24 hours, and that is equal to over 1,000 miles per hour. The circumference of the globe decreases as the rings of latitude move north or south from the equator. Therefore, a point in either direction (north or south) of the equator is traveling at a decreased speed.

The north and south direction of the winds is caused by the movement of warm air at the equator toward the cooler poles, and the movement of cool polar air toward the warm regions at the equator.

The prevailing winds of the Atlantic move in a northeastern direction, which are called 'south westerlies', referring to the direction from which they blow. In the northern regions the winds blow in an easterly direction until they reach the coasts of Europe, where they divide, some moving in a northeastern direction — some swinging in a southerly direction toward the African coast. Near the equator the winds are warmed and begin to move in a southwestern direction, and are called the 'northeast trades'. When the warmed trades reach the coasts of the western hemisphere they swing north along the coast of North America toward the cool polar air. The region between the south westerlies and the northeast trades tends to have calm and light variable winds. [See Fig. 7]

THE COMPASS ROSE

As the art of coastal sailing developed in the Mediterranean area, the mariners identified and named the winds by the direction of the sun at sunrise and sunset, by the nature of those winds, or for the country from which those winds blew. For example, the wind from the north came from the mountains and was termed 'Tramontana.' To the northeast lay Greece and the winds from the northeast were therefore named 'Greco.' The half-wind from the NNE was between 'Greco' and 'Tramontana' and was simply called 'Greco-Tramontana.' Intermediate winds might also be referred to as 'from Greco a third,' 'from Greco a quarter,' or simply 'a little.' [Fig. 8]

By his understanding of these winds the early pilot could gauge his direction even at times when he might be out of the sight of coastal landmarks. He was also able to distinguish the various winds by their temperature, moisture content or strength. The directions of the wind

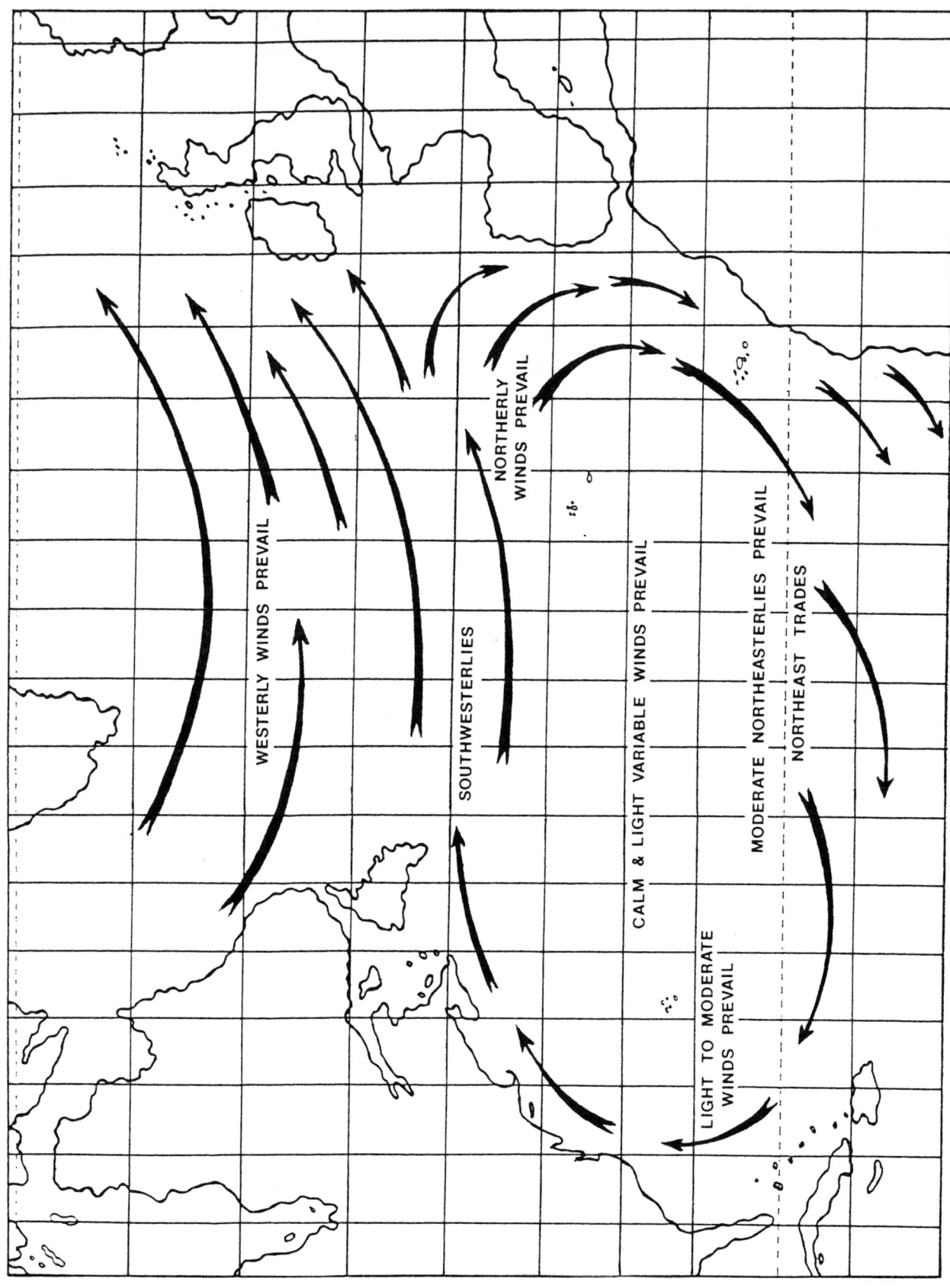

Fig. 7. Wind patterns of the Atlantic Ocean.

was referred to as rhumbs of the wind. From these terms developed the wind rose of the eight principal winds. For an example of the use of the above terms on a sea chart of the time, see Fig. 9.

The wind rose eventually became established as the eight principal winds with their halves and quarters. The nomenclature with which we are now familiar developed in northwestern Europe and eventually took precedence over the old terms from the Mediterranean. The terms based on the four cardinal points (N., N. by E., NNE. by N., NE., etc.) became the pattern and were known to mariners as the 'rhumbs of the wind,' which was shortened to 'rhumbs.' [Figs. 10 & 11.]

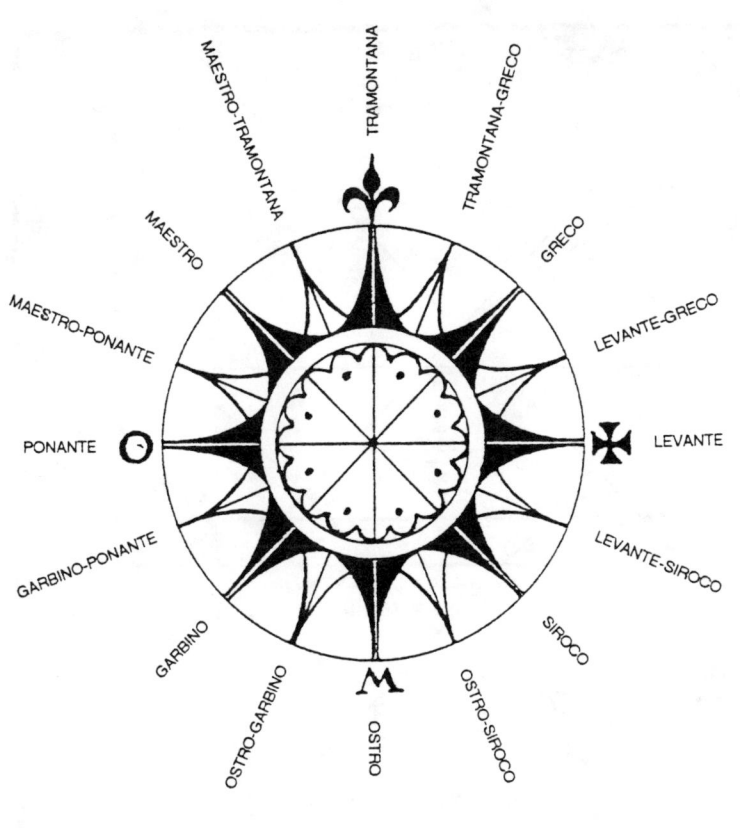

Fig. 8. Mediterranean rhumbs of the wind.

The circle of the sky was divided into 360 degrees by the Babylonians, who were probably the first people to reason out the universe.

They also divided the day into hours, minutes and seconds. Although the known world at that time was very small and they looked upon the earth as a flat disk, they developed a relationship between the sky and earth which allowed the earth to be plotted in relationship to the stars in a coordinated and proportional way.

The Mediterranean practice of referring to the directions as 'winds' continued to be used in the Mediterranean, and was eventually adopted by the northern mariners as well. By the thirteenth century the mariner's horizon had been divided into thirty-two directions, which they called the 'rhumbs of the winds.'

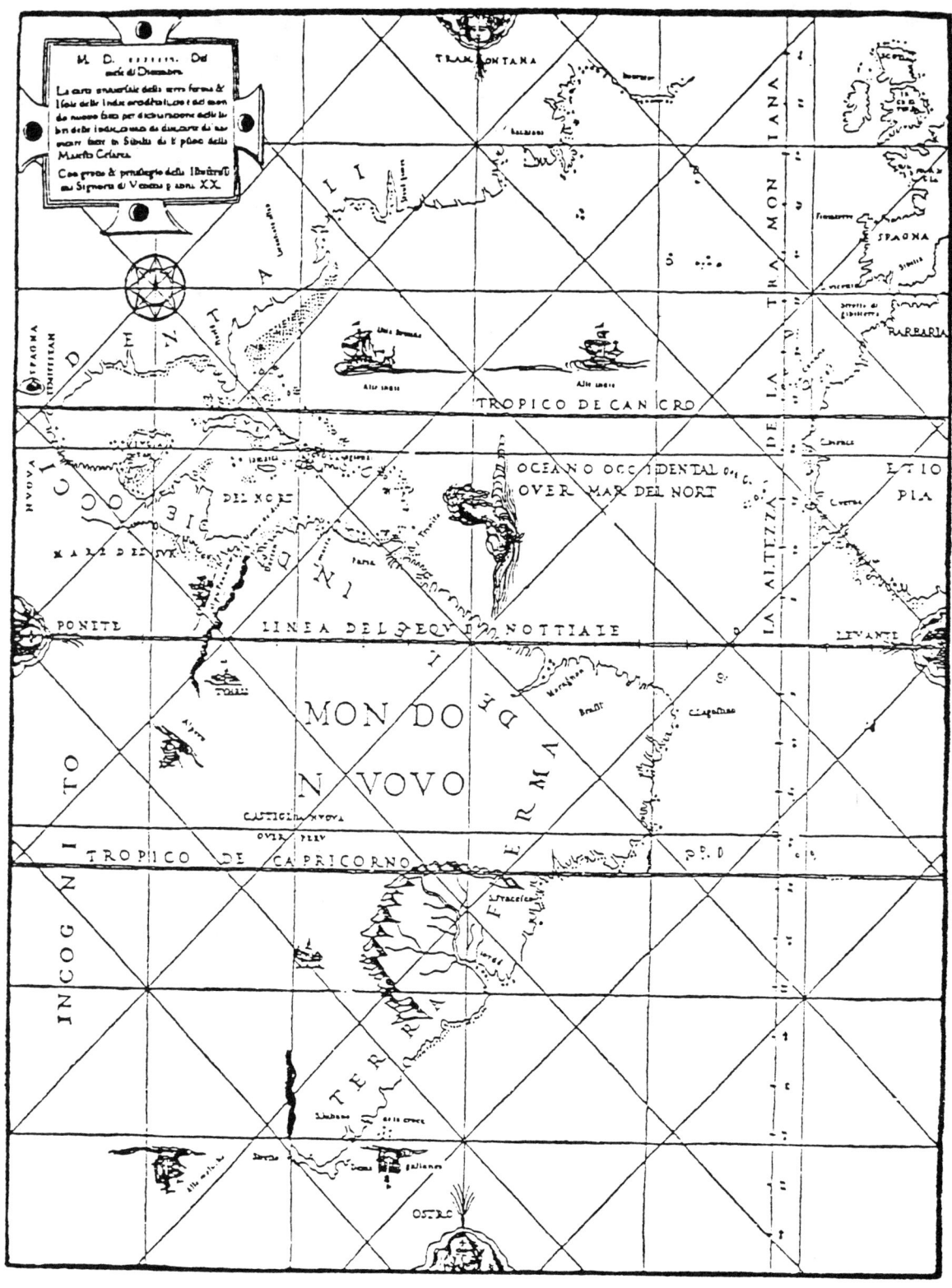

Fig. 9. Map of America, 1534.

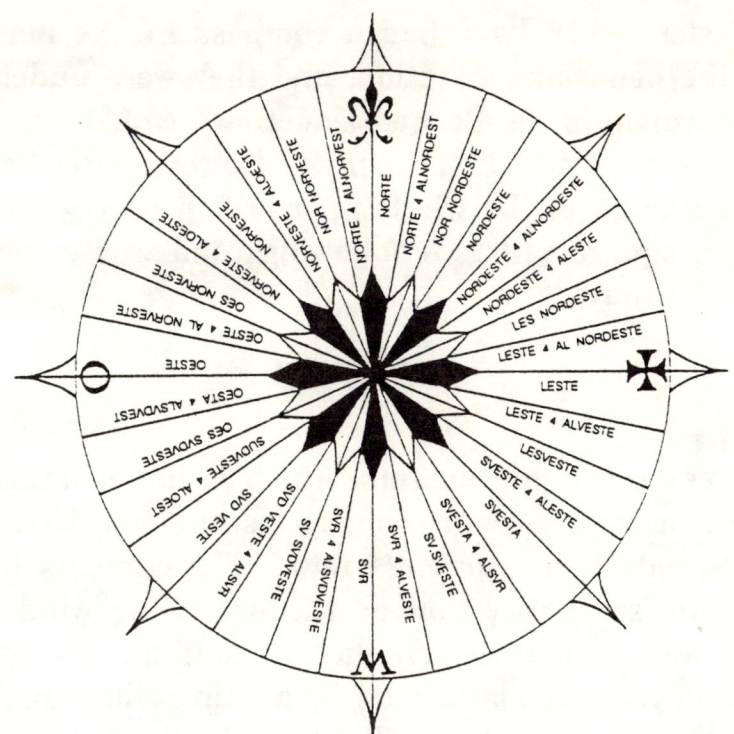

Fig. 10. The compass rose of Cortes.

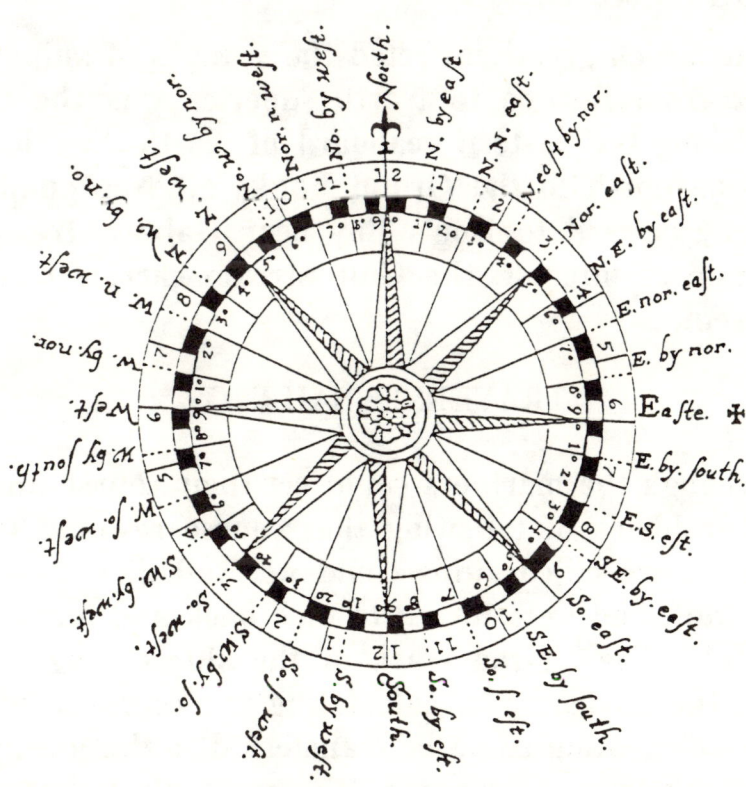

Fig. 11. The English compass rose.

23

The shipmaster would have had a compass by the mast in addition to the one at the helmsman's station, and they were under constant observation. The compass needle was sometimes called the 'Stella Maris' after the polar star to which it turned. However, the basic directions they used were related to the winds upon which they were dependent to fill their simple, square sails. A following wind was essential for them to make good headway.

CURRENTS

A ship moves on a liquid medium which is in constant motion. The currents of the ocean cause any object floating on it to move in the direction and speed of the current's flow. The currents in the Atlantic tend to follow the same direction as the prevailing winds. These currents were not known in the early days of sailing. However, they had a strong effect on the way made good by a ship sailing against or across them. The force of a current is well known by anyone who has tried to row a boat across the running current of a river. The boat will slide in the direction of that current. For a view of the major currents of the Atlantic Ocean, see Fig. 12.

One current which greatly affected the voyages of ships crossing the North Atlantic from Europe to North America was the Gulf Stream, which swings along the eastern seaboard of North America from Cape Hatteras, moving north to the Grand Banks off Newfoundland. From there it swings eastward to Dog's Bay near Galway, Ireland, where it ends. As a note of interest, the Gulf Stream carries more heat than any other current.

TRAVERSE SAILING

Even though the mariners could set their course and know their direction, the problems of following that course resulted from the fact that the large square-sailed ships could not sail directly into the wind (close to the wind), and were forced to tack back and forth, or 'traverse' as it was called. The zig-zag track of the ship's progress had to be worked out by the navigator in calculating the course made good each day before the information could be transferred to the journal (log-book) or the charts. For this purpose a traverse table was needed. Even simple arithmetic was a problem for the majority of sailors in those

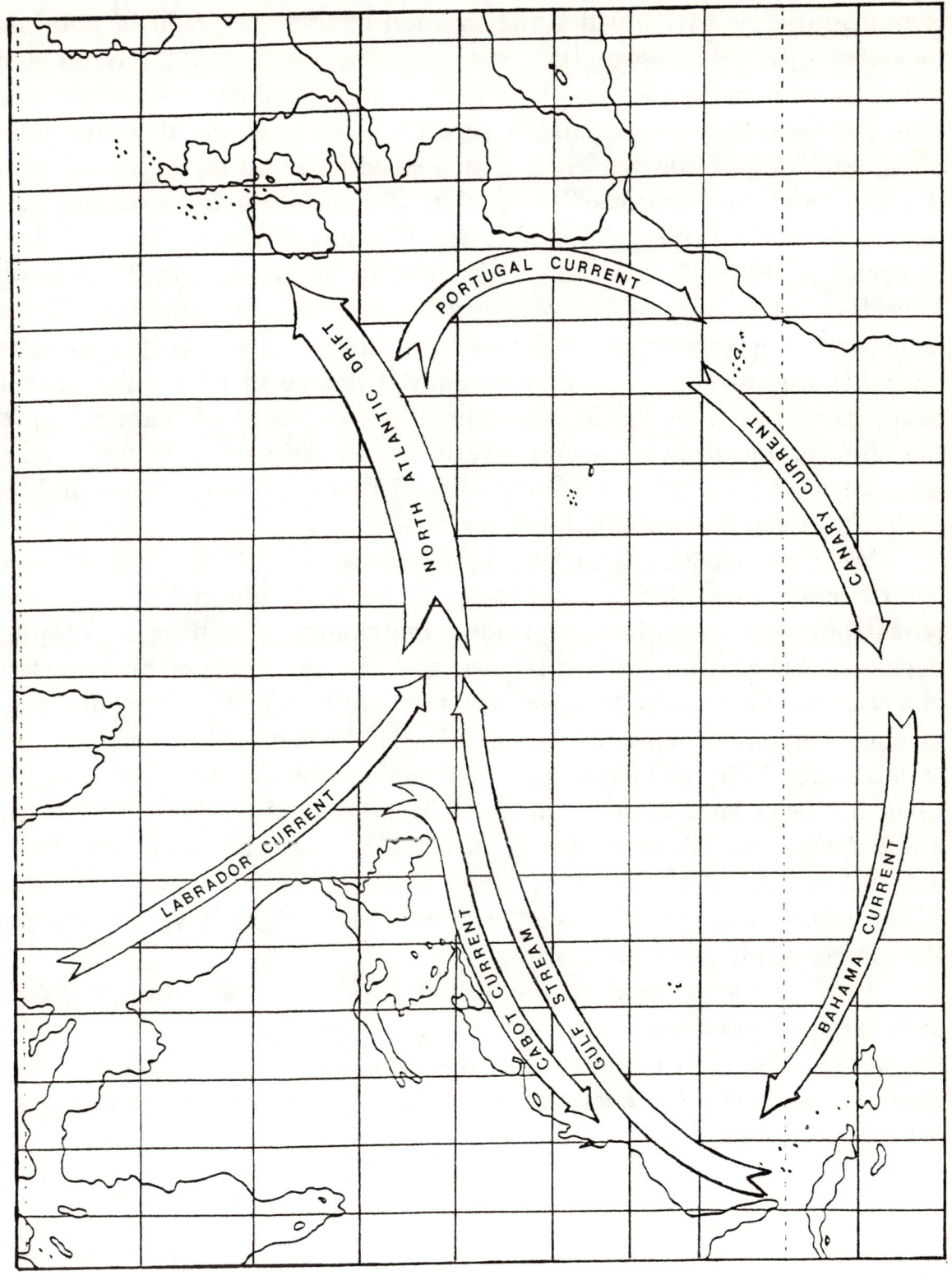

Fig. 12. Currents of the Atlantic Ocean.

early times, which led to the development of the sinical quadrant, a graphical diagram from which the solution of traverse could be obtained. Provided with this information, the early mariners would have had no difficulty in working out the daily course made good and the ship's position, provided they could make a correct estimate of the distance sailed along each leg of the traverse, and a good estimation of the speed of the ship and the leeway of their ship (the position or direction away from that of the wind). All square-rigged ships of the period had much in common, but each was unique and had to be handled in its own way. Therefore, every shipmaster performed his maneuvers slightly different from any other master under the same circumstances. Every shipmaster knew his ship and just how much leeway it tended to have. The seaman could gauge his progress by observing the movement of foam alongside the ship, or by throwing a chip overboard to see how it drifted. Here, as always, the art of navigation depended on the knowledge and experience of the seasoned shipmaster.

We may conclude then that by the late sixteenth and early seventeenth centuries navigation consisted of two fairly distinct arts: pilotage (coasting) and oceanic navigation (instrumental sailing). Pilotage depended primarily upon experience and the observation of terrestrial objects. Oceanic navigation was fundamentally scientific and depended primarily upon the observation of celestial bodies. The navigator had to have the ability to direct the ship's course and fix the ship's position when far from land by instrumental observation of heavenly bodies and mathematical calculation. Using dead reckoning, the navigator kept a detailed account of his heading, speed, winds, currents, weather and state of the sea, leeway, or any other element which might have an effect on the course made good on a voyage.

Today, with his modern navigational aids and education, the ordinary navigator can both pilot and navigate his ship in all the waters of the world. The pilot is almost a rarity. His activities are generally confined to especially treacherous waters in the approaches to important ports.

3. CHRISTOPHER JONES: MASTER OF MAYFLOWER

William Bradford and Edward Winslow were the only Pilgrims to leave accounts of MAYFLOWER and the voyage from England to Cape Cod. The Pilgrims were deeply concerned about their future welfare — not to mention the long voyage to reach their destination. Seasickness probably began to take its toll very quickly among the passengers who were not accustomed to the pitching and rolling of a ship at sea — and certainly not the wave motion created by the North Atlantic as winter turbulence set in.

They would not have been in the mood to put up with the insults and curses of the young sailors who taunted them, and they would have felt even more insecure when the main beam of the ship cracked during a storm at sea.

It is no wonder that the accounts of Bradford and Winslow are filled with negative aspects of the voyage. Their experiences for at least ten years prior to the voyage had been fretful, troublesome and full of doubts. Unfortunately, it has left us with accounts which cannot in any measure give us a true description of that historic voyage across the Atlantic as they prepared to establish the first democratic society in recorded history.

Some authors suggest that MAYFLOWER was a creaking, old ship (based on the fact that a main beam cracked during the voyage). It must be remembered that the Pilgrims were land-lubbers who did not understand the capabilities of the ship as well as its part-owner and master, Christopher Jones. When all of the facts are considered, it will be realized that the choice of MAYFLOWER and its master was a good one.

CHRISTOPHER JONES

Just who was this incredible man of the sea who brought the Pilgrims safely to the New World against all odds? This noble mariner has been given very little credit for the feat he performed.

Christopher Jones is usually referred to as the 'captain' of MAYFLOWER. However, the rank of captain was that used by the British Navy. The skipper of a merchant ship such as MAYFLOWER would have been referred to as Master Christopher Jones.

In 1570 Christopher Jones was born into a seafaring family of Harwich on the eastern coast of England, which is just a short distance north of the Thames estuary. Harwich had been a busy English port for shipping from early times. Many of the fleets of exploration had sailed from Harwich, and the Jones (or 'John') family had long been associated with sea trade. Christopher's grandfather, Morgan John, had been a victualer in Harwich, provisioning ships of trade and discovery. His father (also named Christopher) was part-owner of two ships, and was of citizen rank, which was only one step below the 'gentleman' class.

When Christopher was only eight or so, his father of the same name died. His will was dated 13 October 1578. According to that will, young Christopher inherited one-eighth part and stock for a new ship, CENTURION, to be equally divided between his mother, two brothers and an unborn child. In addition to that Christopher, as the eldest son, was to receive his father's part of a ship called MARIE FORTUNE when he came of age. This was a considerable inheritance for a young lad of eight or nine.

Coming from a family of mariners as he did, Christopher was probably apprenticed to the sea-faring trade at the age of eleven or twelve — possibly as a cabin-boy, which was quite common in those days. When he reached the age of maturity he became master of MARIE FORTUNE, going to France to pick up a cargo of wine and delivering it to Southampton. From this we know that Christopher Jones was familiar with the Southampton docks as early as 1590 — the very docks from which MAYFLOWER would sail thirty years later.

In 1593 Christopher was married in All Saints' Church at Harwich to Sarah Twitt, the daughter of Thomas Twitt who was a shipmaster and whaler. Shortly after 1599 Sarah died of the fever, and in 1603 Christopher was married to Josian Thompson Gray, the widow of his friend, Richard Gray. Richard Gray was the son of John Gray, who had been captain of THE REVENGE, which had sailed from the port of Harwich in the fleet of Drake.

Christopher achieved such prominence in the sea-faring community of Harwich that shortly after his second marriage King James I named him as one of the twenty-four burgesses of Harwich when he established a new charter for Harwich. In accordance with the new charter, Christopher was empowered for life to elect two members of Parliament and to fill vacancies as they occurred.

By the time Christopher Jones was 36-years-old, he had designed and built a strong ship of 240 tuns, which he named JOSIAN OF HARWICH, after his second wife. [A 'tun' is a barrel containing 265 gallons.] JOSIAN was christened in 1606. The King's Admiralty was so impressed with the design and construction of JOSIAN that King James granted Christopher one crown of double rose for every tun of burden (480 crowns).

About 1608 Christopher Jones bought one-quarter ownership of MAYFLOWER and in August of that year he made a trial run to the Bay of Biscay for a cargo of Gascon wine, serving as shipmaster. That same month he sailed her through the North Sea with a cargo of hats, hops and Spanish salt to Trondhjem, Norway, possibly returning with a cargo of herring.

The English trade was beginning to shift from the coastal ports to the London area of the Thames River. Understanding the necessity of shifting his base of operations, Christopher moved his family to Redriffe (sometimes called Redcliffe). Redriffe was just across the bridge from London and to the southeast. It is now called Rotherhithe. Here it was that Jones berthed MAYFLOWER at Redriffe Mill, and from that time the ship was referred to as MAYFLOWER OF LONDON.

Records survive to reveal that Jones sailed from the docks of the London area to the ports of Gascony for wine, Bordeaux for prunes, and Norway with cargoes of taffeta, stockings, hops and salt. In 1615 "Virginia leaf tobacco" was listed among his cargo, and in May of 1620 he brought a cargo of 59 tuns of wine from France into the London docks. How many other trips he made will probably never be known since a great number of records were destroyed in the great London fire of September, 1666. With the sea-faring background of Christopher Jones, it is quite likely that he was a member of the Guild of Master Mariners, however, records to prove this may also have disappeared in the great fire.

By the time the Pilgrim leaders contracted with him to make the voyage to New England, Christopher Jones was a fifty-year-old family man with a wife and five living children — the youngest of whom had just been born in the spring of that year. This veteran of the seas had sailed as master of MAYFLOWER for twelve years. He would have known her ways, her strengths, her weaknesses, her leeward tendencies, her every mood under every condition.

The route Jones chose for that historic voyage in 1620 was not a new one. In 1606 Bartholomew Gosnold had crossed the northern waters of the Atlantic without making the customary stop at the Canary Islands. Thus, he had shortened the voyage by more than a thousand leagues. When Martin Pring crossed the same direction in 1603 he did not stop at the Azores, but set his course straight for 'North Virginia' (New England). And in 1607 the Popham-Gilbert expedition followed practically the same route. A number of other expeditions had already made the course by 1620. Jones was not adventuring across unknown waters to unknown shores with his precious cargo of passengers.

He was a highly qualified, experienced and well-respected man of the sea. This was certainly not an unknown mariner picked at random from some dockside tavern. The Pilgrim leaders had chartered a strong, reliable ship and a seasoned master who understood the art and science of navigation.

4. THE SHIP MAYFLOWER

Before approaching the methods and instruments used in navigating a ship such as MAYFLOWER, it is essential to know something about the vessel itself. We are told that MAYFLOWER was a ship of 180 tuns. But, what does that mean? We are accustomed to thinking in terms of a 2,000 lb. measure of weight when we read the word. However, that is not what the tun of measure meant in the early seventeenth century. A 'tun' was a large barrel or cask for wine equal to a double hogshead (or 265 gallons). An illustration from the period shows four men carrying a tun on their shoulders as they provision a ship. [Fig. 13]

Fig. 13. Sailors carrying a tun.

The size of a merchant vessel such as MAYFLOWER was measured in terms of how many of these barrels could be safely carried in the hold as cargo. MAYFLOWER was capable of carrying 180 of these large barrels. So this was not a tiny ship as some authors in the past have indicated. In fact, she would have been one of the large merchant vessels of her day.

Some authors have also suggested the MAYFLOWER was a dull sailor, making very slow progress in her voyage. This, again, is a misconception. She made the crossing in 66 days, which would average out to about 2 1/2 miles per hour. The fastest clipper ships a century later were only making a speed of about three miles per hour on this same route.

It must also be remembered that in coming from England to Cape Cod MAYFLOWER was sailing against the strong currents of the Gulf Stream as well as the stormy winds of the North Atlantic. As the fishermen of the day knew all too well, September was the time to seek safe harbors for the winter. Undoubtedly, the Pilgrims had been warned of the dangers which they would face in the North Atlantic if they insisted on beginning their voyage at that time of year. However, their money was at an end — not to mention the fact that the English authorities were still searching for William Brewster, who was concealed in the ship. They had no choice but to continue.

On her return trip to England in the spring of 1621, MAYFLOWER made the voyage in 31 days, which would have been an average speed of about 3 3/4 miles per hour. This demonstrates that MAYFLOWER was not a dull sailor for her time. It should be remembered, also, that on her return trip MAYFLOWER was sailing with the currents of the Gulf Stream in fair weather with the wind at her back, and carrying a much lighter burden of cargo, which allowed her to ride higher in the water.

In reading the accounts of the voyage, one is left with the impression that MAYFLOWER was a fragile ship because a main beam cracked during a storm at sea. However, it must be remembered that she had been used in the merchant trade with France and the Scandanavian countries prior to her voyage to the New World. She had endured the pounding waves of the North Sea as she plied the waters between England and Scandanavia, and that is the most treacherous body of water in the world. Because of its shallow bottom, the waves there can reach gigantic proportions during storms. Master Jones knew that if MAYFLOWER were strong enough to brave the North Sea, she was capable of crossing the North Atlantic. This man who designed and built ships would not have ventured to make the North Atlantic voyage in a tiny, creaky, old ship.

SHIP DIMENSIONS

The overall length of MAYFLOWER from stem to stern would have been about ninety feet; her beam (or breadth at the widest part amidships) would have been about twenty-five feet. A ship of these dimensions would have drawn about two-fathom (twelve feet) when loaded — as she would have been on the voyage from England to Cape Cod in 1620. This meant that Master Jones would have had to check his soundings very carefully when approaching landfalls. He had to make certain that the water depth was well over the two fathoms which MAYFLOWER drew in order to avoid the calamitous effects of going aground. Sea-marks in the estuaries, harbors and ports along the coasts of England would have been something Jones knew well. Charts of those areas showed him the soundings and identified the buoyage system then in use. These sea-marks will be discussed in more detail in the section on navigation aids.

DECKS

The middle part of her main deck, which ran the full length of the ship, was exposed to the weather. This open part of the ship was called the 'waist' of the ship, and canvas 'waist cloths' could be rigged to keep out the spray.

Below the main deck was a gun deck with about five feet of head room, and below the gun deck was the hold. The gun deck would have carried several pieces of ordnance. For a cut-away view of a ship, see Fig. 14.

ORDNANCE

At the time MAYFLOWER made her historic voyage the English merchant ships were in bitter competition with both the French and Spanish. We know that there were even untrustworthy English pirates

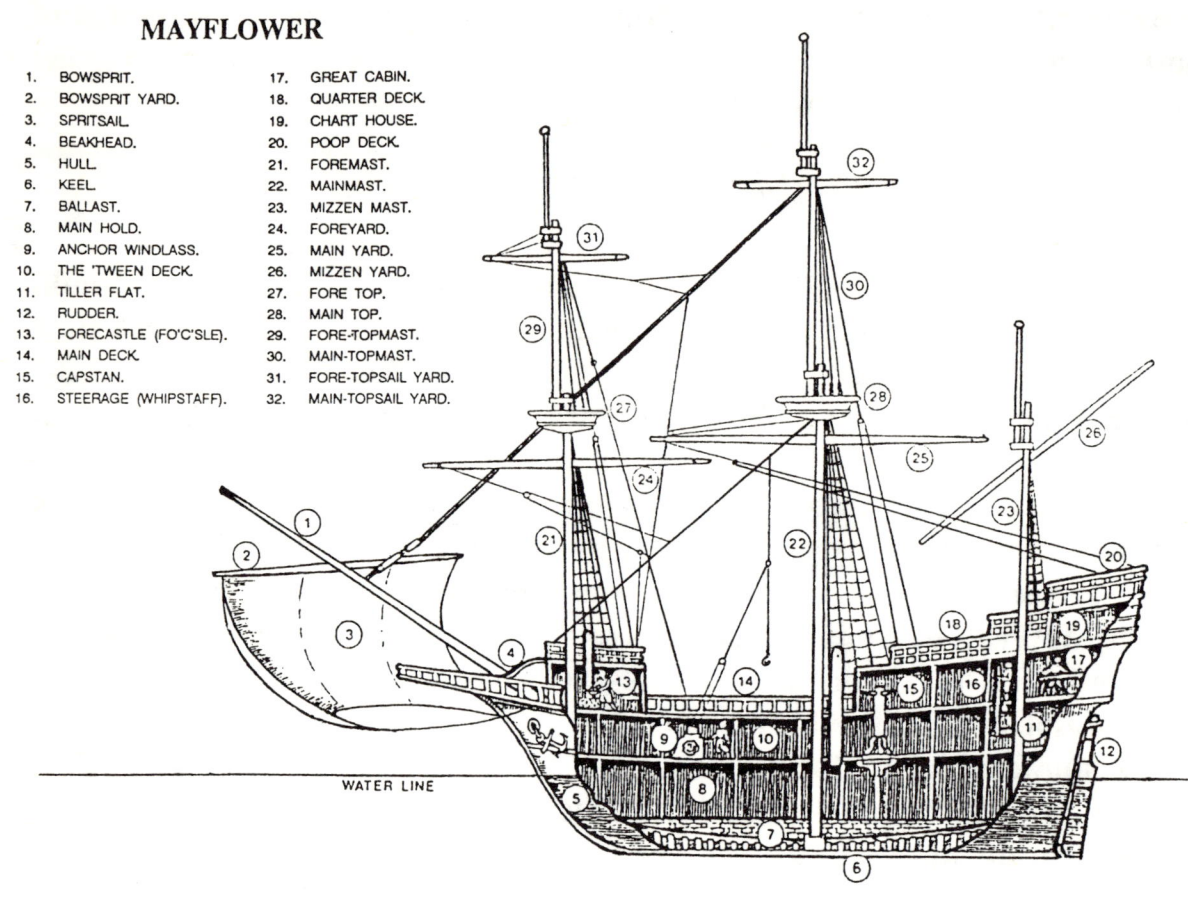

Fig. 14. Cut-away of MAYFLOWER.

along the southwestern coasts of the Channel, who were expert in luring unsuspecting ships into their lairs. The threat of piracy was always on the mind of every merchantship master in those days, and every merchant ship of that day would have been armed, even in time of peace.

MAYFLOWER was no exception. She would have carried several long guns called 'minions,' which fired cannon-balls about 3 1/2 inches in diameter and weighing about four or five pounds. In addition, she probably carried some lighter pieces called 'sakers.' Some of the larger guns were later mounted on the fort at Plymouth. A ship venturing out to sea in those days would have also carried muskets and cutlasses on racks for the men to use in case of a fight at sea.

At each end of the ship were high superstructures. The forward one at the bow was called the forecastle (pronounced 'fo'c'sle') where the crew would have lived under normal conditions, and the cook would have had his galley. The larger sterncastle or 'poop' had two short decks — one above the other. The lower level would have housed the shipmaster and his mates in the 'great cabin'; the upper level would have housed the officers and perhaps the charthouse. In both of these cabins there would have been built-in bunks for the officers and more important persons on board. In this area would have been the 'breadroom,' where the flour and hardtack were stored, because it would have been the driest part of the ship.

The steerage was located on the main deck level between the great cabin and the main mast — partially protected by the upper deck of the poop. Here the helmsman steered the ship by means of a 'whipstaff,' which was a large vertical beam attached to the tiller below. The helmsman's view was obstructed by the mainmast and the forecastle in front of him, and the side walls around him. [Fig. 15] Although he had a compass on the binnacle before him to steer by, he was dependant in large measure upon the commands which were called down to him by an officer on the deck above him, who had an open view. Thus, the helmsman was 'conned' by the ship's master or by one of the two master's mates.

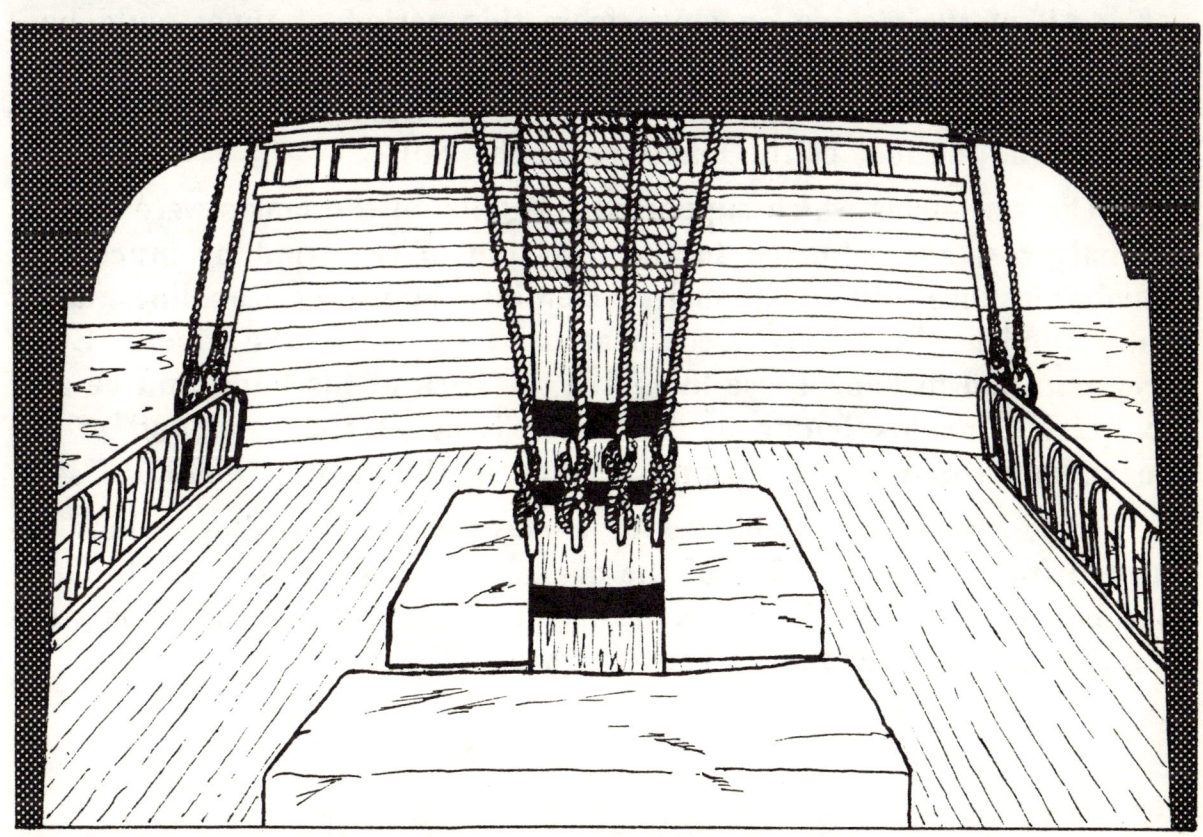

Fig. 15. The helmsman's view.

MASTS

MAYFLOWER would have carried three masts. The mainmast was the middle one, which with its main topmast would have extended about one hundred feet above the water. The mainmast and the main-topmast each carried large, square sails. Above the main-topmast was a flagstaff which carried the British ensign, now called the Union Jack.

The foremast and fore-topmast would have been about twelve feet shorter than the mainmast. These foremasts each carried sails, similar in shape but smaller than those on the main. Topping the foremast was another flagstaff, which would have carried the flag of England, known as the Cross of St. George — a red cross on a white field.

The mizzenmast towards the stern of the ship would have been about sixty feet tall with a forty-foot yard slung diagonally across it. The mizzenmast carried a triangular shaped sail known as the fore-and-aft lateen sail.

RIGGING

All of the rigging on ships from this period of time would have been of hemp. In all there were probably seventy-five different lines in the running rigging of MAYFLOWER. These lines were secured to belaying pins at the foot of the masts or at the rail.

The yard-arms which supported the sails on the masts were hoisted by halyards, and adjusted to the direction of the wind by braces. A number of lines with names such as clewlines, buntlines, leachlines, tacks, sheets and bowlines were used to adjust the sails to the winds. Every crewman had to know these lines like the back of his hand and be able to quickly lay his hands on the right lines at the command of the boastswain (pronounced 'bosun') — even in the dark of night.

The masts were stabilized by a network of heavy lines which extended from the upper part of the masts to the hull of the ship. These shrouds were crossed by ropes (called 'ratlines') which served as steps for the sailors when they needed to go aloft.

5. THE CREW

A merchant ship such as MAYFLOWER would have carried a crew of about thirty or more. These crewmen were ranked from the shipmaster to the lowliest young boys of eleven or twelve years of age who were shipping out to sea for the first time. In John Smith's *Sea Grammar* published in 1627 we are told 'The Master and his Mates are to direct the course, command all the Sailors, for steering, trimming, and sailing the ship. The Master's place is midship.' Master Jones might have been 'midship' as Smith states, or he might well have taken his place on the half-deck of the poop — just above the helmsman, where he could easily order the ship. As already stated, Christopher Jones was an experienced man of the sea, who knew MAYFLOWER well. He understood the complexities of shipbuilding as well as how to command a ship in every situation. He was of good birth from a family which knew the sea, of relation by marriage to well-known mariners, of citizen rank, of the rank of burgess for life, a recognized designer and builder of ships, and of sea training and experience which ranked him high in both Harwich and London.

THE MATES

Smith tells us, 'the Mates are only the master's seconds. Sometimes referred to as the two mid ships men. The place of the ... Mates was amidship.'

THE FIRST MATE

The first mate was John Clarke. Alexander Brown tells us that John Clarke was a native of London, and of the Anglican Church. He was born about 1575 and was a pilot by profession. From surviving records we know that John Clarke was in Málaga, Spain in 1609, and sailed again from London with Thomas Dale for Virginia in March of 1611. Thomas Dale took a fleet of ships to Jamestown with the instructions to create and keep order in that colony. Dale was known to be a strict and even harsh man, and to be a pilot under his supervision would have required a competent seaman.

In the summer of 1611 Clarke was seized at James River by the Spanish and imprisoned. According to his own account, Clarke was seized at Point Comfort, and carried off with his feet kicking in the air. First taken to Havana and imprisoned, he was later transferred to Madrid where he remained in prison for four years. During his interrogations, he readily revealed information about sailing routes across the Atlantic and how to cross the ocean without delay at the Azores, which had been common practice. This testimony in itself reveals his expert knowledge as a pilot.

In 1616 Clarke was exchanged for a Spanish prisoner being held in England. He made another voyage to Virginia with cattle before returning to London, where he was seeking berth at the time Jones and MAYFLOWER were being chartered by the Pilgrims. There is reason to believe that he sailed with the freebooter Captain Thomas Jones in 1619. Azel Ames tells us that John Clarke had been in the employ of the First (or London) Virginia Company, and had just returned to England in June, 1620, from a voyage to Virginia with Captain Thomas Jones in FALCON, when he was employed by Weston and Cushman for the voyage to New England.

From the Minutes of the London Virginia Company of Wednesday, February 13/23, 1621/2, the following information is given concerning John Clarke: "The Master Deputy acquainted the Court, that one Master John Clarke being taken from Virginia long since by a Spanish ship that came to discover the Plantation, that forasmuch as he hath since that time done the Company good service in many voyages to Virginia; and, of late [1619] went into Ireland, for the transportation of cattle to Virginia; he was a humble suitor to this Court that he might be a Free brother of the Company and have some shares of land bestowed upon him." John Clarke was then admitted a freeman to the Company and received two shares.

Azel Ames comments that John Clarke seems to have had the ability to impress men favorably and secure their confidence, and to have been a modest and reliable man. It is possible that he was the John Clarke who was baptized at Redcliffe in 1575. He was probably between thirty and forty-five years of age, thoroughly seasoned, and knew the way to America without stopping at the Azores. He was not mentioned in the affairs of the Pilgrims after he was hired on as 'pilot' on Saturday afternoon 10 June 1620. It was not until the third party of exploration set out that John Clarke appeared as one of the company who put out in the shallop to seek the harbor, which had been described and recommended by Robert Coppin. Coppin was variously called 'the second mate' and the 'bosun.' On this exploration the party narrowly escaped shipwreck at the mouth of Plymouth Harbor and found shelter on an island, which was named in Clarke's honor.

Clarke is not mentioned again in the records of the Pilgrims, although we know that he survived the 'great sickness' in which half of the ship's company died. In November of 1621 he went to Virginia again (as pilot or mate) on FLYING HART, and in 1623 attained command of PROVIDENCE, which sailed to Virginia in April 1623. He died there soon after his arrival.

THE SECOND MATE

Just who served as second mate may never be known. Many authorities seem to place Robert Coppin as second master's mate. However, the answer is yet to be resolved. In telling the story of the third exploration of discovery, Bradford says: 'and there hasted to a place that their pillote (one Mr. Coppin who had bine in the cuntrie before) did assure them was a good harbor, which he had been in, and they might fetch it by night...' A little further in the text, Bradford continues: 'But it came too, the pillott was deceived in the place, and said, the Lord be mercifull unto them, for his eyes never saw that place before and the master mate would have rune her ashore...' This last statement would seem to indicate that Robert Coppin was not a master's mate, since it makes a distinction between the 'pillott' Mr. Coppin and the 'masters mate.' This latter statement could also be interpreted to mean that there was only one master's mate, since Bradford specifically says, 'the master mate,' although it could also be interpreted that only one of the master's mates was present at the time. On the other hand, in *Mourt's Relation* Winslow says that Francis Billington went with 'one of the master's mates' to locate the body of water which would later be known as Billington's Sea. This reference would seem to verify that there was more than one master's mate.

Thomas Clarke may have been the name of the second mate. Thomas was born in 1599, making him twenty-one at the time of the voyage. Thomas Clarke lies buried on Cemetery Hill at Plymouth, Massachusetts. The large grave marker gives his age as 98 at the time of his death in 1697. The marker reads in part: "Thomas Clarke was mate of the Mayflower according to tradition in Plymouth and Connecticut colonies. Arrived in Plymouth in the Ship Anne in 1623." Charles E. Banks believes tradition to be in error about Thomas Clarke's rank on MAYFLOWER.

Much more research needs to be done in finding an answer to this question.

PILOTS

The pilots were responsible for taking charge of the ship when they made landfall, bringing the ship into harbor. Both Allerton and Ellis were hired by the Pilgrims with the intent that they would have charge of SPEEDWELL. Even though that ship was abandoned in England, these two master mariners continued on to New England. The original thought seems to have been that they would have charge of the shallop for fishing purposes.

THE BOATSWAIN (Bosun)

John Smith states: 'The Boatswain was to have charge of all the cordage, tackling, sails, fids and marling spikes, needles, twine, sail-cloth and the rigging for the ship.' As already stated, the Pilgrim records indicate that Robert Coppin served in this capacity on MAYFLOWER in its historic voyage to the New World.

Robert Coppin was listed in the Second Charter of the Virginia Company as a Subscriber who paid 12 pounds 10 shillings. He had been on a voyage to the New England coast sometime before sailing on MAYFLOWER. However, we have no such biography for Robert Coppin as we have for John and Thomas Clarke. The name is an old seafaring one. In Elizabethan Harwich there was a Captain John Coppin, a well known mariner. The Coppin name appears from time to time in several records in connection with the New World.

THE SHIP SURGEON

John Smith tells us that the surgeon was to be exempted from all duties other than attending to the sick and curing the wounded. He further states: 'Good care would be had to have a certificate from Barbers Chirurgion Hall of his sufficiency, and also that his chest be well furnished both for Physicks and Chirurgery, and so near as may be proper for that clime you ago for, which neglect hath been the losse of many a man's life.'

We know the name of the ship surgeon, Giles Heale, only from the fact that he signed the will of William Mullins at Cape Cod. Giles Heale, the young ship surgeon on MAYFLOWER, had been licensed in 1619 by the Company of Barber-Surgeons. Thomas Weston had found him in his own London parish of St. Giles-in-the-Field. He may not have been a 'true surgeon', however, he probably received training in surgery, anatomy and the dispensing of internal medicines as part of his education. Little else is known about him except that he returned to London and set up a practice in Drury Lane until his death in 1652.

THE COOPER

The ship cooper had the important responsibility of constantly checking the casks and barrels in the hold to make certain that the provisions were secure and in good condition. He was also responsible for staving or repairing buckets, baricos, cans, steep tubs, runlets, hogsheads, pipes, butts, etc., which contained the wine, beer, cider, beverages, fresh water or any other liquor. Because wood was in such short supply in England, the cooper was also responsible for seeing that wood was sent back to England on the returning ship to replace any casks and barrels which were left with the colony.

We know from Pilgrim records that John Alden was hired in this capacity. John was a 21-year-old youth at the time of the voyage. There may have been a family connection to Christopher Jones through the Russell-Gardener-Alden family tree of Harwich. It has not been established to the satisfaction of all authorities that John lived in Southampton as some have assumed. His father, who was conceivably George Alden, an arrow-maker, died just before the Pilgrim voyage. It is well known that John signed on at Southampton. He had probably completed his apprenticeship in order to be signed on in such a responsible position.

OTHERS

The remaining crew consisted of the master gunner and his mate who were in charge of the ordnance, shot, powder, match, ladles, sponges, worms, cartridges, arms and fireworks. From Pilgrim writings we know that these officers were among the crew of MAYFLOWER. The boatswaine's mate was in charge of the long boat, which was used for setting of the anchors, weighing and fetching them home, warping, towing, or mooring. Of the ship carpenter Smith tells us: 'The Carpenter and his Mate were to have the nails, clinches, roove, clinch nails, leather, saws, files, hatchets, adzes, etc. They were responsible for caulking, breaming, stopping leaks, fishing, or splicing the masts or yard whenever occasion required.' We have no names for these crewmen, but Smith tells us the carpenter was usually nicknamed 'Chips.'

The ship cook was in charge of feeding the crew in shifts as their duty on watch permitted. Here, again, we have no name, but Smith tells us that the cook was generally nicknamed 'Cookie.'

Other crew members would have included the master mariners, the ordinary seamen, the younkers and the grummets. The younkers were young men between the ages of fifteen and twenty, who were responsible for taking in the topsails, for furling sails, or slinging yards. These were the strong, young men who could easily climb and haul, and were sometimes referred to as the 'foremast men.' The grummets were the young boys between the ages of eight and eleven who were just beginning their lives at sea. Generally, they served as cabin boys and performed menial tasks. The master's mates would have taken charge of overseeing their education. We have no evidence that there were grummets in the crew of MAYFLOWER.

Fig. 16. MAYFLOWER under sail.

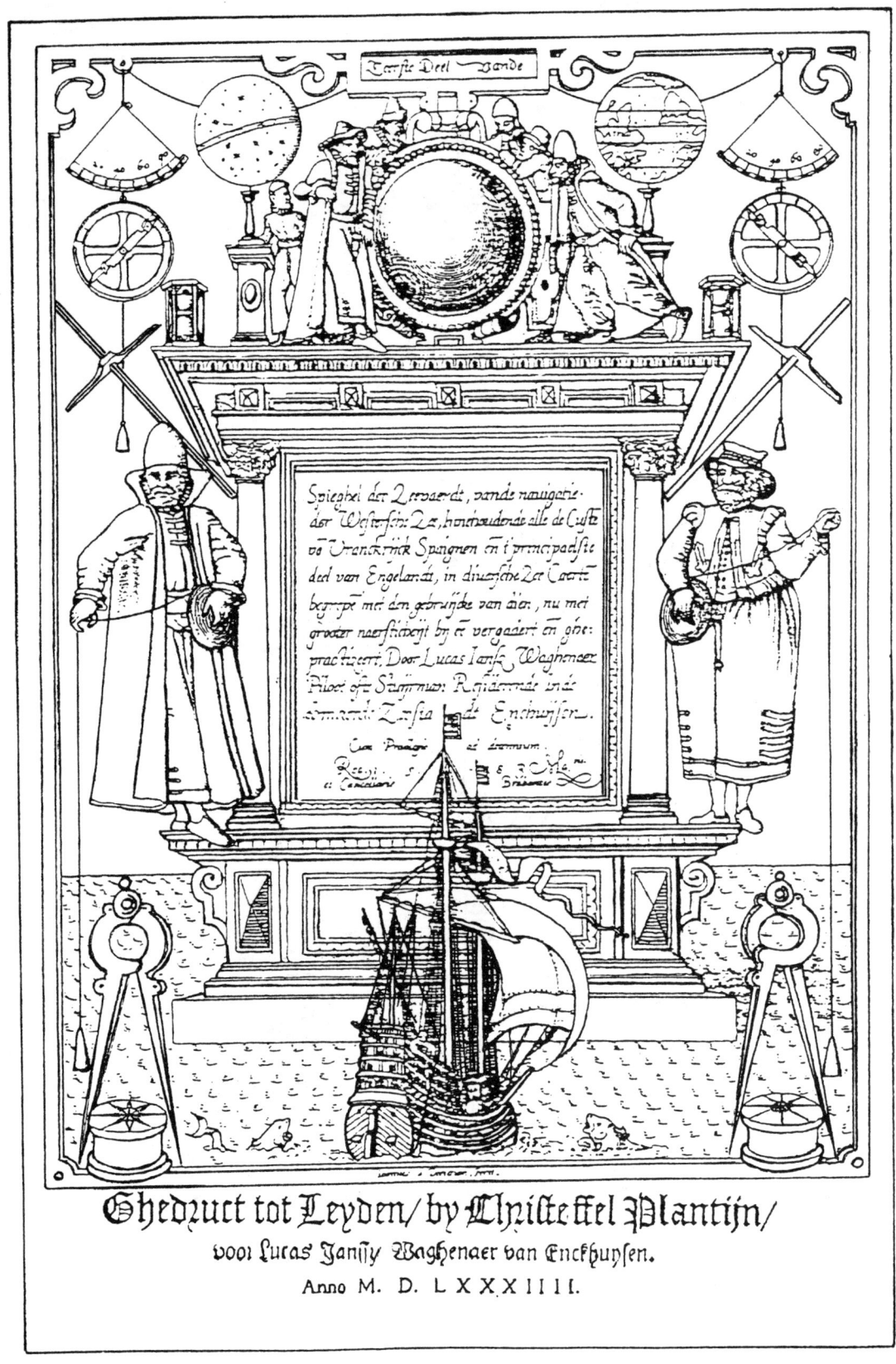

Fig. 17. Title page of *The Mariners Mirrour*, 1584.

6. THE LEAD LINES

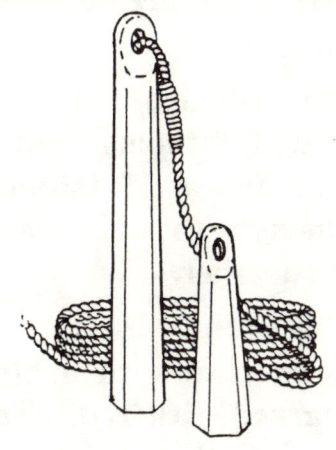

The following sections will concern themselves with the various navigation instruments which were available to the shipmasters, pilots and navigators during the Golden Age of Discovery. A number of these instruments are depicted in the engraving which serves as a title page of *The Mariners Mirrour*, published in 1584 by Lucas Janszoon Waghenaer and translated for an English publication in 1588 by Anthony Ashley. [Fig. 17]

One of the most important things a pilot must know is the depth of the water beneath the keel, especially in rivers, harbors, bays and shallow coastal waters. This information would be of vital importance when entering or leaving port, or when approaching an unfamiliar land mass, to make certain the ship did not run aground.

Probably the most ancient of all instruments used by early pilots was some kind of tool for testing water depth. The early pilots may have used poles or early forms of the lead line to test the water depths. The mariners during the Age of Discovery used two types of lead-lines when approaching an area where the depth of the water was in question.

THE HAND LEAD LINE

The hand lead line would have been used in areas where the water depth was not more than 120 feet or 20 fathoms. [One fathom is equal to six feet.] Capt. John Smith described the hand lead-line in his *Sea Grammar* of 1627 as 'a long plummet, made hollow, wherein is put tallow.' Sir Henry Mainwaring, writing his *Seaman's Dictionary* between 1620 and 1623 (not published until 1644), gave much the same description. For a cut-away view of the lead 'plummet', see Fig. 18.

Both Smith and Mainwaring agreed that the sounding lead (used

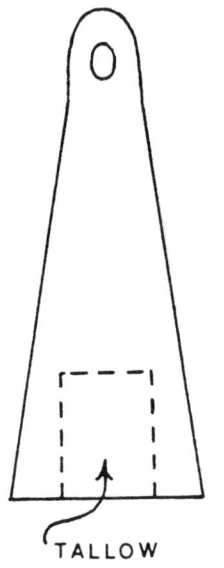

Fig. 18. Cut-away of a sounding lead.

in shallow or shoal water of less than 20 fathoms) was a seven pound weight about a foot long. The weight of the lead may have ranged somewhere between five and seven pounds. The early lead plummets were generally of a conical or pyramid shape, but there are also examples from the period which are six-sided as in Fig. 22.

In its early form the hand lead line was marked at 2 fathoms and 3 fathoms with a black leather, at 5 fathoms and at 15 fathoms with white cloth, at 7 fathoms with a red cloth, and at 10 fathoms with a leather.

The later line differed only in the 13 fathom mark, which was marked with a blue cloth, and 17 fathoms marked with red. The 20 fathom mark was two knots in a piece of string or 'house line' as Smith called it. [Fig. 19] Some later lead lines seem to have added a mark at 25 fathoms, indicated with one knot.

The hand lead line for 20 fathoms was marked as follows:

    2 fathoms: two strips of leather.
    3 fathoms: three strips of leather.
    5 fathoms: a piece of white cloth (usually cotton).
    7 fathoms: a piece of red bunting (usually wool).
  10 fathoms: a piece of leather with a hole in it.
  13 fathoms: a piece of blue serge.
  15 fathoms: a piece of white duck.
  17 fathoms: a piece of red bunting.
  20 fathoms: a piece of 'house line' with two knots.
  25 fathoms: a piece of 'house line' with one knot.

The markings were placed on the lead line when it was wet, and the accuracy was checked regularly to detect any changes in the length of the line. Sometimes the lead lines were marked at each foot near critical depths for the vessel with which it was used in order to further insure that they did not run aground.

When the marking nearest the surface could not be seen by the leadsman from his position in the chains, the distance from the hand (or waist level) of the leadsman to the water's surface had to be deter-

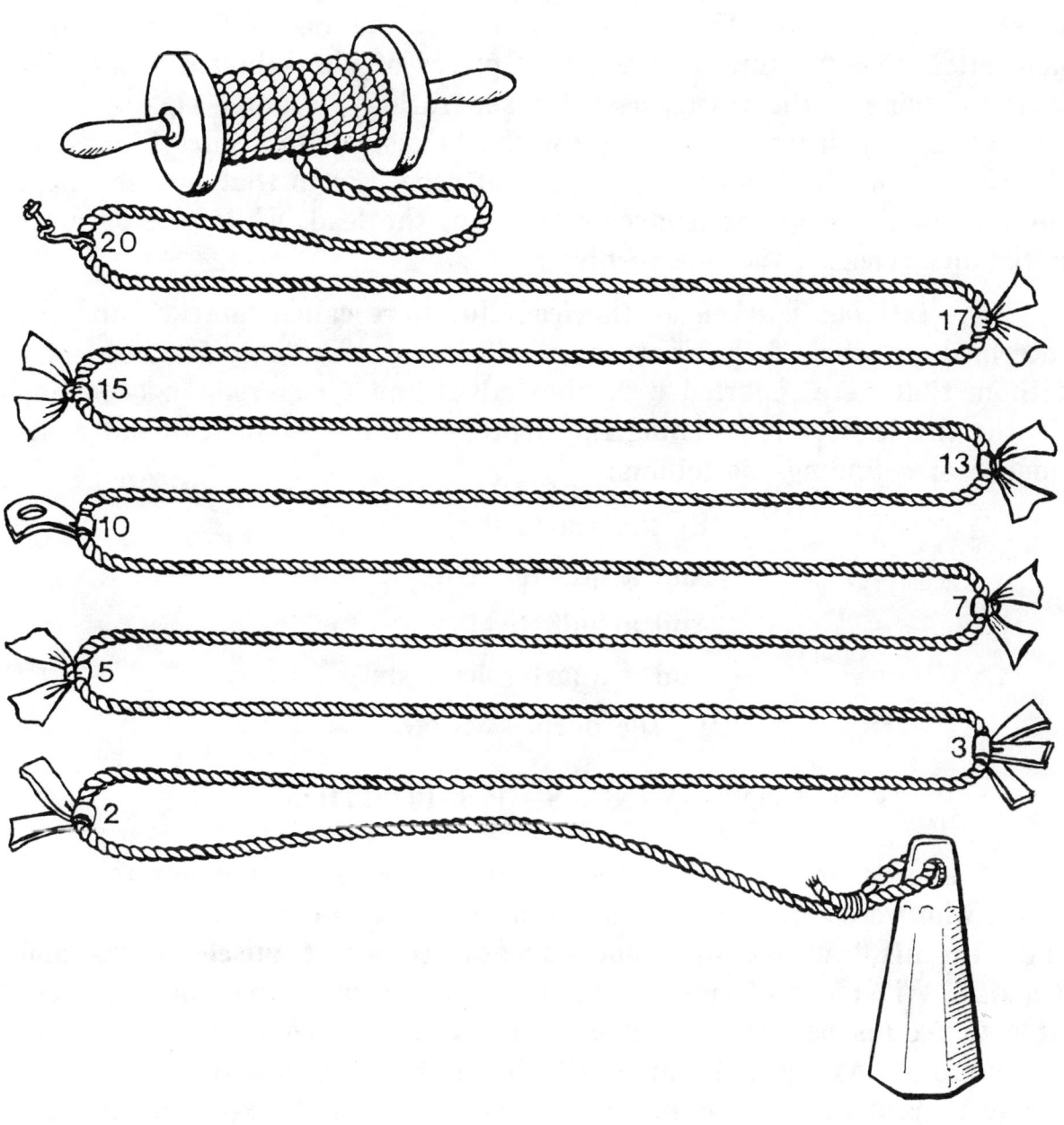

Fig. 19. Markings on a hand lead line.

mined so that the correct allowance could be made for an accurate sounding.

The leadsman's station when taking soundings was in the chains as shown in Fig. 20. The 'chaines' was a shortening of the term channel-wailes. The Channels were broad pieces of plank bolted lengthwise to the outside of the vessel, used for separating the lower rigging. For his own safety, it was customary for the helmsman to secure himself to the shrouds or deadeyes with a length of rope. From that position near the bow of the ship the leadsman cast out the lead, while one or more assistants released the line to him.

The fathoms marked on the lead line were called 'marks', and the intermediate whole fathoms were called 'deeps'. The only fractions of a fathom that were reported were the halves and quarters. In reporting depths the leadsman watching the depth markings would call out a sequence of soundings as follows:

>'By the mark, five!'
>
>'And a quarter, five!'
>
>'And a half, five!'
>
>'And a quarter less, six!'
>
>'By the deep, six!' etc.

CONFIRMING SHIP'S POSITION

A knowledge of the sea bottom was extremely important to those pilots who were sailing the opaque waters of the northern seas. By testing with his lead-line the pilot was able to locate unseen rocks and shoals. When out of sight of land or on overcast days the pilot was able to fix his position by detecting the contours, color and texture of the bottom. As the fishermen still do in those waters, the pilot could locate himself by the contours, color, smell, taste and texture of the seabed.

In order to bring up samples of the type of seabed over which the ship was sailing, a cavity was drilled into the bottom of the sounding lead. Into the cavity in the bottom of the lead weight was placed a hard, white tallow — except when it was used on a soft, oozy bottom. In the event of ooze the weight was 'armed' with white woolen cloth which had been saturated with yellow tallow.

Fig. 20. Leadsman using the sounding lead.

When MAYFLOWER began her historic voyage and sailed from her mooring at Rotherhithe down the Thames River, Master Jones would have picked up an official pilot at Gravesend, who would have command of the ship as she passed over the dangerous shoal waters of the Thames estuary. That pilot would have known (by sight) all of the land and sea marks. In addition he would have been familiar with the range bearings which he must maintain in the channels. Range bearings consisted of two or more landmarks which he had to keep lined up in his sight in order to maintain a safe course between the shallows. In addition to this, the leadsman would have been calling out the depths as the ship threaded her way toward open water. Once MAYFLOWER was safely piloted to open water, the pilot of MAYFLOWER would have taken command, and the official pilot of the Thames estuary would have disembarked.

Every shipmaster or pilot provisioned himself with a pilot book, or rutter, which included charts of the areas in which he was accustomed to sailing. On the charts would be indicated the soundings and type of sea bed to be encountered.

MAYFLOWER's pilot was undoubtedly a man with a thorough knowledge of the English channel. As MAYFLOWER made her way south and west to the ports of Southampton, Dartmouth and Plymouth, the pilot could confirm his position by the depths of the soundings and the type of seabed beneath him by comparing the samples to those listed in his charts.

As she proceeded westward through the Channel, MAYFLOWER would have passed over seabeds described in the pilot books as 'pobbles (pebbles) bygge as beanes' at 30 to 40 fathoms, 'dyntes and cliftes in the talowe lyke small threade' at 35 to 60 fathoms.

In the areas south of Plymouth the samples would have come up as 'small blacke sand' at 50 to 60 fathoms.

Sailing south of the Scilly Islands, the leadsman may have brought up samples of red sand, or (if closer to shore) 'stones and shells'. If the sample came up 'stones and fine sand', Master Jones would have known that MAYFLOWER had come near the point at which the Channel pilot could be relieved. As she reached the western extremity of the Channel and approached the edge of the continental shelf, the leadsman on MAYFLOWER would have drawn up samples of 'fine blacke speckled sands' as the ship proceeded into the open waters of the Atlantic.

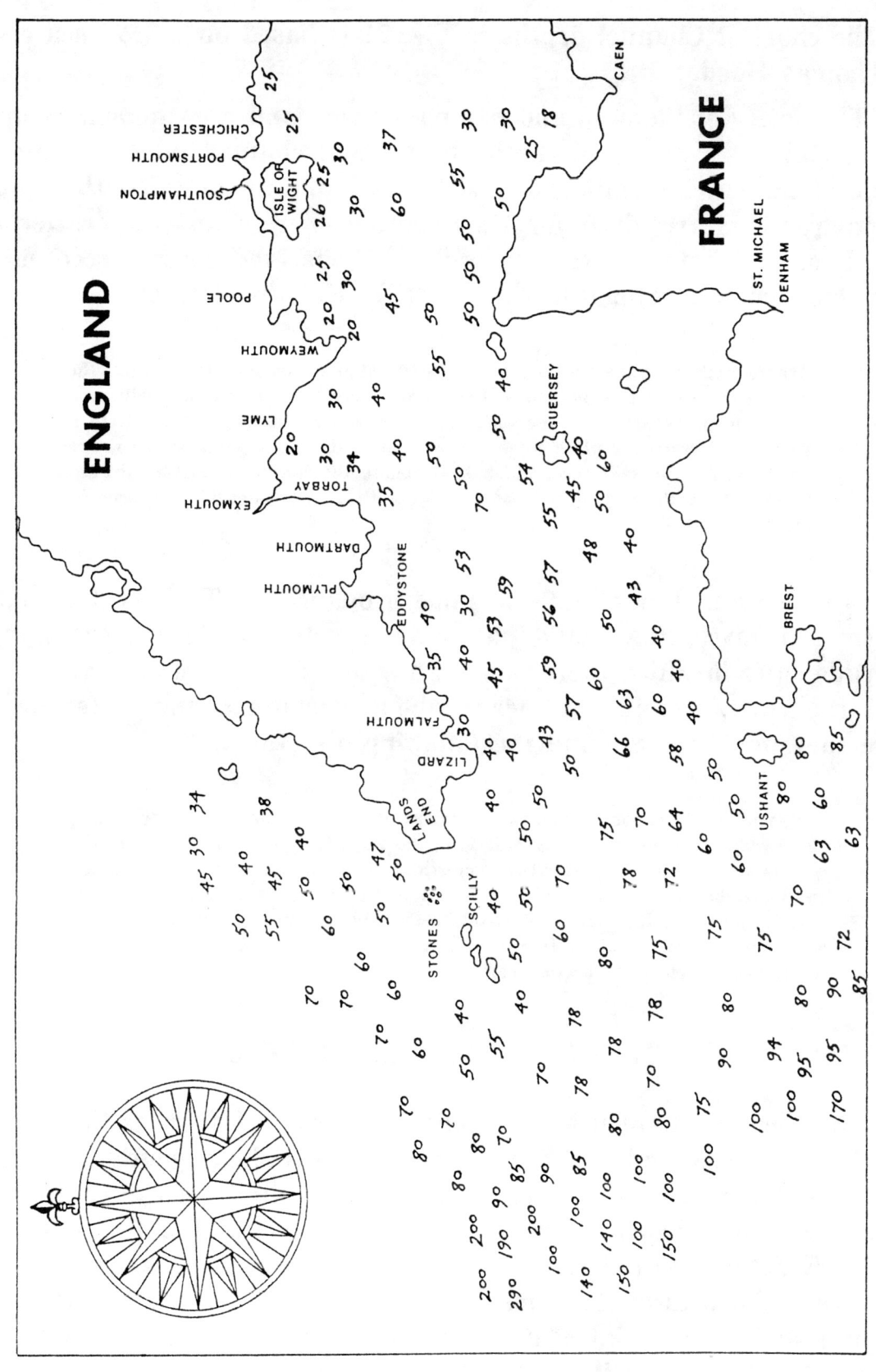

Fig. 21. Chart of the English Channel.

The chart of Channel depths in Fig. 21 is based on a 1596 sea chart by Thomas Hood.

The safety of the ship and her passengers and crew depended upon the careful observations of the leadsman and channel pilot. As an example of the specific sailing directions available to the pilot, the following instructions are given for Dartmouth haven in an early rutter (or pilot book). Master Jones may well have observed these directions as they returned to Dartmouth with SPEEDWELL in distress.

> "There lyeth a blinde rock on the east-side of the haven of Dartmouth, the markes to sayle out of the danger thereof are these, there is a redde point east of Dartmouth which upon the water is black, and in the redde there lyeth a white stone, when the white stone is over against the black point, then you are right against the said rock, which lyeth before the haven of Dartmouth, but when you see the Kaye [quay] of the village then . . . you shall not sayle by the stone."

As Master Jones and the pilot brought MAYFLOWER into the Dartmouth haven they would have been careful to observe the sample of redde sand in which there was a white stone. They would, also, have read the rutter carefully to learn about anchorage and water depth. Here they would have found the following directions.

> "To sayle into Dartmouth when you come out of the west, you must sayle so long about east, or along by the west-side until the Kaye [quay] of the village, (which lyeth on the west-side of the haven) commeth in the middle between both the lands, and be readie with your boat, if the winde should change to whirle, that you might towe in, and then turn on the west-side before the brewhouse and anchor at 10 or 12 fathome, for within it is a wide haven, and you may as well anker before the village as before the brewhouse."

THE DEEP SEA LEAD LINE

The English Channel is on a continental shelf, known as the 'soundings.' Between Ireland and Brittany the Channel slopes gently to a depth of about 100 fathoms (600 feet). At the outer limits of the continental shelf the bottom drops abruptly to immense depths. For this reason it is clearly defined by the 100 fathom lead and line. This knowledge was of extreme importance to a mariner approaching the edge of the continental shelf. The point of demarcation is only ten or twenty miles off the coast of Spain and Portugal. At other places it is hundreds of miles to the seaward. From the Lizard it lies 200 miles on the arc of the southwest quadrant.

For the deep sea (pronounced 'dipsie') lead line the lead weight or 'plummet' was attached to a line 150 fathoms in length, marked first at 20 fathoms and then every 10 fathoms with so many small knots in strings fixed to each mark. Sir Henry Mainwaring, writing about the lead line in his *Seaman's Dictionary*, gave the weight of the plummet as 14 pounds, but gave the line length as 200 fathoms. The longer line would have been more useful to those mariners who were sailing the western end of the Channel as they departed or returned from the Atlantic. For a comparison of the leads for the dipsie line and the sounding line, see Fig. 22.

The hand lead line could be used for soundings while the ship was under way because it was short. However, to use the deep sea ('dipsie') line for sounding, the ship was hove-to, and the sounding was taken either from a small boat, or was taken from the forward chains of the ship.

The line was coiled at intervals along the weather side of the deck or poop. One of the crew was stationed at each coil. Under the watchful eye of the shipmaster the lead was cast overboard. As the coil ran out at each location along the deck, the crewman called out to the next man behind him, "Watch, there, watch!"

When the line ceased to run out and came to a full stop, then simply bounced up and down when lifted and dropped, the depth was taken. If the line ran its full length without stopping, the call went out, "No bottom!"

Once MAYLOWER had passed beyond the western edge of the continental shelf, the lead lines would not have been used until Master Jones believed he was in range of the New World.

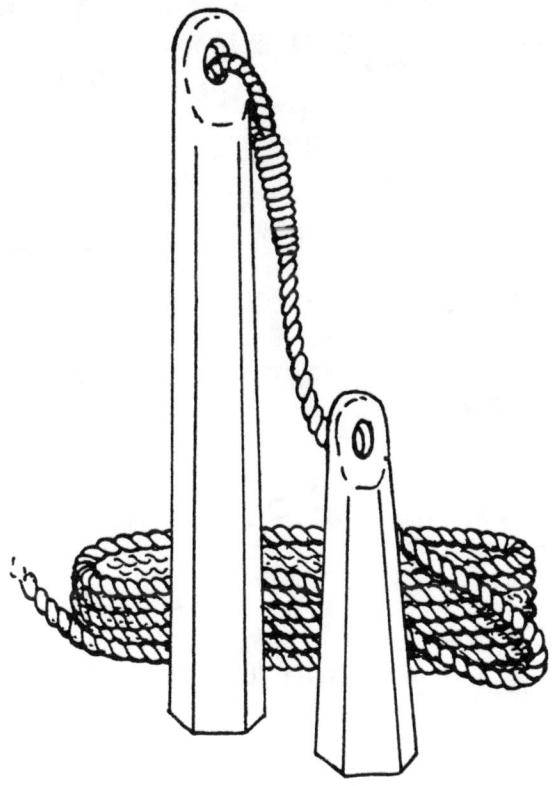

Fig. 22. Dipsie lead (l.) and Hand lead (r).

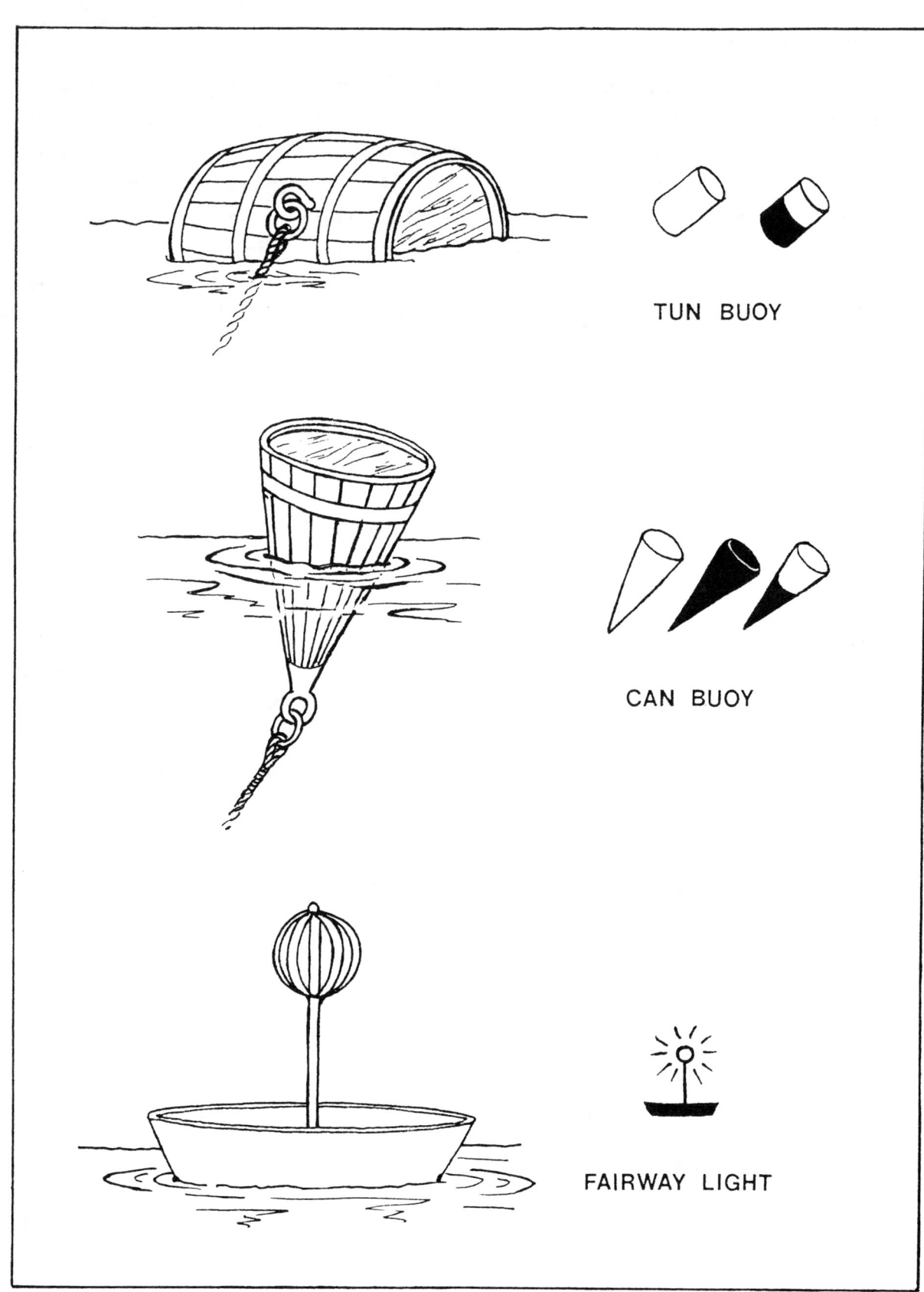

Navigation aids and chart symbols.

7. NAVIGATION AIDS

During the Age of Discovery, the merchant ships of Europe sailed year round. Those shipmasters had braved the autumn storms and winter gales of the English Channel for generations, carrying vintage wines from Bordeaux and the Bay of Biscay. As a result, they had become inured to the hardships of the sea in all seasons.

Some merchant shipmasters specialized in their various cargoes. The shipmasters of Southampton and Bristol traded chiefly to the southwest with the French and Spanish Biscay ports as well as the ports and islands of Spain and Portugal. Some of the Southampton shippers also traded cross-Channel, while ships from London were trading with the Netherlands. The men of the east coast ports of Harwich, Yarmouth, Kingston-upon-Hull and Newcastle-upon-Tyne occupied themselves mainly with the fish-carrying trade between Scandanavia, Iceland and the Netherlands in addition to what little trade there was in the Baltic area.

From lifetimes of experience the shipmasters and pilots of the English ports knew the coastlines, landmarks and seamarks which they would encounter in their regular sea routes. The meanings of the navigation aids on their routes were as familiar to them as their own spoken words. They depended on their knowledge of the natural contours of the shorelines with all of their unique features, such as rolling hills, woods, steep cliffs of various colors, rocky coastlines or sandy beaches. Beyond the natural features of the coastlines, there were the man-made features, such as church steeples, castles, or any number of other constructions, which were easily and quickly recognized.

Navigation aids were not new to the shipmasters in the age of Henry VIII and his successors. A Mediterranean sea guide from about 1250 details the use of buoys in the region of Seville and Alexandria, etc. It begins: 'First, from Cape St. Vincent to the mouth of the river of Seville by river is 9 miles. If you wish to take a ship into the river Seville, first take soundings and mark the buoys, and when the tide rises, follow the buoyed channel.' Later we find the following: 'Coming from Cape Finisterre sailing NNE, if you have 80 fathoms you are 20 leagues from the shore and the ground is small black stones with great red sand . . .' Notice that such references also give us the information that soundings with 'armed' leads were being taken at that early period.

MARITIME ORGANIZATIONS

The pilot's profession is not much younger than that of navigation. The Bible tells that Hiram of Tyre (I Kings 9:27) provided pilots for King Solomon. In the first century A.D. fishermen of the Gulf of Cambay, India, were meeting seagoing vessels and guiding them into port.

In England organizations of shipmen were formed in early times for overseeing the welfare and conduct of their fellow mariners, and to supervise the selection and work quality of pilots in the various ports.

In 1514 Henry VIII licensed the Corporation of the Trinity House of Deptford Strand for the purpose of advancing navigation and commerce. The Trinity House of Deptford was established as the authority for navigation aids, to train, license and regulate the English pilots, and to supply pilots as ships made their way into the Thames estuary and upriver to the London docks. The first dry-dock in the world was built at Portsmouth in 1495. Other than that, the royal dockyards were all on the Thames or on the Medway which flows into the Thames estuary.

The licensing of Trinity House was done to safeguard both royal and merchant ships from damage and loss. However, it was learned that these measures needed strengthening. Inspired by the example set by the mariners who established Trinity House of Deptford Strand, the mariners at Newcastle-upon-Tyne applied for a similar charter.

In 1541 the Trinity House of Kingston-upon-Hull was chartered as a guild exclusively for shipmasters similar to those at Deptford and Newcastle-upon-Tyne. The Trinity House of Hull was authorized to license any mariner who sailed from Hull (according to his competence), and to certify the ports to which he was entitled to sail. All outbound shipmasters were also required to provide the Trinity House with an account of the number of their mariners and, upon returning, to evaluate the behavior of those mariners on the voyage. Furthermore, seamen from other ports were not to be employed at Hull without certification.

England then had three incorporated Trinity Houses which were distinct and independent of one another. There was also an unincorporated guild at Dover. The Trinity House of Deptford Strand was of greatest importance and exerted a strong influence over the others because it was so closely allied with the Royal Navy. Although the charter for Trinity House of Deptford Strand was not renewed by Elizabeth I, the Trinity Houses of Newcastle and Hull received new charters under Edward VI, Mary and Elizabeth I upon their accession to the throne. The charter for Trinity House of Deptford was redrafted and renewed by James I in 1604. It is unfortunate that the many records of Trinity House of Deptford were destroyed in a series of disastrous fires.

LANDMARKS & SEAMARKS

In the eighth year of Elizabeth I's reign (1565) 'An Act concerning Sea-marks and Mariners' was passed. Since the master wardens and assistants of Trinity House of Deptford Strand were the major experts and governors of ships, they were charged with the responsibility of overseeing the building and maintenance of ships, the regulation of all men who traded by water, and the conducting of ships from the Royal Navy.

The Act of 1565 expressed concern over the destruction of certain landmarks in England and Wales, such as steeples, woods, beacons and other identifying marks on the shore which the mariners had used to determine their positions and avoid the dangers of wrecking on shoals, etc. Trinity House was given authority to set up and maintain as many beacons, marks and signs for the shores, heights, and approaches to the ports anywhere on the coasts of England and Wales — and especially the port and river of the Thames — as it was deemed necessary for the safe conduct of shipping. These marks were to be supported out of the shipping dues which Trinity House was entitled to levy. The Act went one step further by prohibiting the destruction of conspicuous landmarks such as steeples, great trees or any other structure which had long been used by mariners for coastal, estuary and port identification.

Some of the navigation aids, which the early seventeenth century shipmaster would have had available to him as he arrived or departed from the Thames estuary, are found in the sailing directions provided by Lucas Janszoon Waghenaer in 1586:

> 'If you will sayle from Margate into the Thames shape your course by North the Foreland to West South West: then on alongst the coast west and west by north to the Reculvers where a ship that draws water must staie for the tide to pass over the Shoaldes called the Lastes, between a buoy and a beakon where is there three fathoms depth. From the buoy set west north west and west by north towards the beakon standing northward (on the Spaniard).'

[See chart in Fig. 23.] Compare these directions with those given for the same area by Jacob Colomne in 1637:

> 'Sayle on so west all alongst the shore until that the Reculvers (which are two steeples in one church) come one in the other and then you shall run in sight of the first buye [buoy] of the Lastes which lieth upon the foresaid marks of the Reculvers; being by it you can also see the other buy [buoy] which lieth like as the first also on the north side, and over against on the south side standeth a beakon (on the Horse); there you must saile thro' betwixt them both. From thence you may with little shippes and shippes of little draught at high water run over the Swallow (Swale) on west north west towards Sheppei for it is there Shoale water. When you come by Sheppei runne within two cables length alongst by it for to avoid the tail of the Spaniard until that you be past Quinboro. To saile with shippes of great draught you must when you be past ye buyes upon the Laste sayle thro Fischer's deep towards Black Tayle, which lieth from the second buye upon the Lastes unto the first buye in Fischer's deep (N.W. and N.W. by W.) which lieth upon the north side of the sand men do call the Spaniard, The second buye in the Fischer's deep you must leave on the Starboard side and the buye on the Spaniard on the Larboard. Being past that you come against the Black Tayle and to the Southwards of the Shoe Beken into the Right deepe.'

For coastal routes through the Thames estuary, see the chart in Fig. 24, which is based on charts by Robert Norman in 1580 and Robert Borough in 1588. One of the important landmarks for this route was Reculver Castle, which still stands today. [Fig. 25]

BUOYAGE

In addition to land-marks and beacons at the various ports of England, the shipmaster had buoys to mark his way. The responsibility for the laying and maintenance of buoys rested with the Lord High Admiral who represented the Crown. He was given authority to levy 'buoyage' and 'beaconage' to defray the cost involved.

The wooden buoys were of two types. The 'tuns' were very large barrel-shaped buoys which were floated on their sides. The 'can-buoys'

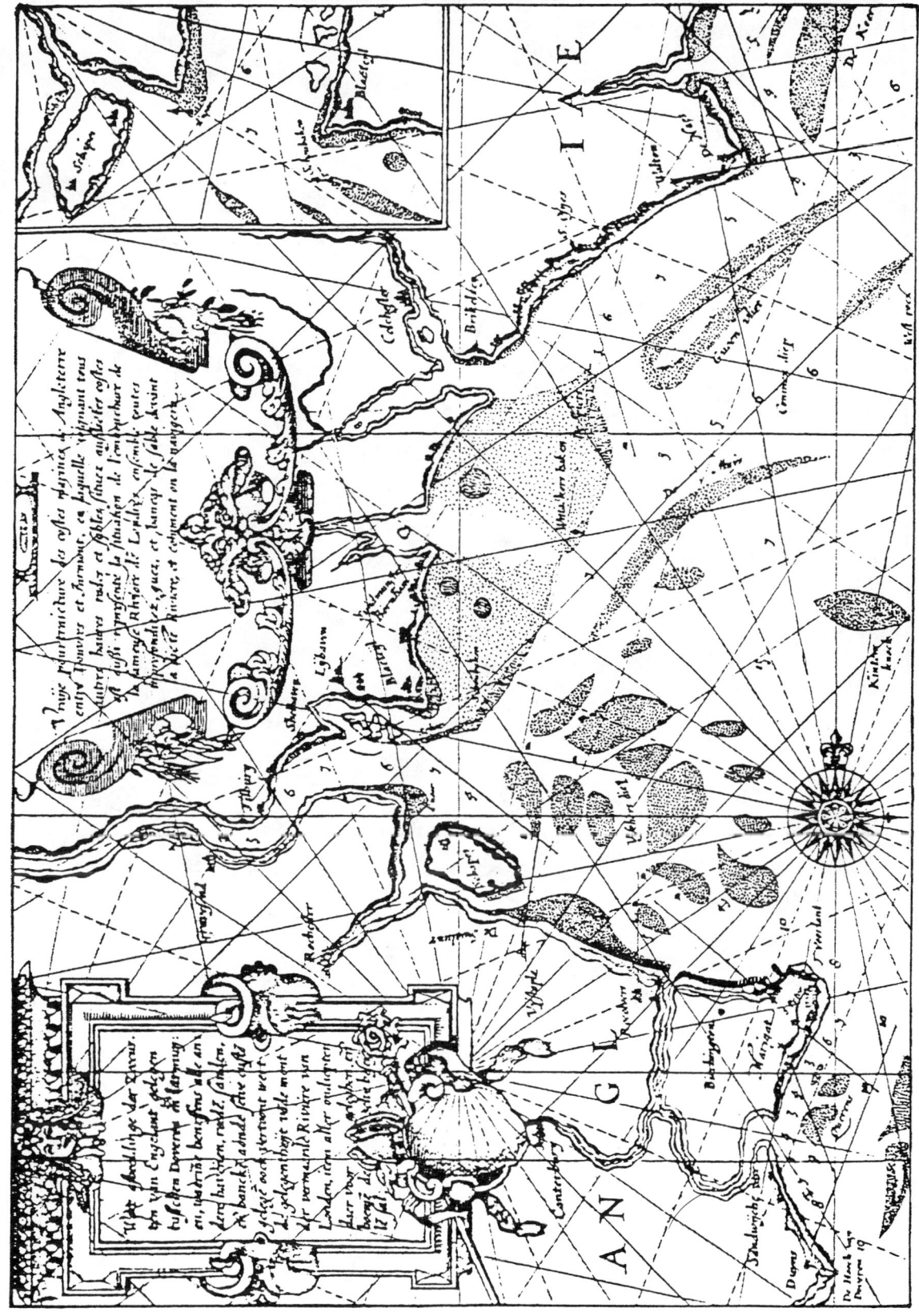

Fig. 23. Chart of the Thames estuary.

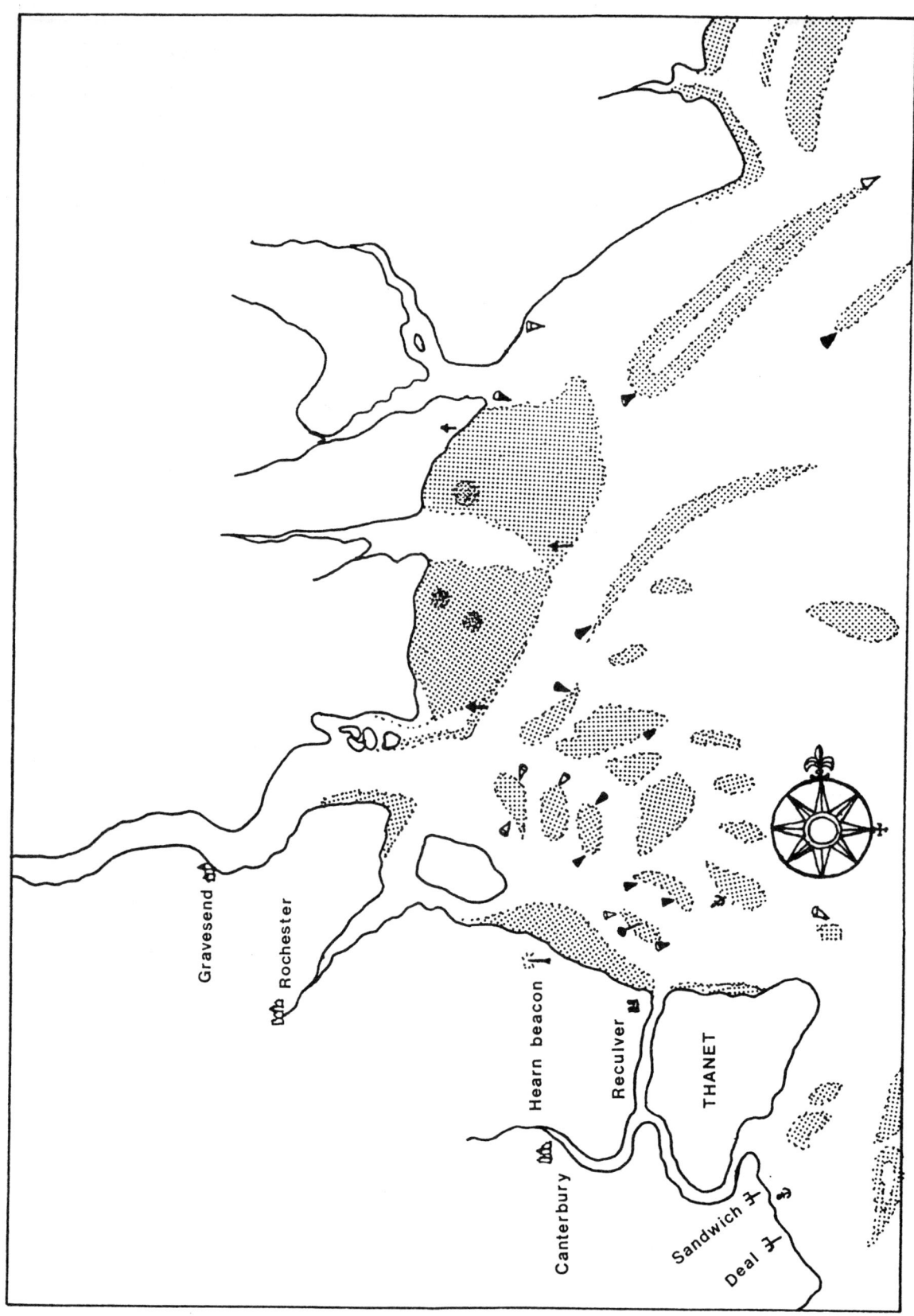

Fig. 24. Navigation aids and routes in the Thames estuary.

Fig. 25. Reculver Castle, Kent.

were large cone-shaped buoys which were placed point down since the apex was the strongest part for attaching to their moorings.

Wagenhaer's book published in 1582 gives 'A Shorte Instruction of the forms and fashion of Buyes, Beakons, and other markes' which was arranged to show the sands, shoals or hidden rocks off the coast of Holland, Friesland, Zeeland and the Thames, along with charts to show their representations. This seems to be the earliest printed description of these kinds of navigational aids. This work gives us a date at which the system of buoyage as charted was in force. It also gives the information that the charted depths were given in fathoms along with information on tidal ebbs and floods. The English navigators adopted Wagenhaer's cartological symbols to denote the various types of terrain, buoys, seamarks, safe anchorages and dangerous rocks which might be hidden by water.

Examples of navigation aids and the manner in which they were depicted on charts of the time can be seen in Fig. 26.

CHANNEL CLEARING & BALLASTAGE

In addition to supplying pilots for the Thames estuary, the Deptford Trinity House was also granted the rights and emoluments of ballastage in the Thames. This ensured that ballast was removed from the riverbed of the Thames and from the beaches, which would in turn assure the widening and deepening of the shipping channels by dredging. The dredger-lighters were manned by teams of men who began working at half ebb and continued until the flood lifted their lighters too high. They worked with long poles, called 'spoons', with an iron framework and a leather bag attached which was in turn attached to the lighter. When the flood tide lifted them too high to continue their work, they proceeded to the ships requiring ballast. There they loaded the ships before the ebb began, which would carry them back to their work stations.

LIGHTHOUSES

The earliest known lighthouses were the towers constructed by the Cushites and the Libyans along the Mediterranean coast of Egypt where the beacon fires were maintained by the priests. At Sigeum in the Troad a lighthouse was built before 660 B.C. The most famous was the lighthouse called Pharos of Alexandria, which was one of the seven wonders of the ancient world. Built in the third century B.C., it may have been between 200 and 600 feet tall. Since that time the word 'pharos' became a general term for lighthouses, and can be found on some sea charts of the time.

By the first century A.D. there were well-known lighthouses in Italy, the best known being those at Ostia, Ravenna and Messina. Probably the oldest known lighthouses in western Europe were those built in the first or second century by the Romans at Dover and Boulogne. The earliest light tower built at Cordouan, a rock in the Gironde estuary, was built about A.D. 800, and was the first known lighthouse to be built at sea.

Fig. 26. Chart symbols.

FIRST ENGLISH LIGHTHOUSE

The ordinances of the Trinity House of Newcastle-upon-Tyne gave it authority to set up and maintain two towers — one on either side of the port entrance — with a perpetual light which was to be maintained nightly. Thus, during the reign of Henry VIII, the first English lighthouse was established at the entrance to Newcastle-upon-Tyne in 1536. However, it was not until the seventeenth century that the number increased.

By the early seventeenth century the mariners had a large number of familiar capes, bays, church steeples, conspicuous trees and other structures to lead them into estuary channels and ports. They also had a growing number of artificial beacons of timber or stone along the coast. The addition of more beacons had been hotly debated in the reign of James I. Opponents to the additional beacons believed that they would facilitate the sudden invasion of the enemy. Examples of beacons and lighthouses of the period can be seen in Fig. 27.

Until about 1600 the English navigation aids — buoys, seamarks and beacons — were of use only in the daytime. The only lights on the English coast for the assistance of mariners were the two maintained by Trinity House of Newcastle-upon-Tyne. These 'firebeacons' were of 'firecoals' as might be expected in a region known for its coal. Instead of being burned continuously at night as had originally been stipulated, they were lighted at night only from half-tide to quarter to half-tide. The purpose was to assist in safe passage of shipping during those tides as ships passed a dangerous shoal in the lower reaches of the river. The beacons were lighted on two stone towers which stood at different levels and some distance apart — the lower one being to the seaward of the upper one. This placed the lights in transit (a range bearing), when the shoal was passed to the southward.

In about 1600 the entrance to the Tees began to be marked nightly by a single light because of the increasing coal trade. About that same time two lights began to be seen at Caister on the northeast coast of Norfolk. It is not known whether these later lights were of coals or candles. However, a few years later, two candle-lights were set up at Lowestoft by the Trinity House of Deptford Strand for ships which made the dangerous passage through the channels lying close inshore between Lowestoft and Winterton.

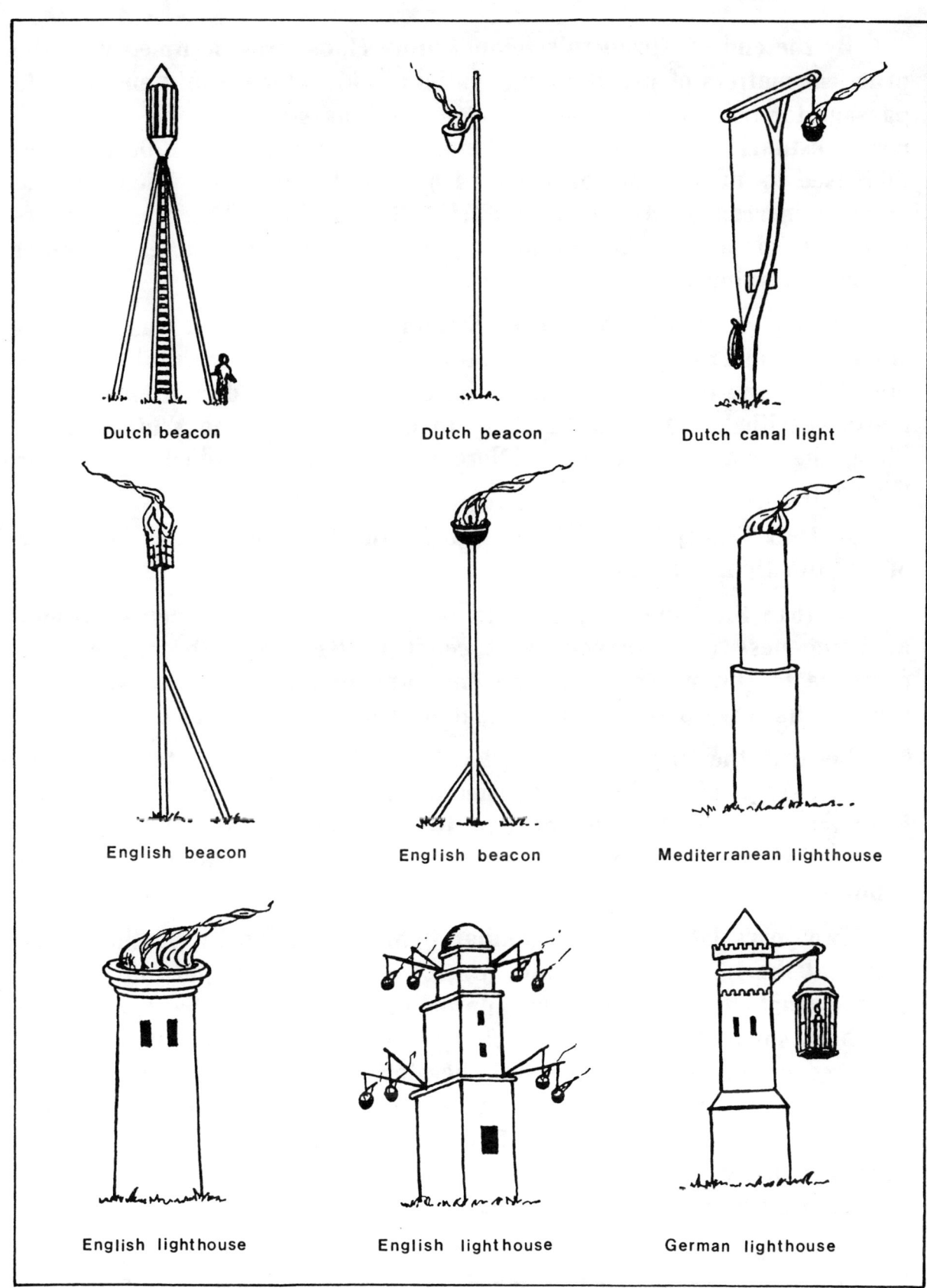

Fig. 27. Examples of beacons & lighthouses.

By the end of Elizabeth's reign Trinity House was occupied with the practical matters of providing navigational aids which would ensure safe passage for both domestic and foreign ships passing into and out of the rivers, estuaries and ports of England. Between 1600 and 1700 England increased its number of lighthouses from one to fourteen, which was the greatest increase of any country during that period. This was a reflection of England's rapidly expanding sea-trade and an increased effort to prevent shipwrecks.

In 1605 a certain Ponnyl, of Stroud on the Medway, was commissioned by the Trinity House of Deptford to repair and maintain 8 buoys and 3 beacons (or 6 buoys and 5 beacons) with the dimensions of the buoys specified. The beacons were to be erected at the Whitaker, the Shoe, the Last and the Nore [Nore was originally spelled 'Nower' or 'Noure'].

In 1609 Trinity House of Deptford Strand took over the maintenance of the two lights at Caister.

In 1615 Sir Humphrey Howard began to exhibit an open coal-light at Dungeness (on the southeast coast of Kent) which marked the entrance to Dover Strait. Its purpose was to warn deep-sea shipping, working its way up the Channel, that it was in the vicinity of the coast.

Because the trade on the east coast of England was steadily growing as a result of the increased demand for coal, three more lights were established on the Norfolk coast in 1617 by Sir William Erskine. The one at Winterton was of coals while the two at Wintertonness were of candles.

Two years later [1619] a similar light was set up by Sir John Killigrew at the Lizard in Cornwall, which was the most important landfall on the English coast for ships approaching from the Atlantic. There had been some objections from Trinity House on the basis that the area was free of outlying dangers and therefore it was not needed. There was also some thought that such a light would only assist enemies and pirates. What is more, the local residents were openly hostile because such a lighthouse might diminish the benefits they had been reaping by plundering the numerous shipwrecks on their coast.

In December of 1619 Killigrew wrote that 'the Light and Tower on the Lizard is, I prayse God, finished and I presum speaks itself to most parts of Christendom . . .' By the spring of 1620 Killigrew wrote that a ship had 'perished thro nott having notice that anie such light was there mentayned and the men Drunk being confessed by them that are saved.' However, some local seamen noted that it could not be seen in hazy weather. Much to Killigrew's distress the cost of maintaining the light at the Lizard was exceeding his ability to support it. The light was not maintained with regularity until 1621. In 1623 the King ordained that the Lizard lighthouse should remain a lighthouse forever on that coast.

If MAYFLOWER passed within sight of the Lizard during the nighttime hours, this beacon may well have been one of the last major landmarks of their homeland to be observed by the Pilgrims as they began their historic voyage.

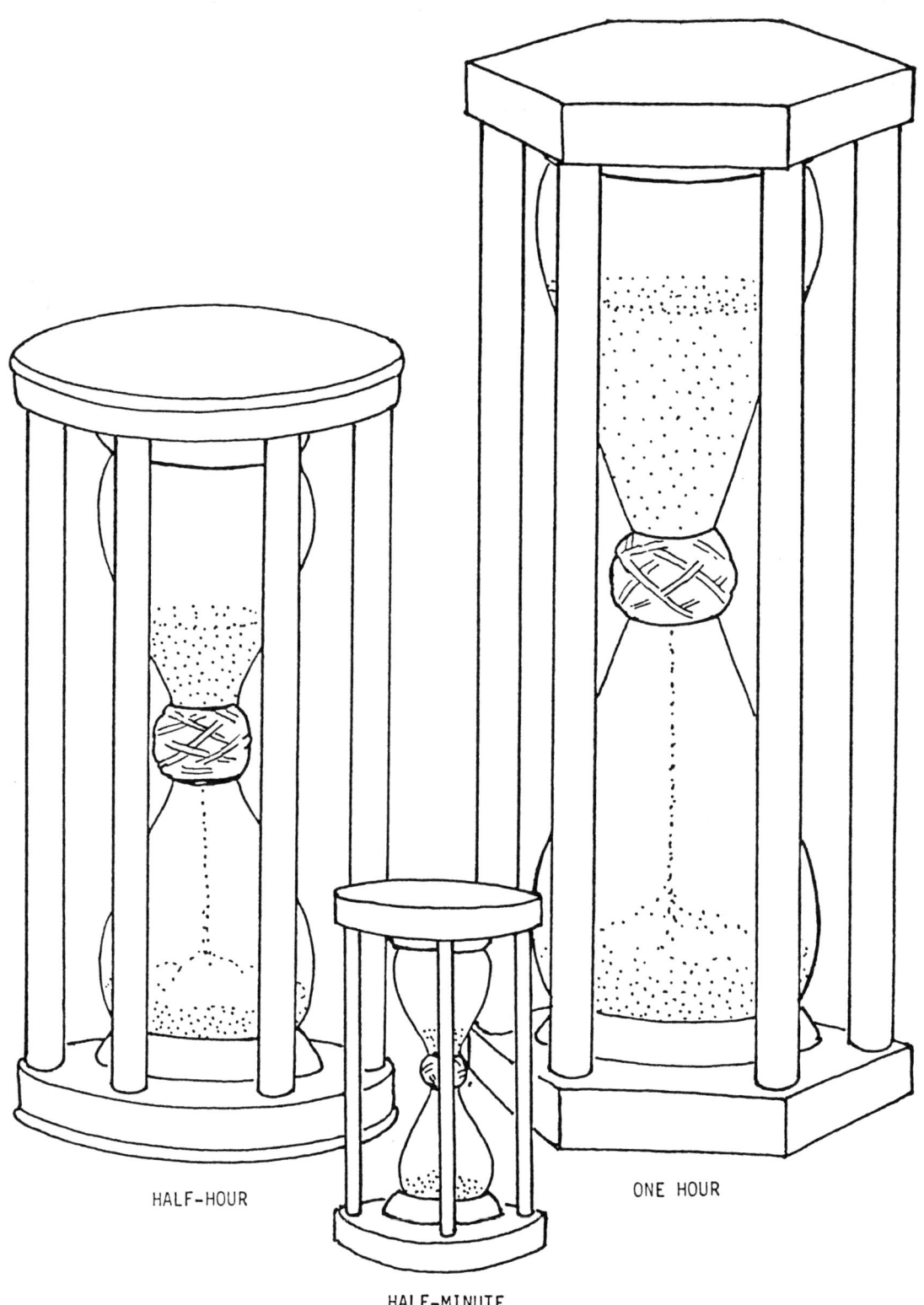
HALF-HOUR

HALF-MINUTE

ONE HOUR

8. TIME-KEEPING

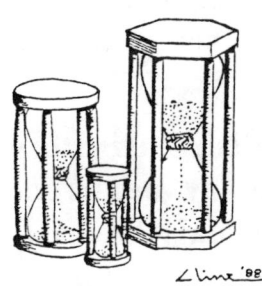

Some method of keeping time was of extreme importance to shipmasters and navigators. The determination of speed depended on the number of feet they traveled in a given time. The length of time spent on duty by the mariners during their watches had to be set. When approaching a port, they had to be able to determine the time of tidal ebbs and floods. Tides in the Mediterranean are not so extreme. But, the rise and fall and the changes in direction of flow in tidal streams on the Atlantic — and around England — were of great importance to shipmasters sailing those waters. As time went on the navigators depended on time-keeping to assist them in determining their longitudinal position. Some method of keeping time was imperative to those men of the sea.

Few ports had public clocks, and where there were clocks, they might be in error by as much as an hour in a day. Public clocks had to be corrected daily with the aid of a sun dial.

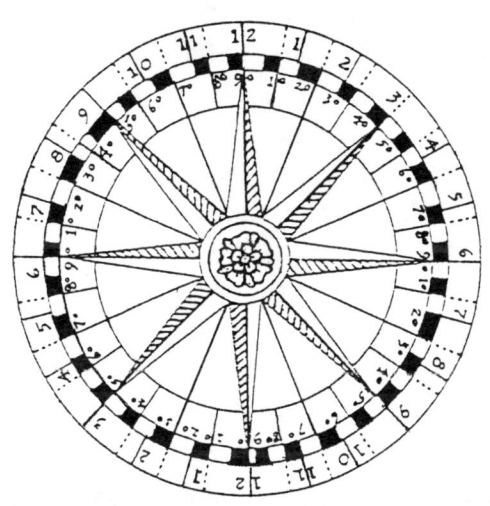

Fig. 28. The compass clock.

The shipmaster could use his compass rose as a rough time-piece — a practice which developed because mechanical clocks and early watches were extremely unreliable. As will be seen, even sand-glasses could be unreliable over any length of time. It was an ancient custom to divide the compass into 24 equal parts or hours, by which they distinguished time. [Fig. 28] Even today the 24-hour clock is still observed aboard ships.

The compass clock could be used

on sunny days, but its horizontal position made it extremely unreliable in the northern latitudes. For navigators of the time the most obvious times in the 24-hour day were sunrise and sunset. The sun rose due east and set due west at six o'clock at the times of the equinoxes in March and September. These were the east and west points of the mariner's compass. Mid-day, when the sun was at its zenith, was south by his compass points. In summer when the sun was in its greatest north declination, the sunrise would be somewhat past 7 o'clock (ESE by his compass) and at a southeast sun it would be past 10:00 o'clock. In midwinter the sun rose at eight, south of east, and set at four, south of west.

Up to the close of the seventeenth century English navigators frequently recorded the time of day for some noteworthy occurrence in terms of bearing of the sun — entering in their journals 'at east sun' instead of '6 o'clock in the morning.' They were using the long-established practice of finding the time of day by taking a bearing of the sun with the compass, and of expressing the time in terms of the rhumb upon which the sun bore instead of in hours and minutes.

HOURS AND MINUTES BY THE COMPASS-CLOCK AT EQUINOX

RHUMB	HOUR	RHUMB	HOUR
N	Midnight	S	Noon
N. by E	0:45 AM	S. by W	12:45 PM
N.N.E	1:30 AM	S.S.W	1:30 PM
N.E. by N	2:15 AM	S.W. by S	2:15 PM
N.E	3:00 AM	S.W	3:00 PM
N.E. by E	3:45 AM	S.W. by W	3:45 PM
E.N.E	4:30 AM	W.S.W	4:30 PM
E. by N	5:15 AM	W. by S	5:15 PM
E	6:00 AM	W	6:00 PM
E. by S	6:45 AM	W. by N	6:45 PM
E.S.E	7:30 AM	W.N.W	7:30 PM
S.E. by E	8:15 AM	N.W. by W	8:15 PM
S.E	9:00 AM	N.W	9:00 PM
S.E. by S	9:45 AM	N.W. by N	9:45 PM
S.S.E	10:30 AM	N.N.W	10:30 PM
S. by E	11:15 AM	N. by W	11:15 PM

Sun-dials were used aboard ships of that early period. However, they were impractical to a large measure. The passage of time was measured at sea by half-hour or one hour intervals by the turning of a sand-glass.

SAND-GLASS

It is not known when or where sand-glasses were invented. They were probably developed for use aboard ships sometime in the eleventh or twelfth century. Cook Lorell's *Book* of **1515** records that on board ship 'one man kepte ye compas, and watched ye glasse.' Columbus carried half-hour glasses on his voyages for his log recorded a day and night as forty-eight 'ampolettas,' or sand-glasses.

The sand-glass consisted of two pear-shaped globes attached neck-to-neck in a frame of wood or metal with a thin metal disk between the two globes. Until the eighteenth century, sand-glasses were blown from a thick, heavy, semi-transparent glass. In the metal disk between the globes was a small hole just large enough in diameter to allow the filling material to flow from one globe to the other by gravity. Various types of filling material were used. The most common material was probably sand — hence the name by which we know them. However, iron filings, marble dust and ground egg shells were also used in some glasses. The size of the hole in the diaphragm between the two bulbs was gauged according to the fineness of the filling material.

The joint between the two globes was sealed with wax or putty — sealing wax was never used — then strengthened by a wrapping of coarse linen, finished off with a binding of leather and finally a decorative winding of thread in a braid-work finish matching a 'turk's head' knot. To protect the sand-glasses from the many shocks to which they would be subjected aboard ship, the glass globes were kept from actual contact with their bases by a collar of leather which rested on the frame and supported the globe. To add further protection maritime sand-glasses were sometimes encased in square wooden boxes fitted with horn or glass windows.

Sand-glasses were made up for various time periods. A 'watch-glass' to measure the four-hour watch might measure a foot in diameter and be two feet in height. With the weight of its filling material in addition to the actual glass and framework, it could weigh several pounds and require two hands to turn. Even the half-hour glass would seem large by comparison to our modern counterparts. It is interesting to note that there were some pocket sand-glasses which were enclosed in cylindrical leather cases, a section of which was open to allow observation of the glass. A one-minute glass of this pocket type might have been carried by the ship's surgeon for timing pulse.

Sand-glasses were prone to develop problems due to moisture in the sand, or an enlarged hole in the diaphragm caused by the wear of sand as it passed from one globe to the other. Because of this chance for error, the prudent navigator turned two or three glasses simultaneously. Sometimes a group of four glasses were carried in one frame. This simultaneous turning of a battery of glasses enabled the navigator to take the mean reading of the glasses in the event they did not register the same passage of time. Another arrangement was to have a battery of four glasses in one frame which registered one hour, three-quarter hour, half-hour and quarter-hour intervals. [Fig. 29] The latter arrangement gave the helmsman a more accurate way of determining the time of any event which might occur between the normal turning of the glass at the half hour.

The frames for sand-glasses used aboard ship were generally oak with round, hexagonal or square top and bottom disks which were supported by four to eight upright legs. The sand-glass used by the helmsman generally had holes drilled in the top and bottom plates of the frame through which cords were threaded and tied into a bight from which it could be suspended near the binnacle. This prevented the glass from being knocked about and broken. The hexagonal and square bases allowed the glasses to be laid on their sides when not in use since the round bases tended to roll with the motion of the ship. [Fig. 30]

A sand-glass was hung in the binnacle where it could easily be seen by the helmsman. For his purpose, a half-hour glass was used. The sand-glass — or 'running glass' — was started at noon when the sun was due south and appeared highest in the heavens.

Fig. 29. Four sand-glasses framed together.

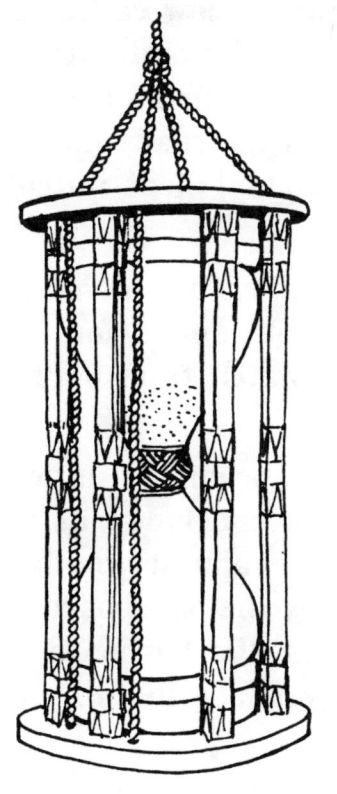

Fig. 30. Helmsman's sand-glass

This, too, was not always easy to determine because the slow movement of the sun made it difficult to detect its highest point — especially in summer when it is at its highest declination. With the noontime turning of the glass the new day began aboard a ship at sea. While in port, the mariners generally observed land time — in which each new day began at midnight. However, at sea, each new day began at the noon shooting of the sun. This point can cause some confusion is reading the old ship journals, since we are not accustomed to thinking in terms of two dates for one period of daylight — the morning being one date, while the afternoon becomes the succeeding date.

Each time the sand ran out, the helmsman marked the time by ringing a bell — one stroke for every half-hour that passed during a four-hour watch. 'Watch-bells' were listed in the inventories for ship's furnishings as early as the fifteenth century.

Captain John Smith stated in his book *A Sea Grammar* published in 1627 that a shipmaster should provision his ship with a good quantity of sand-glasses of various time lengths because there was great breakage during the course of a voyage. He tells us that the day was divided into 'watches' for the ship's crew, writing that each squadron was on duty '...for eight Glasses or foure houres.'

The earliest explanation of the rotation of the watches appears to be that recorded by Thomas Hariot in his *Mathematical Papers* published probably before 1595. Time was measured in 'whole watches' of four hours and 'half watches' of two hours as well as in half-hours.

John Smith tells us that the ship's company was divided into two parts: one was the 'starboard watch' which was under the charge of the shipmaster; the other was the 'larboard watch' under the supervision of the first mate, or 'right hand mate' as he was called. ['Starboard' refers to the right side of the ship as one faces forward toward the bow:

'Larboard' refers to the left side of the ship, and is now called 'port'.] These two 'watches' worked 'turn in turn' to serve as lookouts, trim sails, work the bilge pumps and attend to all of the duties during a four-hour watch. At times when the ship was in harbor or in the roads [sea lanes] only a 'quarter watch' [one quarter of the company] kept watch at a time.

The 'first watch' beginning at 8:00 PM was taken by the 'starboard watch' on the first day at sea, which completed its duties for the day by taking the 'last dog watch' which was a half watch from 6 PM to 8 PM.

On the first day at sea, the 'larboard watch' began its duties with the 'second watch', which began at midnight, and concluded its day by taking the 'look out watch' from 4 PM to 6 PM — another 'half watch' of only two hours. The second cycle was begun as the 'starboard watch' began its duties with the 'last dog watch.' Thus, the 'larboard watch' began the next 24-hour period with the 'first watch'. In this manner the watches were alternated on a daily basis.

POCKET SUN DIALS

Sun dials were in use aboard many ships. The sun dial had been used to determine the hourly divisions of the day for about 4,000 years. The time was indicated by the shadow of the sun cast by a gnomen (upright indicator) on a circular dial below.

There are a number of examples of pocket-type sundials, which have been retrieved from shipwrecks dating from the Age of Discovery. Many of them have built-in compasses, which would have aided the sailor in positioning the dial for a more accurate reading. At best, the time could only be a rough approximation — especially on the tossing deck of a ship at sea. Examples of pocket-type sun dials can be seen in Fig. 31.

THE DIPTYCH SUN DIAL

A very popular variation of the sun dial during the sixteenth and seventeenth centuries was the diptych sun dial. The name diptych originated in the Latin and late Greek word for a pair of folding writing tables. The diptych was small enough to conveniently carry in the pocket. Thus, they were a type of pocket sun dial, and a sort of predecessor of the modern pocket watch.

THE CYCLE OF WATCHES AND BELLS

FIRST WATCH
(8:00 PM to Midnight)
8:00 PM - 8 bells
8:30 PM - 1 bell
9:00 PM - 2 bells
9:30 PM - 3 bells
10:00 PM - 4 bells
10:30 PM - 5 bells
11:00 PM - 6 bells
11:30 PM - 7 bells

SECOND WATCH
(Midnight to 8:00 AM)
Midnight - 8 bells
12:30 AM - 1 bell
1:00 AM - 2 bells
1:30 AM - 3 bells
2:00 AM - 4 bells
2:30 AM - 5 bells
3:00 AM - 6 bells
3:30 AM - 7 bells

DAY or MORNING WATCH
(4:00 AM TO 8 AM)
4:00 AM - 8 bells
4:30 AM - 1 bell
5:00 AM - 2 bells
5:30 AM - 3 bells
6:00 AM - 4 bells
6:30 AM - 5 bells
7:00 AM - 6 bells
7:30 AM - 7 bells

FORENOON WATCH
(8:00 AM to Noon)
8:00 AM - 8 bells
8:30 AM - 1 bell
9:00 AM - 2 bells
9:30 AM - 3 bells
10:00 AM - 4 bells
10:30 AM - 5 bells
11:00 AM - 6 bells
11:30 AM - 7 bells

AFTERNOON WATCH
(Noon to 4:00 PM)
Noon - 8 bells
12:30 PM - 1 bell
1:00 PM - 2 bells
1:30 PM - 3 bells
2:00 PM - 4 bells
2:30 PM - 5 bells
3:00 PM - 6 bells
3:30 PM - 7 bells

LOOK-OUT WATCH
(4:00 PM to 6:00 PM)
4:00 PM - 8 bells
4:30 PM - 1 bell
5:00 PM - 2 bells
5:30 PM - 3 bells

LAST DOG WATCH
(6:00 PM to 8:00 PM)
6:00 PM - 4 bells
6:30 PM - 1 bell
7:00 PM - 2 bells
7:30 PM - 3 bells

The Last Dog Watch ended at 8:00 PM with eight bells, and the First Watch began a new sequence.

Fig. 31. Pocket-type sundials.

Between the two covers of the diptych sun dial was a string or wire, which cast its shadow on the hour dial below. The diptych included a compass to aid in achieving the proper orientation, and thus a more accurate reading of the time of day. The string could usually be adjusted to different positions, depending upon the latitude in which the instrument was being used. The various markings were generally in the range of 42° to 54°. There were also corresponding circles drawn on the horizontal tablet. The vertical tablet listed a number of important towns where the user might find himself. [Fig. 32]

THE EQUATORIAL SUN DIAL

The equatorial sun dial consisted of a meridian ring with latitude markings on its lower quadrant, a style (indicator rod) with a bead at its center suspended across the axis, and a semi-circular hour scale with hours marked on its inside surface. This unit sat atop a small column which was positioned on a base that was marked with the major points of the compass. [Fig. 33]

The equatorial sun dial could be used at any latitude because its hour-ring was set parallel to the Equator and the style (indicator rod) was set parallel to the Earth's axis. Since the equatorial sun dial does

Fig. 32. The diptych.

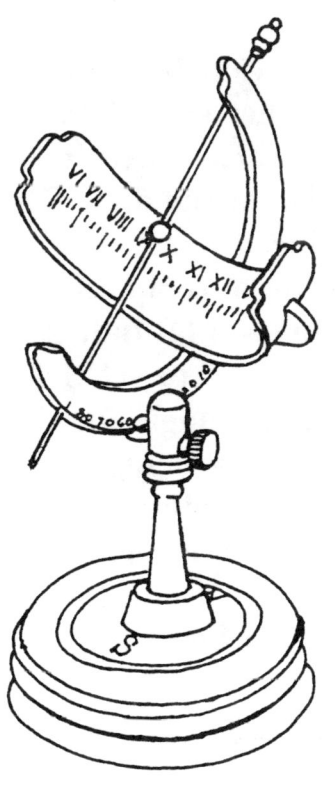

Fig. 33. The equatorial sun dial.

not include a compass, the unit had to be turned in the approximate direction of the geographic north pole. A compass could be used to help determine the proper orientation. However, it must be remembered that there is a variation between the magnetic north and the geographic north, and the direction must be determined on the basis of local error. The problem of variation will be discussed in more detail in a later section.

The sun dial on this instrument indicated the local solar time, which may differ from clock time by as much as six minutes either way, except at the four times a year when the mean time and solar time are the same (two equinoxes and two solstices).

THE UNIVERSAL RING DIAL

Whereas the sun dial marks the passage of time by casting the shadow of a gnomen (upright indicator) on the hour dial, the universal ring dial registered the time by means of a tiny shaft of sunlight shining through a pin-hole located in a sliding scale at its center. [Fig. 35] The universal ring dial has been attributed to William Oughtred, the English instrument-maker, who developed it about 1600. What made this timepiece a very popular and widely used instrument was the fact that it could

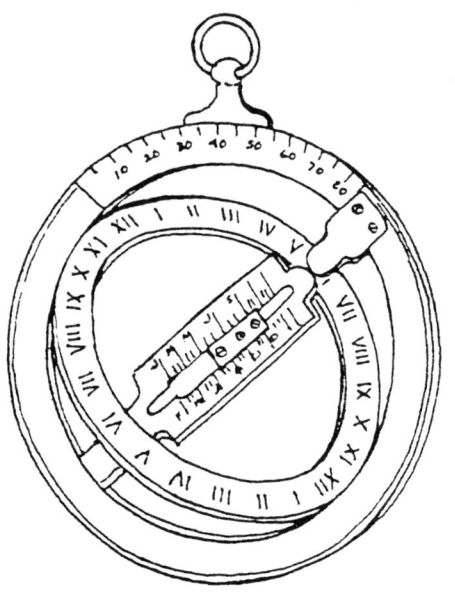

Fig. 34. The universal ring dial.

be adjusted to any latitude except the Arctic and Antarctic.

The suspension piece at the top of the outer ring could be set in accordance with the latitude in which it was to be used. When the ring dial had been adjusted for the proper latitude, it had to be adjusted for the approximate date. This was done by sliding the index (containing the pinhole) along the scale of months. The whole instrument was then rotated on its vertical axis until the sunlight passed through the central pin hole and cast a ray of light on the inside surface of the outer ring with its hour markings. The correct time could then be read.

THE UNIVERSAL EQUINOCTIAL SUN DIAL

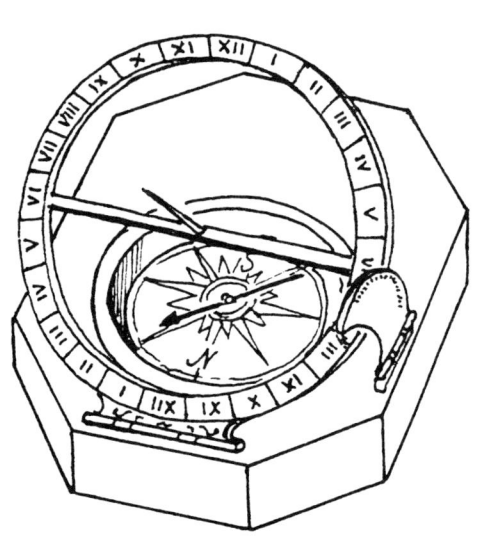

Fig. 35. The equinoctial sun dial.

As previously mentioned, some of the pocket sun dials included a compass, which aided in the proper orientation of the dial. The universal equinoctial sun dial was also fitted with a compass. This dial also includes a latitude scale, which allows the user to set the hour dial at the proper angle for the latitude in which it is being used. When the gnomen (indicator point) at the center is in an upright position, the time is read from the shadow it casts on the hour dial. [Fig. 35]

THE NIGHTTIME CLOCK

At night the favorite time indicator was the constellation Ursa Minor — Little Dipper or Little Bear — with its alpha star — Polaris — sometimes called the Pole Star, Lode Star, etc. Each night this constellation swung counter-clockwise around the axis of earth, pivoting around the Pole Star. This aspect of time-keeping will be discussed in further detail in the section dealing with nocturnals.

Both methods of determining time by the sun clock and star clock were rough approximations. The nocturnal readings could be off by as much as a quarter of an hour. The timekeeper which was most important in the daily routine aboard ship was the sand-glass. With it the shipmaster could judge his speed and estimate the time of his expected landfall. Sand-glasses were prone to error due to their construction, but they were easy to use and to keep close at hand — daytime or nighttime. An added factor in their favor was the fact that their use did not depend on weather conditions, which might conceal the sun or the constellations.

Fig. 36. Various types of nocturnals.

9. THE NOCTURNAL

The nocturnal, or nocturlabe as it was sometimes called from the French, was a device for reckoning the time at night. The nocturnal was described in sixteenth century texts, and examples dating from about 1500 are still in existence. With the nocturnal it was only possible to determine a rough estimation of the time — within a quarter of an hour.

Until the latter part of the sixteenth century the English mariners could judge the time of night by the stars, but had to do so on the basis of their own experience and knowledge of the movement of the heavenly bodies. Both shepherds and mariners were accustomed to memorizing the stellar positions for every month by observing easily recognized stars. The knowledgeable shipmaster prior to the sixteenth century probably memorized the rules giving the positions of the Guards (or 'two brothers') of the Lesser Bear during the year as they circled around Polaris, and may have been able to reckon the time within an hour at most seasons. A human figure with outstretched arms marked the quarters of the sky in an early version of the nocturnal. [Fig. 37] In Pierre Garcie's *Grand Routier* published in 1483, the Guard is accompanied by a table of twenty-four half-monthly midnight positions of the Guard. Garcie's book was later translated and used by English mariners. A Portuguese sea manual from about the same period of time gives a bi-monthly table which had to be learned.

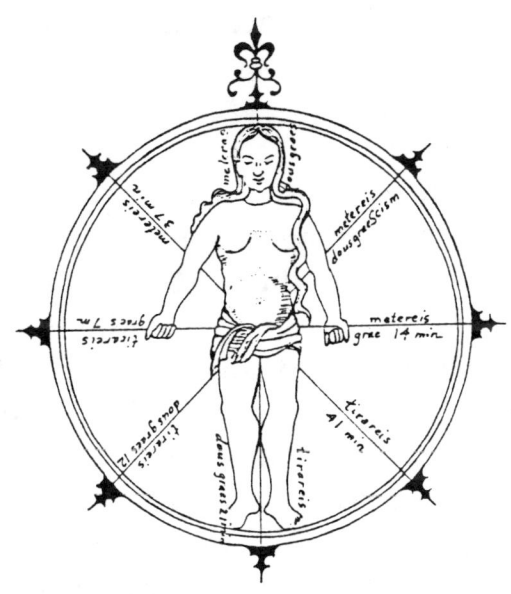

Fig. 37. The 'guard.'

From the middle of the sixteenth century the mariners could have used an almanac which contained the rules for reckoning time. They could use their compass dial in reckoning time at night, but it was not until the latter part of the sixteenth century that they had the nocturnal, which the more sophisticated southern mariners used. Although the nocturnal may have come into use at an earlier date, it was not mentioned until the sixteenth century. Robert Norman, an Elizabethan compass-maker, described a rather crude form of nocturnal which could be made by the ship's smith. His suggested nocturnal was composed of an iron hoop fitted with equally spaced spikes around the rim to represent the 24 hours of the day and a small ring held in the center of the hoop by four equally spaced pieces of line.

To an observer the sun seems to rotate in the stellar system, but also seems to have a slower movement, making a complete rotation in one year. The solar day appears to slip back a little each twenty-four hours. According to the solar time, the sidereal (or day measured by the stars) is three minutes and fifty-six seconds shorter than the solar day. For an observer the Pointers appear in a slightly different position each night, having slipped back slightly in their circuit. In early March the Pointers (α and β) of Ursa Major are in a line and high above Polaris at midnight. By June they are due west of the Pole Star at midnight. In early September the Pointers are in line directly below Polaris. In the course of a year the Pointers appear to make a complete circuit counter-clockwise around Polaris. By sidereal time the Pointers appear to lose an hour every fifteen days according to mean (solar) time.

USE OF THE NOCTURNAL

The operation is based on the fact that the stars, while remaining fixed relative to one another, appear to rotate about Polaris (the Pole Star or North Star), which lies along the axis of the earth's rotation. It is, of course, the earth which is rotating, while Polaris remains fixed. As the other stars appear to rotate, their position at any moment indicates the time. [Fig. 38] The mariners referred to Polaris (α Ursae Minoris or 'Stella Maris') as the Lodestar. It is thought that the name 'lodestar' is derived from the old English word 'lad', meaning leader, giving it the meaning of 'leading or guiding star.' The word 'lodestone' comes from the same source, giving it the meaning of 'leading or guiding stone.'

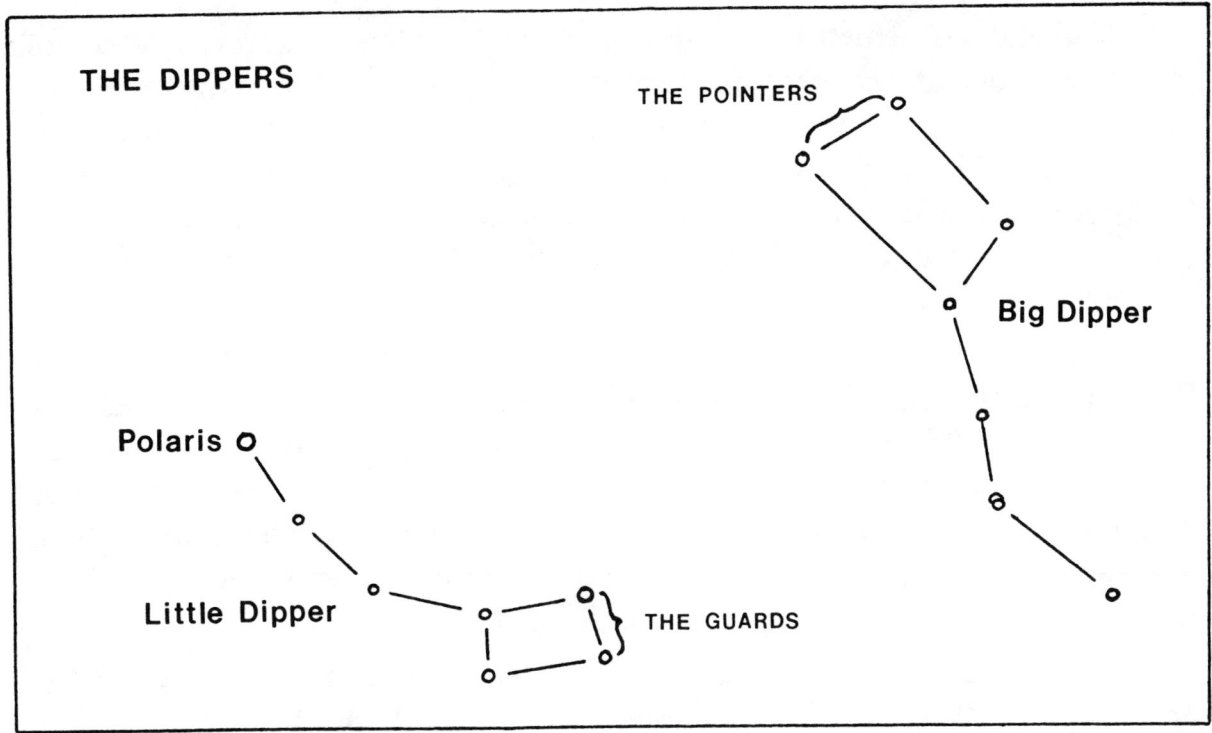

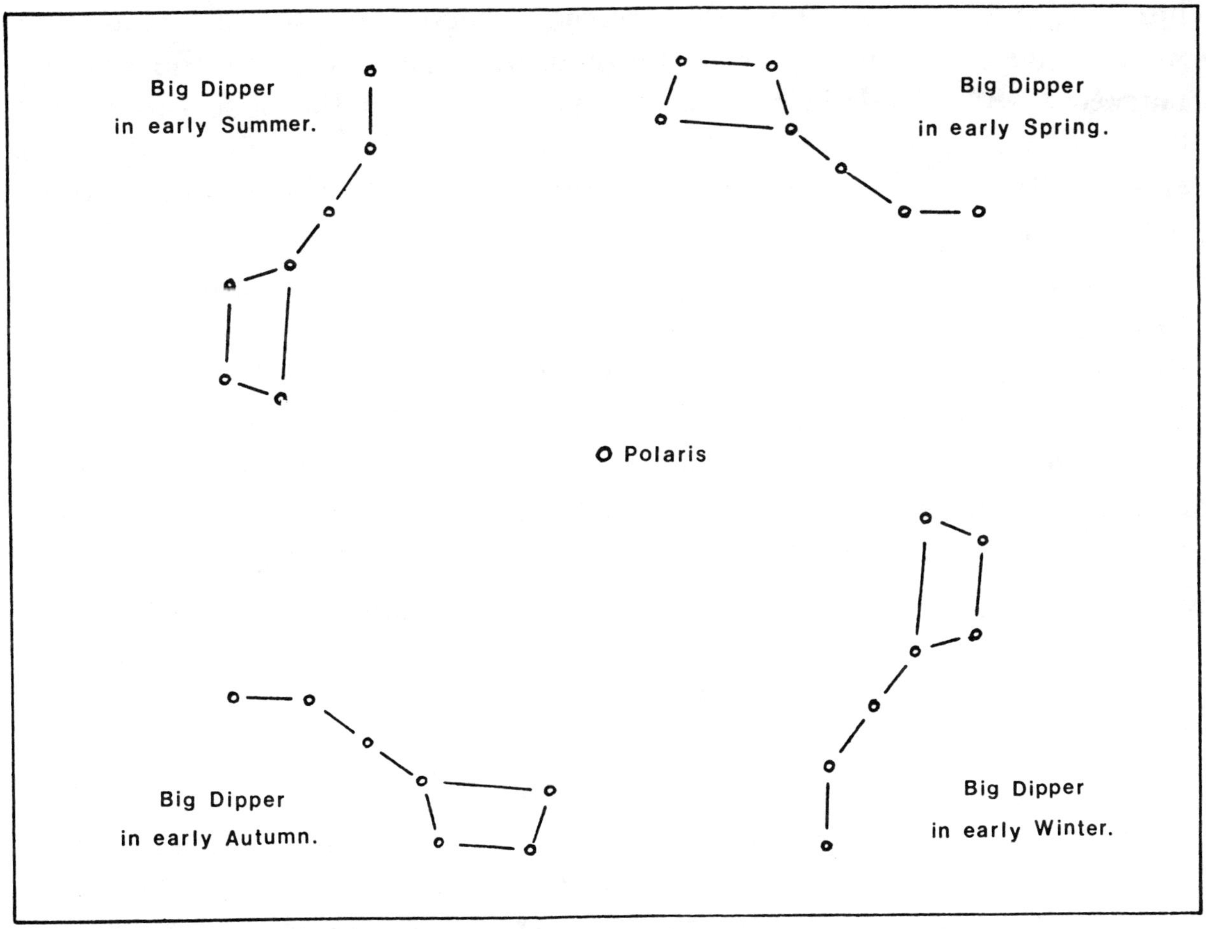

Fig. 38. Movement of the constellations around Polaris.

A nocturnal, which is circular in form, consists of several pieces of metal or wood, attached at the center so they can rotate relative to one another. [Fig. 39] Most of the nocturnals from the seventeenth century, which were made by professional instrument-makers, were made of hardwood. At the axis of rotation there is a hole. When in use, the nocturnal is held upright by the handle until Polaris can be sighted through the center hole.

The long arm of the device is then turned until it lies along the Pointers of the Big Bear. That is the line made by the two brightest stars α and β in the constellation Ursa Major, which is also known as the Great Bear, Big Dipper, or Plough. These two stars are often used as pointers because they are easily seen and they lie along a line which passes close to the Pole Star. The bright star in the Little Bear (Little Dipper) can also be used in the same way.

Some nocturnals were made to be used with either the Great Bear or the Little Bear, and were many times labeled "Both Bears" on the handle. [Fig. 40] In these dual purpose nocturnals, if the Great Bear were to be used, the inner dial would be turned so that the pointer marked "GB" would lie against the date on which the observation was being made. By doing this, the correction was automatically made from sidereal time to solar time. The solar time is an average of four minutes longer than sidereal time.

After setting the inner dial to the correct date, the nocturnal was held up and Polaris was sighted through the center hole. The long indicator arm was then turned until the two brightest stars of the Great Bear were lying along it. The time was then read from the scale on the central dial — as though the indicator arm were acting as a hand on a clock. The hour positions were sometimes notched on the dial to make it possible to read the time in the dark by feel. [Fig. 41]

If the Little Bear were to be used, the method was essentially the same. However, the dial would be set with the pointer "LB" against the date, and the indicator arm would be lined up with the bright star of the Little Bear constellation.

Thus, the navigators on MAYFLOWER were able to tell the time of night — if the weather were clear. The problem was that in foul or cloudy weather, when the sky was obscured, they had no way of knowing the exact time except by the running of the sand-glasses. Spring-wound watches were being made at this time in history, but they were expensive and unreliable time-keepers. We have no references to indicate that any watches were on MAYFLOWER.

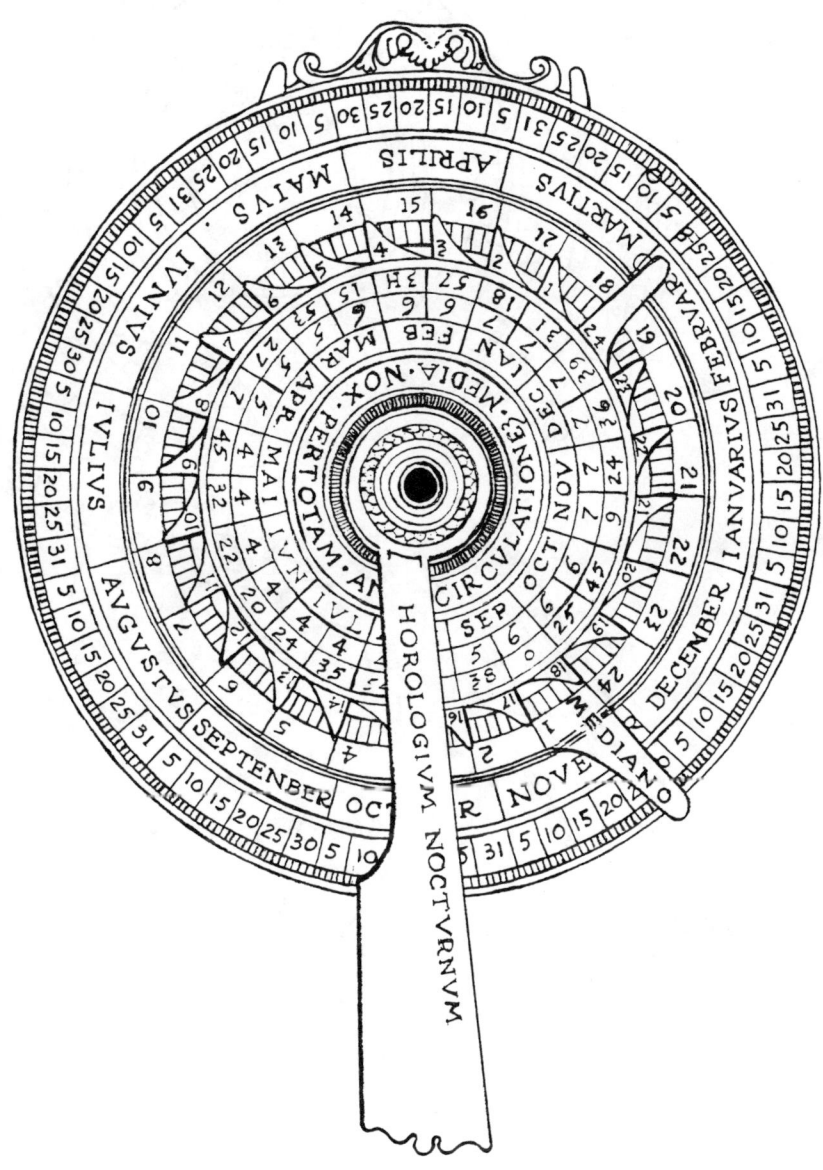

Fig. 39. A nocturnal.

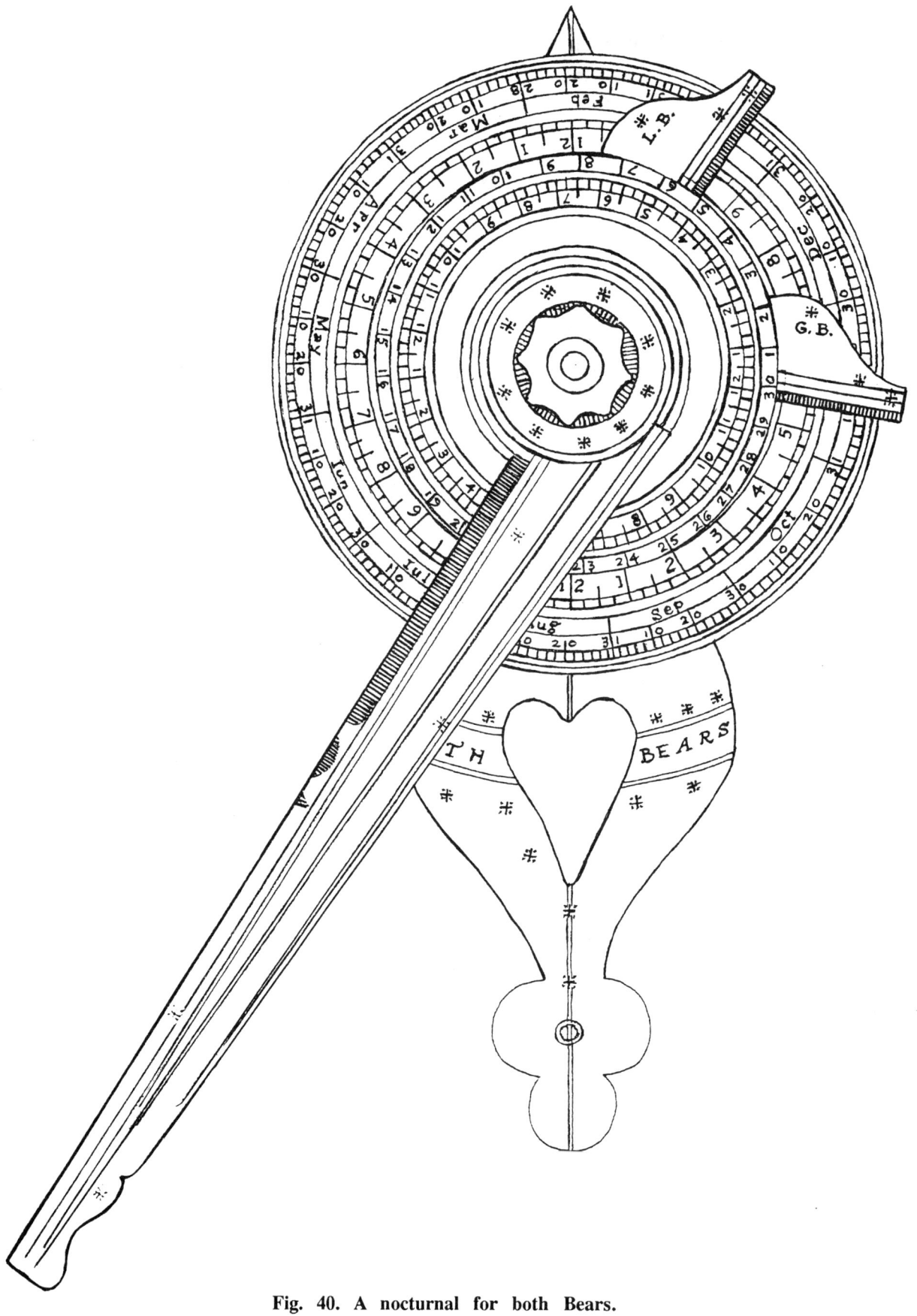

Fig. 40. A nocturnal for both Bears.

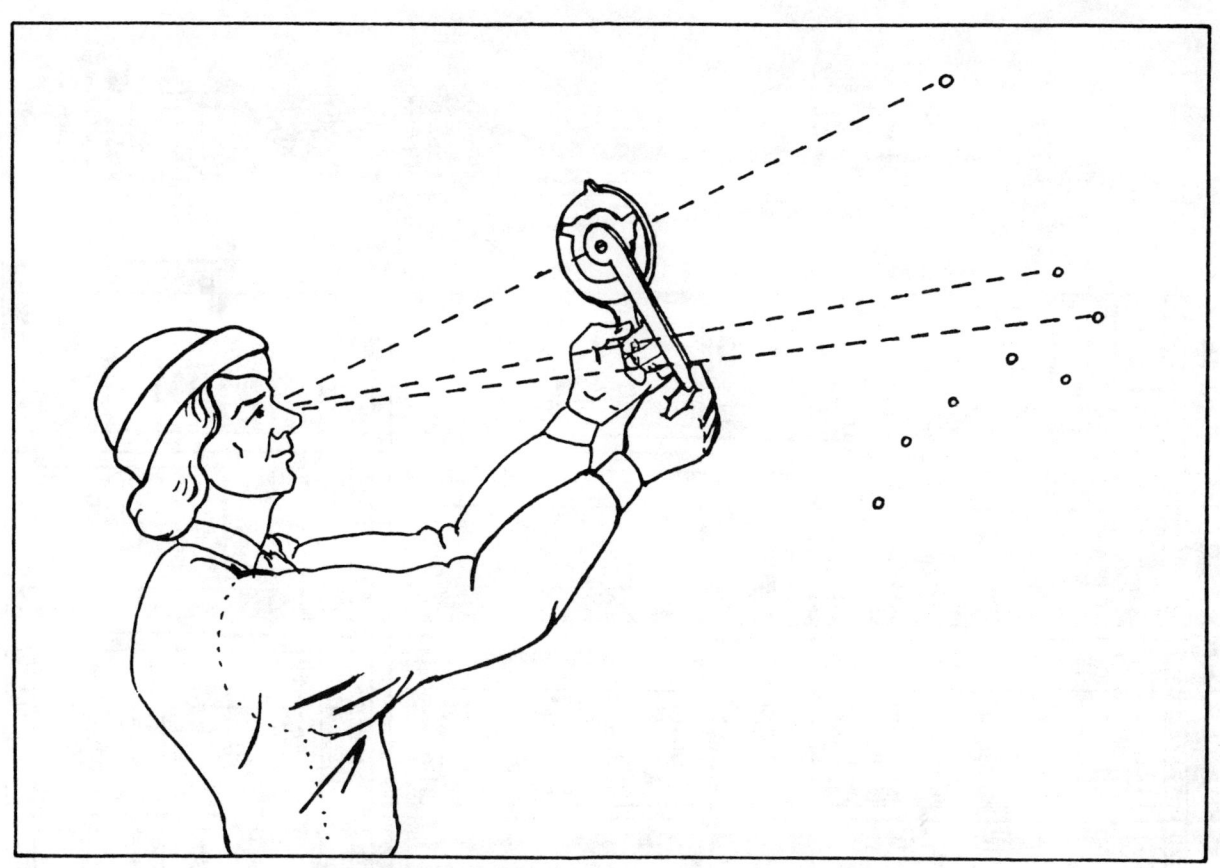

Fig. 41. The nocturnal in use.

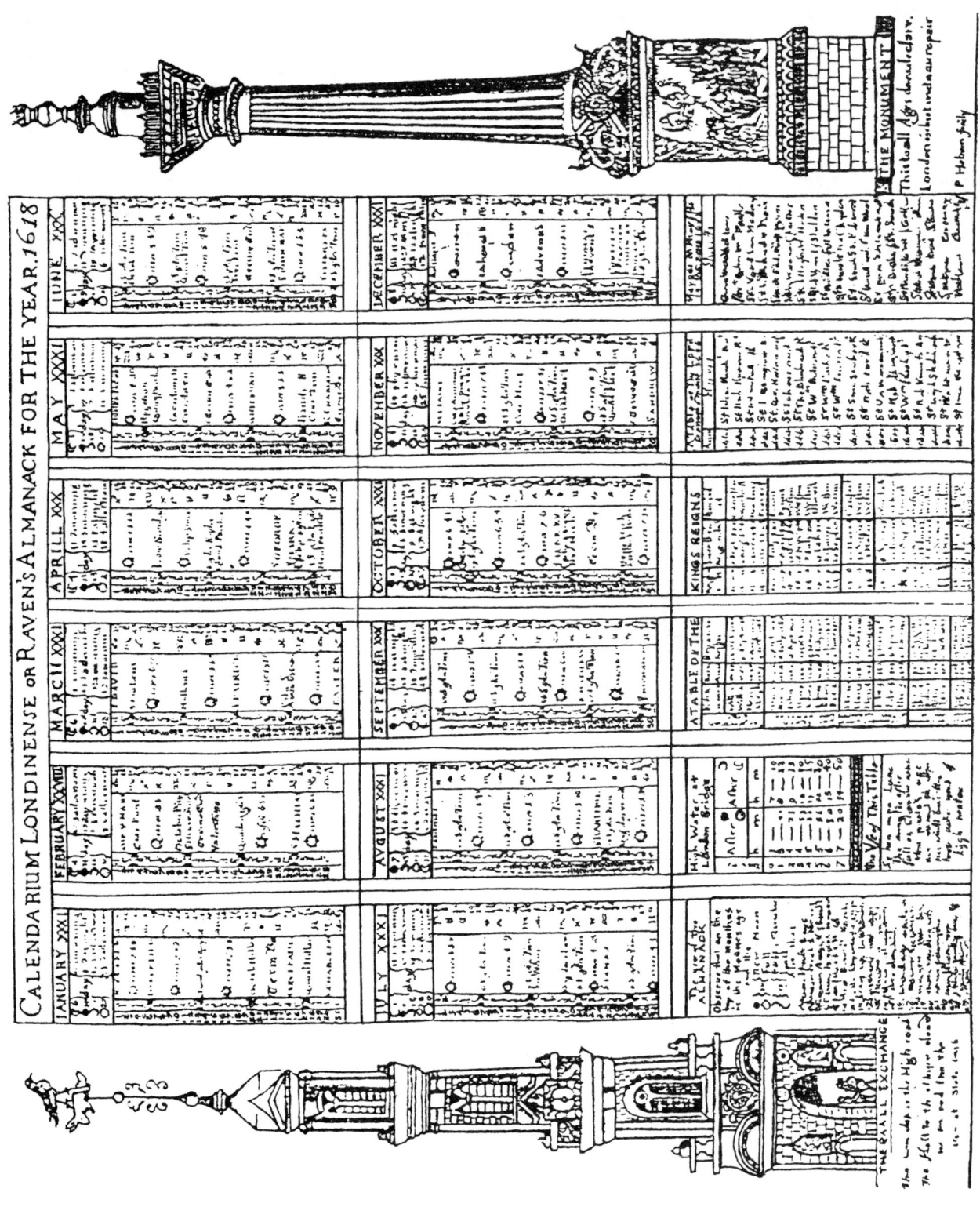

Fig. 42. A broadsheet almanac.

10. ALMANACS and CALENDARS

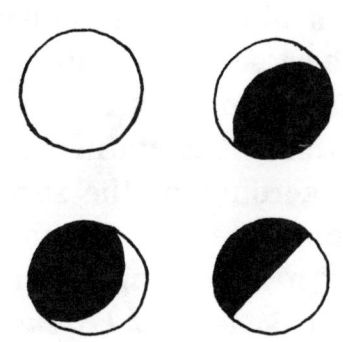

Among the other navigational aids needed by the shipmaster and his pilot or navigator was an almanac or calendar, which gave him the phases of the moon, in order to judge the tidal influences on water depths at the ports he intended to visit.

The most important of the Continental astrologers was the Laet family who were Flemish astrologers and physicians. Based on the work of the Laet family, France produced the *Kalendar of Shepherdes*, which was a large perpetual calendar containing religious and moral advice as well as rules for good health. The English editions were at first translated abroad and printed at Antwerp, then shipped to England.

When the English printers became aware of the possibilities, almanacs began to be printed in England. The first printed almanac in England made its appearance in 1503 under the title *The Kalendar of shypper's*. It was actually a crude translation of the French work, which included a description of the universe and numerous moral precepts. Because of its great popularity it went through several editions. In 1520 Richard Pynson, the king's printer, organized the translation of Laet's prognostications, which was chosen because of the popularity of his earlier works and because of his reputation as 'an expert master in the science.'

Simpler almanacs were printed as broadsheets for use by mariners and the less educated. [Fig. 43] These simple broadsheets were in a form which could be posted on a bulkhead aboard ship or posted on a wall. They contained a calendar showing the light and dark times of the moon and some weather forecasts. Pocket almanacs contained the same type of information as the broadsheets, but with more complete information. For all of these calendars and almanacs the year began with the vernal equinox — March 11 — and each day began at noon.

The true almanac was a larger work which elaborated on the major astronomical events of the year which might have an influence on terrestrial events. Information included in these almanacs would be the times of conjunction and opposition of the sun and moon, tables of declination, the position of some of the stars, and the rule for using the Pole Star. Sometimes a number of years were included in one volume. The first combined calendar and almanac was published in 1539.

As early as 1541 the English edition of Laet's almanac contained tide-tables for London, Sandwich and Bristol. Robert Askham's annual almanac printed in 1553 was the first English almanac to start the year on January 1, and though it did not include tide-tables, it contained the rules for reckoning time by the stars. A detailed account of the sun's position month by month through the year was published by Anthony Askham in 1555. Hubrigh's 1565 edition contained a blank page facing the calendar for each month. The following year *A Blanke and Perpetuall Almanack* appeared with blank pages on which the reader could note debts, expenses or any events he wished to remember. By 1566 a perpetual almanac gave tide-tables for over thirty harbors throughout the British Isles and the English Channel. In 1569 Hubrigh's almanac added notes to assist navigation from Portland Bill to Berwick with notable landmarks, locations of dangerous shoals and other impediments to shipping. Tide-tables became a standard part of almanacs, especially for the Thames — very often for other areas as well.

The early almanacs contained prognostications concerning governments and heads of states, which produced some concerns in those quarters. They were not certain just how much these prognostications might affect their destinies. It is not surprising, therefore, that when the Company of Stationers was incorporated in England the government had some supervision of the press. The royal injunctions of 1559 set up a system of licensing for the press in an effort to control prognostications. In 1562 — with governmental controls in place — twenty booksellers were arrested for selling a prognostication by Nostradamus. The editions of Nicolson for 1563 and Stephens for 1569 carried the assurances that they had been examined and allowed according to the injunctions.

Beginning in 1571 the publication of annual almanacs in England was controlled by a patent which confined their issue to two London printers — Watkins and Roberts. This arrangement continued until the death of Watkins in 1599, after which almanacs were published by the assigns of Roberts until 1603. During Elizabeth's reign the printed almanac quickly took its standard form. Grossenne's almanac of 1571 contained road directions for England, and a table of kings since the Conquest.

James I issued a new charter which gave the Company of Stationers a complete monopoly on the publishing of almanacs, which they retained until the late eighteenth century. By this time the almanac took on a set form which then included the ecclesiastical calendar, times for bloodletting and purging, zodiacal influences on the anatomy of man, tables of the position of the moon in the zodiac, phases of the moon, fair dates for all of England, and a sort of atlas which gave the distances of various towns from London. In addition to all of this there would be a prognostication of the weather and other events which might be under the influence of astrology.

During the sixteenth and seventeenth centuries the almanac became such a popular item that it could be found in just about everyone's pocket. These early editions had a close relationship to our modern pocket diaries — some even included blank pages for personal notes. [Fig. 44] Of particular interest to the mariners were those editions which included the ebbs and floods for various coasts along the English Channel.

The second *Booke of the Sea Carte* not only included prognostications and tide-tables, but added information about winds, thunder, lightning, rainbows and the look of the sea in such homely quotes as: 'A sudden calm in the sea after great wind signifieth the wind to change, or then the same wind to increase and grow;' or of the sea: 'The rock and sands of the sea, making a murmur, or sounds without, and not on shore, signifieth great storm to come...The sea froth appearing in divers places, bellowing of the water signifieth evil weather for many days after.' This kind of information was of great importance to everyone who ventured out upon the waters.

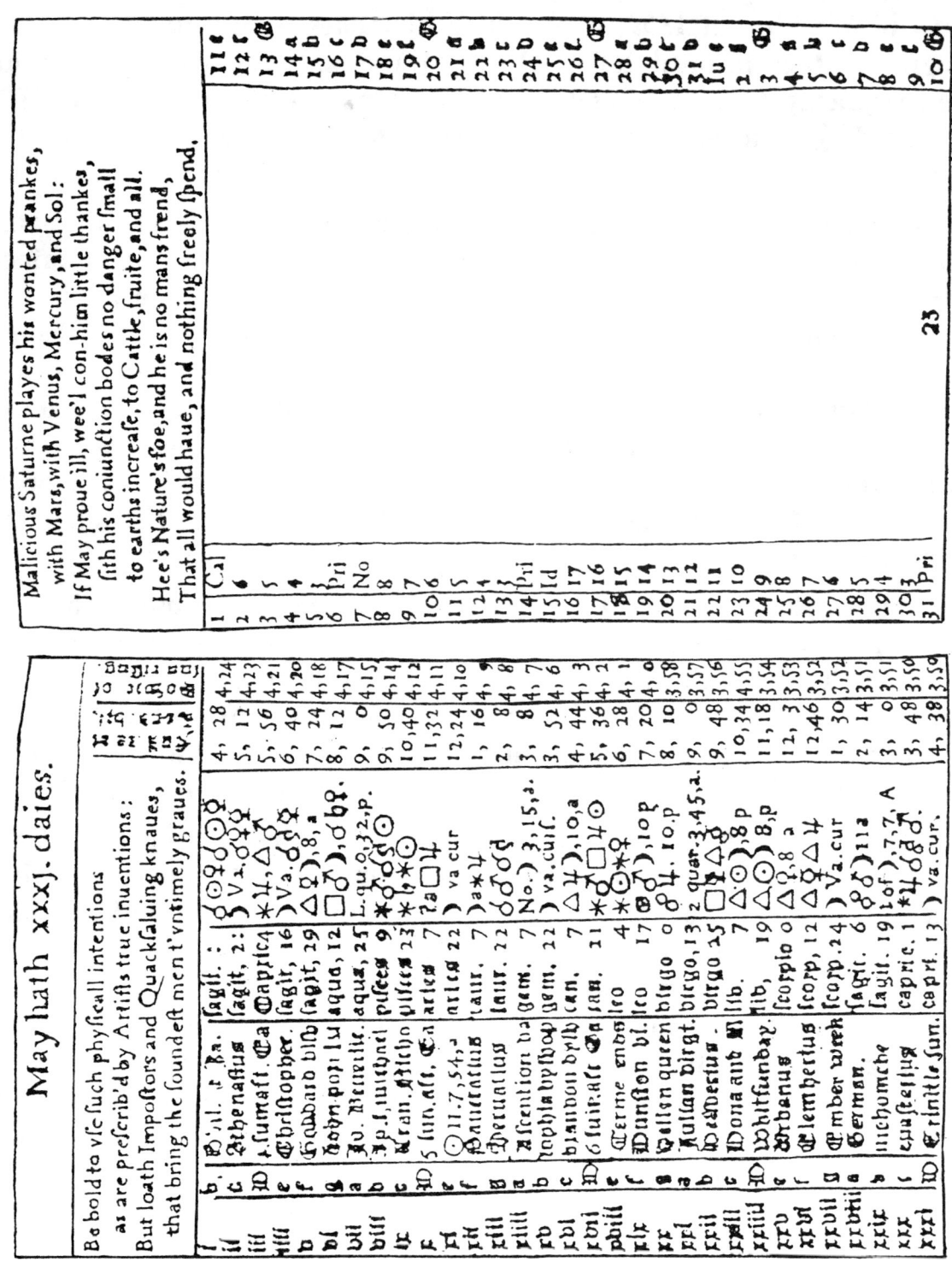

Fig. 43. Page of a pocket-type almanac.

11. TIDE TABLES

Of extreme importance to the shipmaster was the matter of tides. Tides are the alternate raising and lowering of water levels along the coasts. The ancient writers of Greece and Rome give little mention of the phenomenon. This is understandable, since the Mediterranean is an almost tideless sea. Therefore, the range of tide levels was not as important to shipmasters in the Mediterranean trade as it was to those who sailed the northern waters around the coasts of England and northwest France, where the range of water levels could be as much as five fathoms (30 feet).

A shipmaster on the northern waters had to know as precisely as possible just when the flood stream would occur in order to sail safely into a given port. Any misjudgment on the part of a shipmaster or pilot could cause his ship to run aground or to strike underwater rocks and shoals during the ebb tide. Therefore, tide tables or notes in his pocket notebook (or 'rutter') would be carefully consulted before a shipmaster dared approach too closely to any port of call.

Pliny described the rising and falling of the waters in A.D. 77, when he wrote his *Natural History*. By the eighth century it was understood that the movement of water was related to the moon. The philosophers who wrote about the relationship between the tides and the moon were probably informed of this phenomenon by unnamed mariners. Those who had to navigate tidal waters would most certainly have been aware of the daily and monthly variations, and used their experience in their daily work — even though the causes were beyond their understanding.

TIDAL PREDICTION

As early as the thirteenth century a tide table had been compiled by the monks at St. Albans. In it is found the times of high-water at

London Bridge for each day of the moon's age. The determination of the information contained in a tide table is known as 'tidal prediction'. A tidal prediction demands a knowledge of the laws of the tides — and their correlation with astronomical variables — for each location where a tide table is being constructed.

FLOOD AND EBB TIDES

When a current is moving in toward the land, or up an estuary, it is called the 'flood' current. When a current is running away from the land, or down an estuary, it is called the 'ebb' current.

RANGE OF TIDE

The range of tide is the difference in level between successive high and low tides. Generally, the high water is about as much above the mean level of the sea as the following low level is below it. However, the range of tide may vary from day to day, and at most places the high tide reaches its maximum height only once in two weeks — reaching its minimum height at times midway between two maximum heights. Christopher Jones would certainly have been aware of tidal range. MAYFLOWER was being moored at Rotherhithe — just across the Thames River from London. At London Bridge the average tidal range in a two-week period was 21 feet, and the least range in the same length of time was 14 feet 11 inches. MAYFLOWER would have to ride at anchor in such a manner as to accommodate this tidal range twice a day.

SPRING AND NEAP TIDES

The waters around England reach their maximum range of tide a day or so after the new and full moon, and are known as 'spring tides'. The highest tide of the lunar month is caused by the combined effect of the moon and the sun on the waters of the seas. About the time of the equinoxes [March 21 and September 22] the spring tides are generally larger, while at the time of the solstices [June 21 and December 22] the spring tides are generally smaller than usual. During Christopher Jones' time, it was too difficult to determine the mean sea level to which a tidal range could be related. Therefore, the sea guides (or 'rutters') of the day rarely made mention of the difference between the water depth at spring tides.

The 'neap tide' is the lowest level of high tide, or a high tide lower than usual. It occurs every two weeks when the moon is at the first and third quarters. At those two points the sun's attraction counteracts the moon's influence, causing the high tide to be smaller than usual. The range of tide usually reaches its minimum a day or so after the quarters. By 1569 indications were being made for neap tides and full seas — as well as the effect of wind on the tides.

TIDAL INTERVALS

The water level at most coastal locations reaches its highest level approximately twice a day. The times of high water have an intimate relation to the positions of the moon and the sun. The average elapsed time between two successive high waters is 12 hours and 24 minutes. That period of time is half that of the moon's apparent revolution around the earth. However, this interval may vary considerably, depending on the location.

The length of time between the moon's crossing the meridian of a given location and the next high water there is known as the 'high water interval' for that place. The length of time between the moon's crossing the meridian and the next low water is called the 'low water interval'.

THE ESTABLISHMENT OF PORT

The 'establishment of the port' refers to the average value of the high water interval [the time between the moon's crossing the meridian and the succeeding high water] on the days of the new and full moon. By the first half of the sixteenth century tide tables began to appear in almanacs, giving shipmasters handy guide to the establishment of port for many places. The establishment of port for Rotherhithe, where MAYFLOWER was docked before beginning her historic voyage, is 1 hour and 58 minutes — a fact which Master Jones would have known well.

HIGH AND LOW TIDE DOUBLED

At most places on the ocean coastlines the time taken by the tide in its rising is almost equal to the time taken in falling on the same day.

There are places where the high waters are 'doubled'. This means that the water reaches a maximum height, falls a little, and then rises to a maximum height again before receding into a low tide. At other places it is the low tide that is 'doubled'. Southampton is one of those places where the high waters are doubled — a phenomenon quite familiar to Master Jones, who had sailed into this port a number of years prior to the 1620 departure.

CURRENT DIRECTION

The tidal current in a strait or narrow sea generally flows in one direction for about six hours and twelve minutes, and then in the opposite direction for about the same time. At the point when the current reverses itself, there is a period of time when the water comes to a rest — commonly referred to as 'slack water'. In estuaries the current flowing downstream may do so in about a quarter length of the time it took to flow upstream. In the open sea waters the directions of the current may take in all points of the compass within a tidal period, making a complete revolution in that space of time.

CURRENT SPEED

There is a great range in the speed of tidal currents from one place to another. At one place the speed of the current may reach seven knots, while in others, such as the North Sea, it may only reach a speed of one knot. When the tidal current reaches some distance up certain rivers the water may spread over flat sands in a roaring surf and become almost a wall of water, commonly called a 'bore'. Any experienced mariner knew the effects of current direction and speed. Christopher Jones would have been no exception, especially since he sailed the North Sea to Norway with cargo, and returned to London by way of the Thames estuary and river. No rutter of the time recorded the strength of the tidal stream until the eighteenth century when that information began to be included in sailing directions.

DIURNAL INEQUALITY

In England and Ireland there is a fairly regular tidal movement, making it possible to provide fairly simple tables, which relate to the transit of the moon. The day to day advance in time of high water is fairly uniform, and the variations in the height of high water and the changes in low water are predictable since they relate to the transit of the moon. Creating a tide table is relatively simple when necessary corrections are made — taking into consideration the changing distances of the moon and sun.

With this apparent simplicity in the tide waters surrounding England, the English mariners thought that similar methods could be used in all waters. However, at many places outside of the Atlantic the height of two successive high or low tide waters might be considerably different. This phenomenon is known as 'diurnal inequality'. English mariners might have had more difficulty when navigating in waters where there was diurnal inequality in the tides.

TIDAL COMPUTATION

It had been established that the time of high water was always the same on the day of the new moon. Time-keeping was still a problem for the seaman who used sand-glasses and his compass clock to record the passage of time. In order to simplify the tide tables for mariners the times of high-water at various ports on the days of the full and new moon were given in terms of the compass bearing of the moon at high-water. However, in some rutters the time of low-tide was given instead.

Haphazard arrangement of information in various rutters could prove confusing to a shipmaster who was visiting an unfamiliar port. Using the compass clock, a port might be listed as 'North-North-West and South-South-East', which indicated that the full and new moon occurred at 10:30 PM and 10:30 AM.

Of special interest to Christopher Jones was the information that at Dover the moon was South at high tide, which indicated at noon and midnight. As trouble developed with SPEEDWELL and they were forced to turn into Dartmouth, Jones would have consulted his rutters to learn that high water occurred on days of full and change at ports on the English coast between Start and the Lizard at a West Southwest moon, which meant 4:30 PM and 4:30 AM.

The shipmaster knew that successive high tides normally occurred at intervals of 12 hours 24 minutes. Therefore, there was a complete cycle of tides during a lunar month of 29 1/2 days. Within the 24-hour solar day there was a retardation of 48 minutes or 4/5 of an hour. However, that was not a convenient figure for the northern seamen to

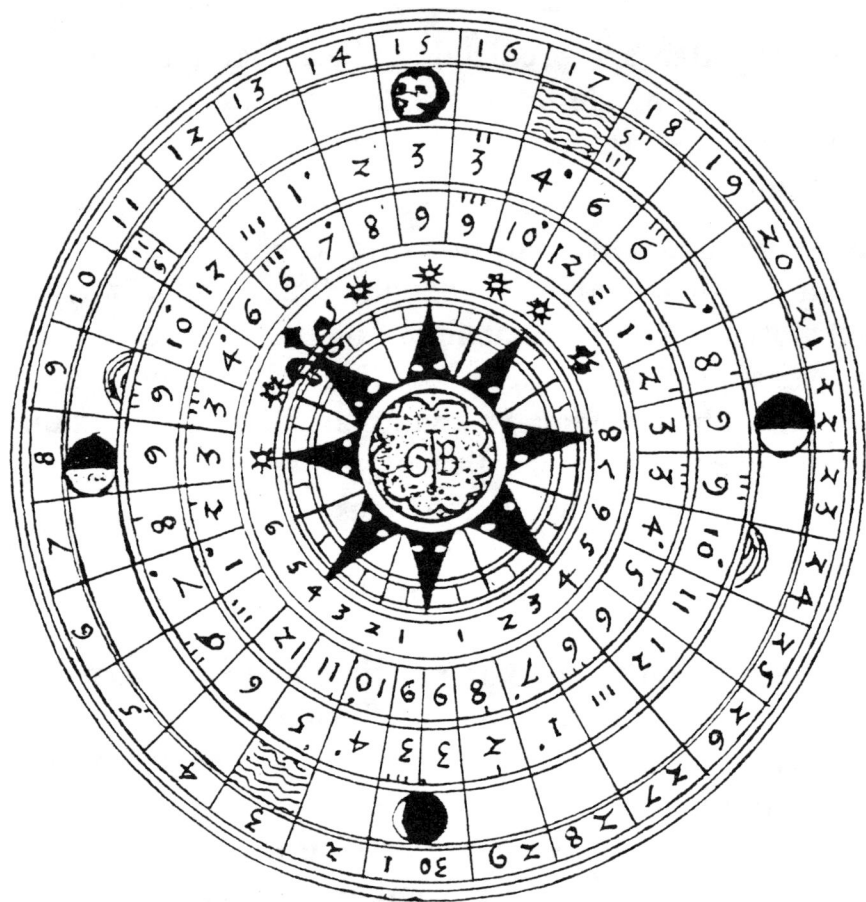

Fig. 44. The rose calendar by Brouscon for calculating tides of high & low water.

compute with the aid of their compass of 32-points. To facilitate computation a mariner often adopted the daily retardation of 45 minutes. Using that figure, he was able to calculate accurately enough for practical purposes the daily change in the time of high-water. Each point on his compass had the value of 45 minutes.

After verifying from his tide table the times of high tide for the port which he was entering, he consulted his almanac to find the age of the moon. Then he was able to subtract one point of his compass for every day of the moon's age. The only problem was that by using the 45-minute (or one point) calculation, the compass was off by three minutes per day. This error could then be corrected by starting on the same point on the sixteenth day.

Breton tide-tables of the fifteenth and sixteenth centuries were more elaborate. Lines on these charts ran out from the points of a compass-card of rhumbs to the various seaports, according to the hour of establishment [the time of high water on the day of new and full moon]. [Fig. 44]

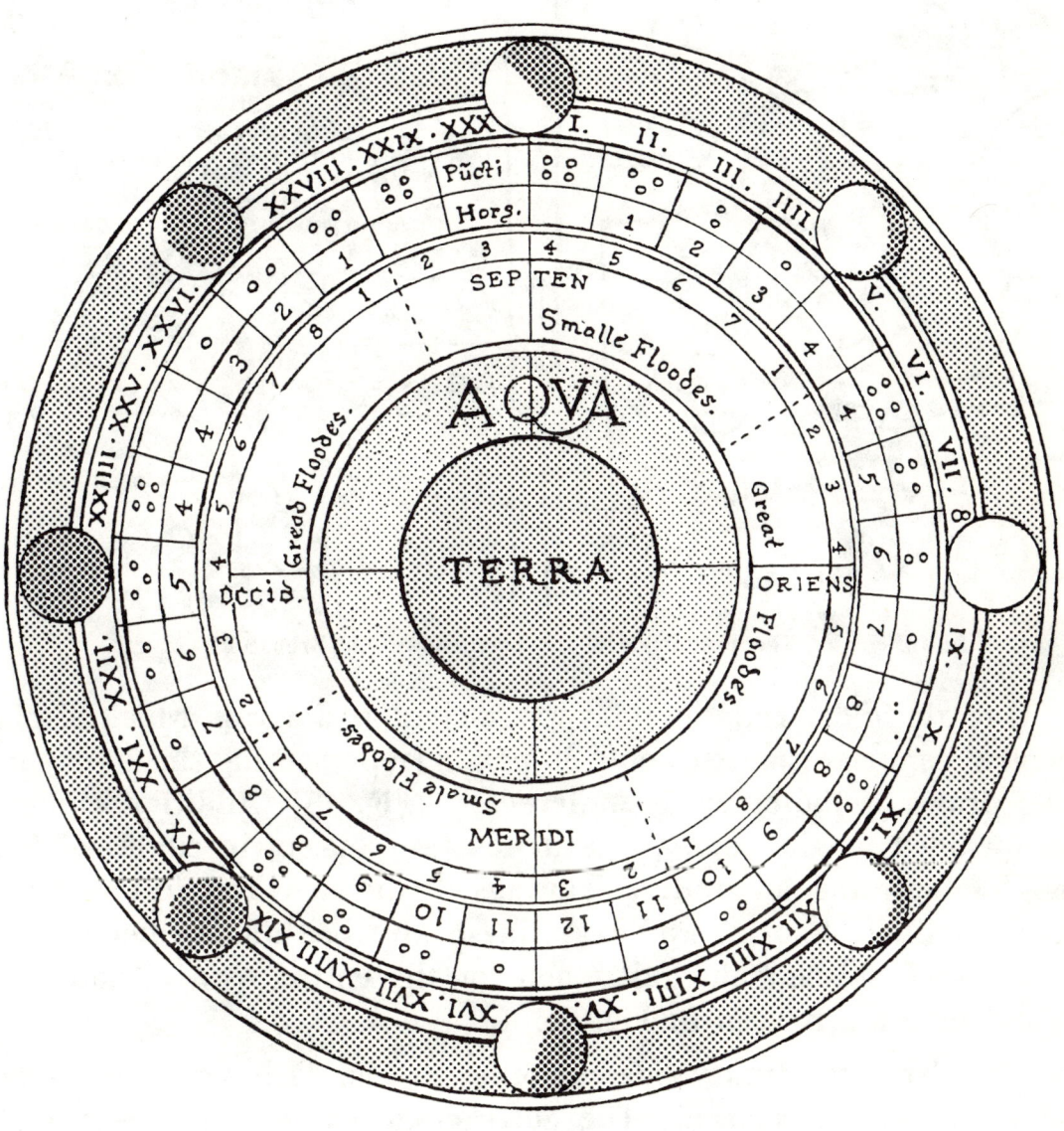

Fig. 45. Thirty point rose calendar for calculating tide.

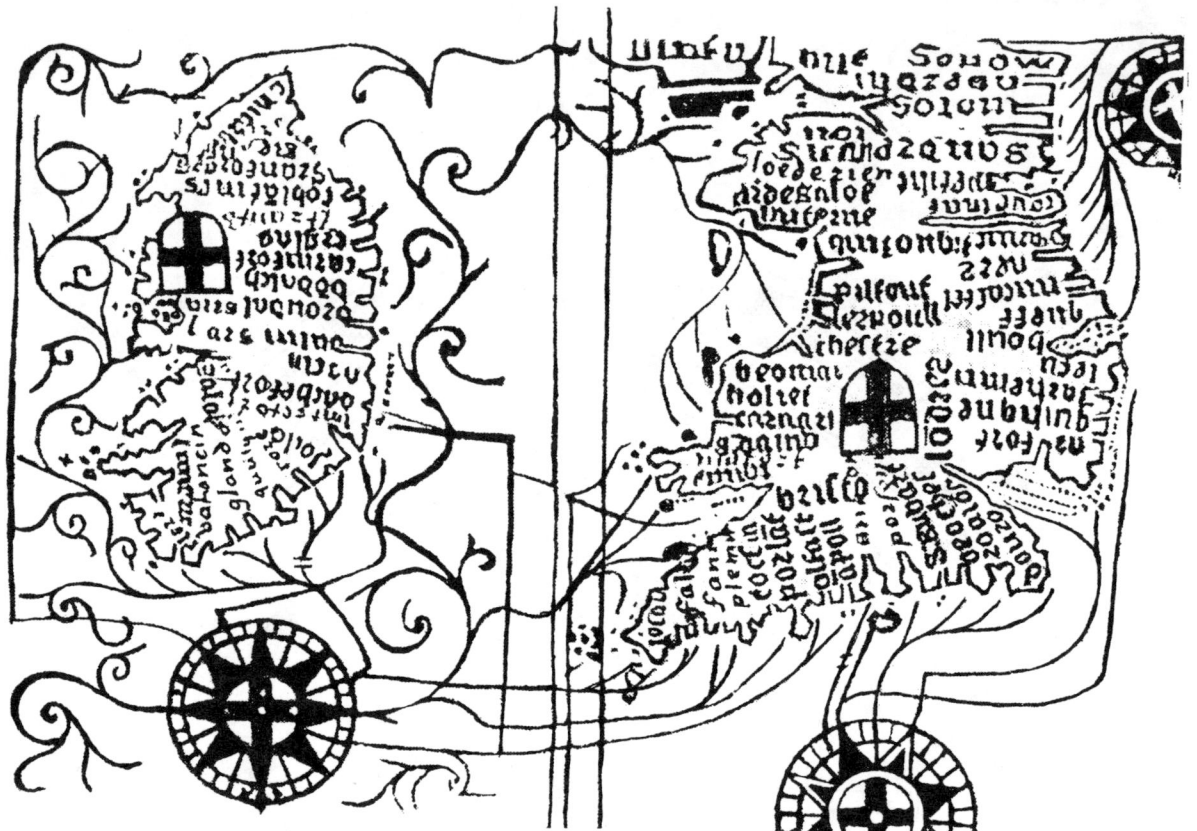

Fig. 46. The establishment of port shown on Brouscon's chart.

One aid in determining tides was a circular diagram which displayed a central compass-rose with only 30 points (representing the 30-day lunar cycle) drawn to the outer circumference. [Fig. 45] Additional information included on the compass-card was two concentric circles of hours, times of high and low water, drawings of the new and full moon, and representations of spring and neap tides. Attached was a calendar giving the dates of the new and full moon for the entire year. Another type of tidal diagram is seen in Fig. 46.

The sixteenth-century tide computer in Fig. 47 is based on the concept of the compass-clock. The outer circle carries the 24-hour clock dial and the mariner's equivalent of rhumbs. The middle disk with pointer carries the 29 1/2 days (representing the age of the moon), which allows it to be set to the establishment of any port. The inner dial (when set to the age of the moon) indicates the time of high water on that day for the designated port.

Because tidal information was so incomplete by modern standards, it was not uncommon for ships to run aground — even in well-known ports. An experienced mariner, such as Christopher Jones, knew the dangers and was more likely to avoid problems caused by the tides.

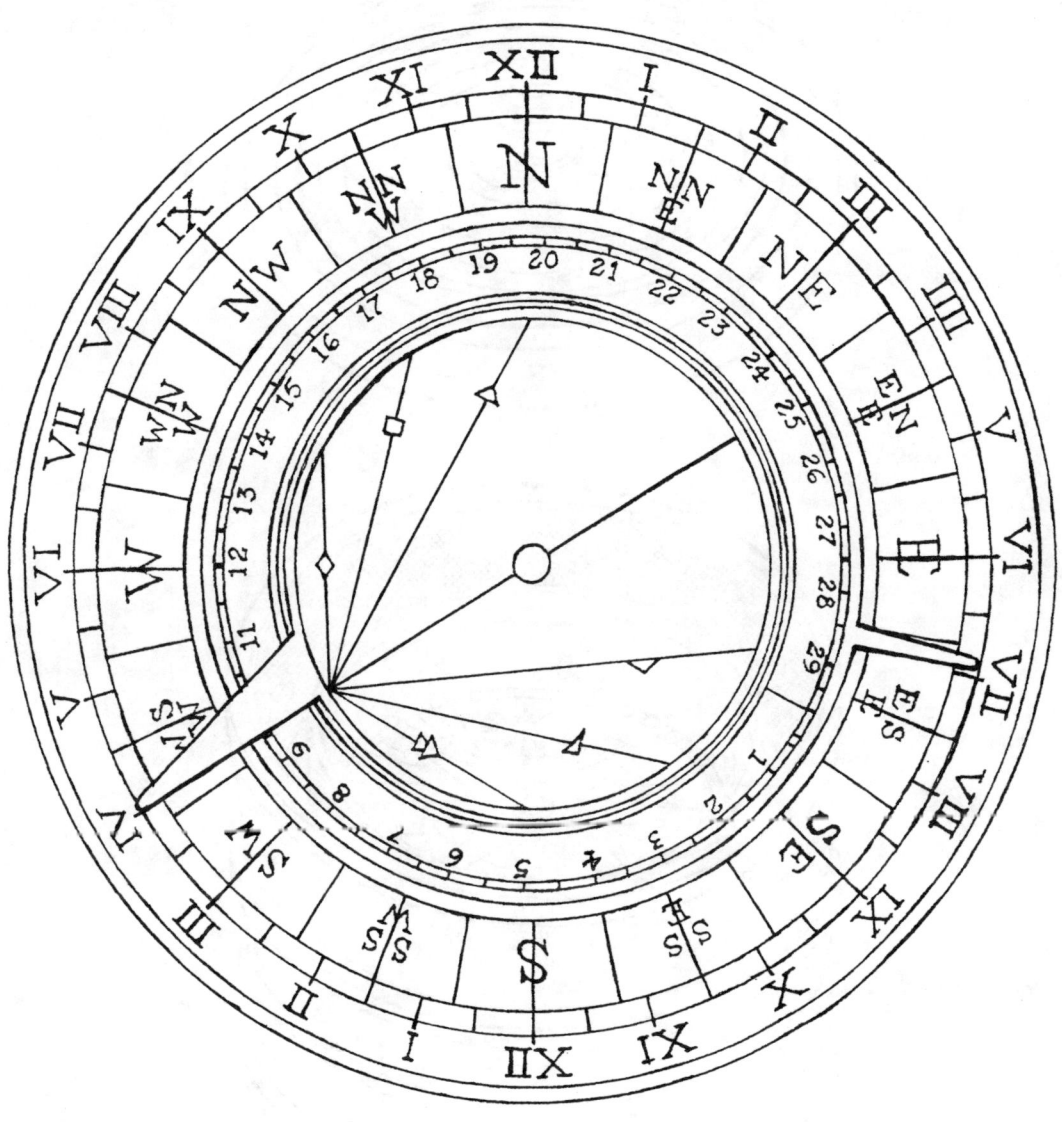

Fig. 47. A sixteenth century tide calculator.

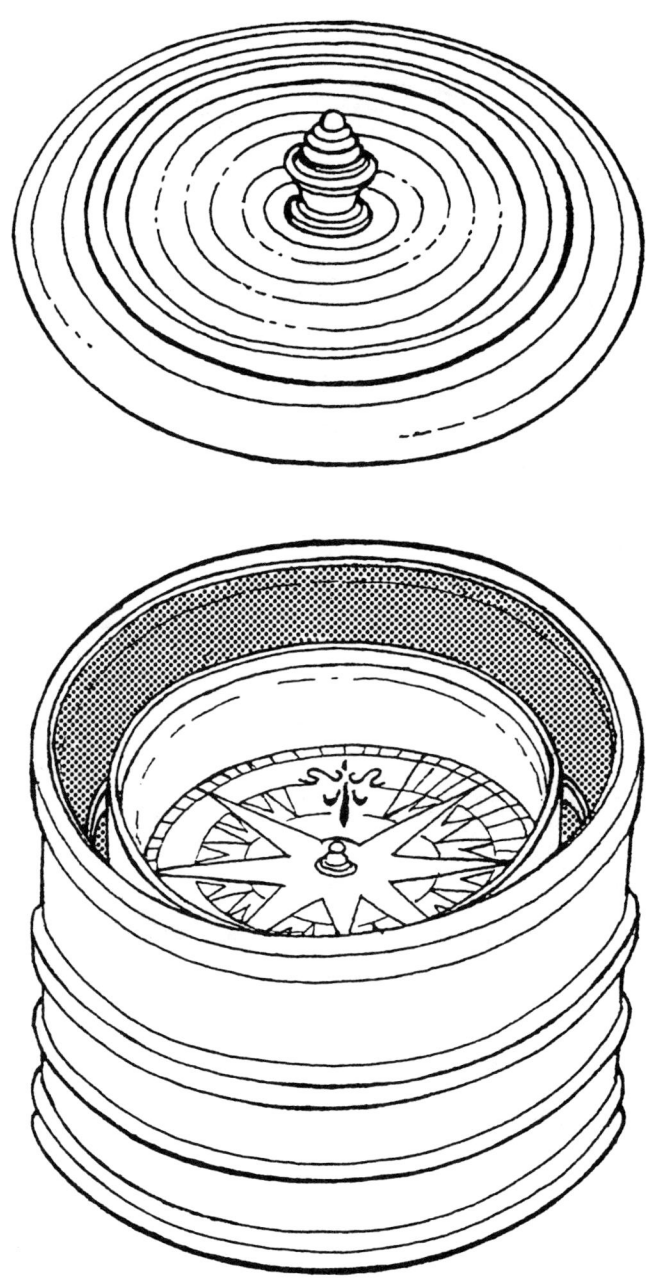

12. THE MARINER'S COMPASS

One of the oldest navigation instruments made available to shipmasters was the compass — probably second only to the hand leadline. Until the compass came into use at sea, the mariners were dependent upon the winds to give them an indication of direction. These directions were based on the 'rhumbs of the wind', and were simply referred to as 'rhumbs'.

The magnetic compass is based on the natural forces of geomagnetism — or the magnetism of the earth. The earth has a magnetic field around it much as though it had a powerful bar magnet embedded in its center. The mariner's compass is a term which is commonly used to describe the magnetic compass used at sea.

It was a marvel of the time, when the discovery was made that the lodestone [magnetic oxide of iron] would point to the north when freely suspended. That discovery has been attributed to the Chinese. Although, the discovery of the magnetized needle, which became the central feature of the mariner's compass, seems to have been developed independently in the European region.

THE LODESTONE

The term 'lodestone' is thought to have come down to us from the old English 'lad,' which meant *leader* or *guide*. Therefore, magnetic oxide of iron became known among mariners as the 'guiding stone'. Over a period of time it was discovered that a magnetized needle, if it were free to dip and turn, would align itself with the magnetic field of the earth, pointing in a northerly direction — the direction of the North Star, which was the sailor's guiding star at sea. The North Star is also known by a number of other names, such as Polaris, the lodestar, the Pole Star and 'Stella Maris' ['Star of Mary'].

DEVELOPMENT OF THE MARINER'S COMPASS

There are many theories about the origin of the magnetic compass. However, it appears that it probably developed in the Mediterranean or European regions. There are indications that the compass was in use by mariners in the year 1187 — and, the first mention does not refer to it as being a 'new' development. Guyott de Provins, a French poet, described the nautical use of a compass when the Pole Star was hidden from view. However, it may have been in use as early as 203 B.C. when Hannibal set sail from Italy with Pelorus as his pilot.

A needle stuck through a straw and floated in a bowl of water seems to be the earliest recorded version of the mariner's compass. In use, the shipmaster or pilot pointed a lodestone at the floating needle to attract it to the stone, then moved the stone round and round, faster and faster until with a sudden movement he withdrew the stone. When done properly the floating needle pointed to the Pole Star.

By 1248 Hugo de Bercy described a new compass construction in which the needle was supported on two floats. Early in the thirteenth century the needle for use at sea was being mounted on a pivot rather than floated in a bowl of water, which had been a problem for mariners on vessels tossed about by the waves.

THE COMPASS ROSE WITH NEEDLE

It was only a matter of time before the needle was actually being 'touched' and then glued under a wind-rose. Adoption of the wind rose as a compass card, or 'fly', has generally been assigned the late thirteenth or early fourteenth century. There are traditions which attribute this development to Alavio Gioja, who attached a sliver of lodestone or a magnetized needle to a card and set it on a pivot. Surviving sailing directions from about 1250 were given in half-points of the compass of the horizon, which suggests that a boxed compass with a fly was already available to mariners in the Mediterranean waters.

The wind-rose had become established as the eight winds and their halves and quarters. The term 'compass' originally denoted the nautical division of the circle of the horizon into its 32 points of 'rhumbs.'

THE BINNACLE

Apparently the officer of a medieval ship used a magnetic compass that was only four or five inches in diameter in a box of brass or wood. [Fig, 48] The compass used by the helmsman who steered — or 'conned' — the ship would have been kept in, or on, a small wooden cupboard near the whipstaff. This small cupboard, called the binnacle (or 'bittacle') also held what Capt. John Smith called a 'dark lanthorne' [a lantern closed on all but one side] in order to see the compass at night. The 'dark lanthorne' cut down on excess light, and allowed the helmsman a better view of the stars, which he might be using as a guide.

GIMBALS

We are told that English sailors used the needle and stone during the fifteenth century, when they sailed the six-day voyage to Iceland. A reference from sixteenth century literature proves that early in that century the compass aboard ships was also hung in gimbals in an outer box. The use of brass gimbal rings permitted the compass to remain in a horizontal position as the ship rolled over the waves.

THE LUBBER'S LINE

The lubber's line was a mark on the compass box which was aligned with the keel of the ship, and indicated to the helmsman the position of the bow of the ship in relationship to the compass fly. Prior to its introduction, the helmsman simply used the masts or the stem of the ship as a reference. In 1269 Petrus Peregrinus de Maricourt described the use of a 'lubber's line' equipped with sights for taking bearings. Cortes did not mention the use of a lubber's line in his writing, but it was mentioned again in the Spanish navigation manual written by Zamorano in 1581. This work was translated into English in 1610. Thus, the English mariners were definitely aware of its use by the beginning of the seventeenth century.

EARLY COMPASS CONSTRUCTION

By the late sixteenth century the mariner's compass had developed into an instrument very much like those of today. In 1596 Martin Cortes described the construction of a mariner's compass in his work, *The*

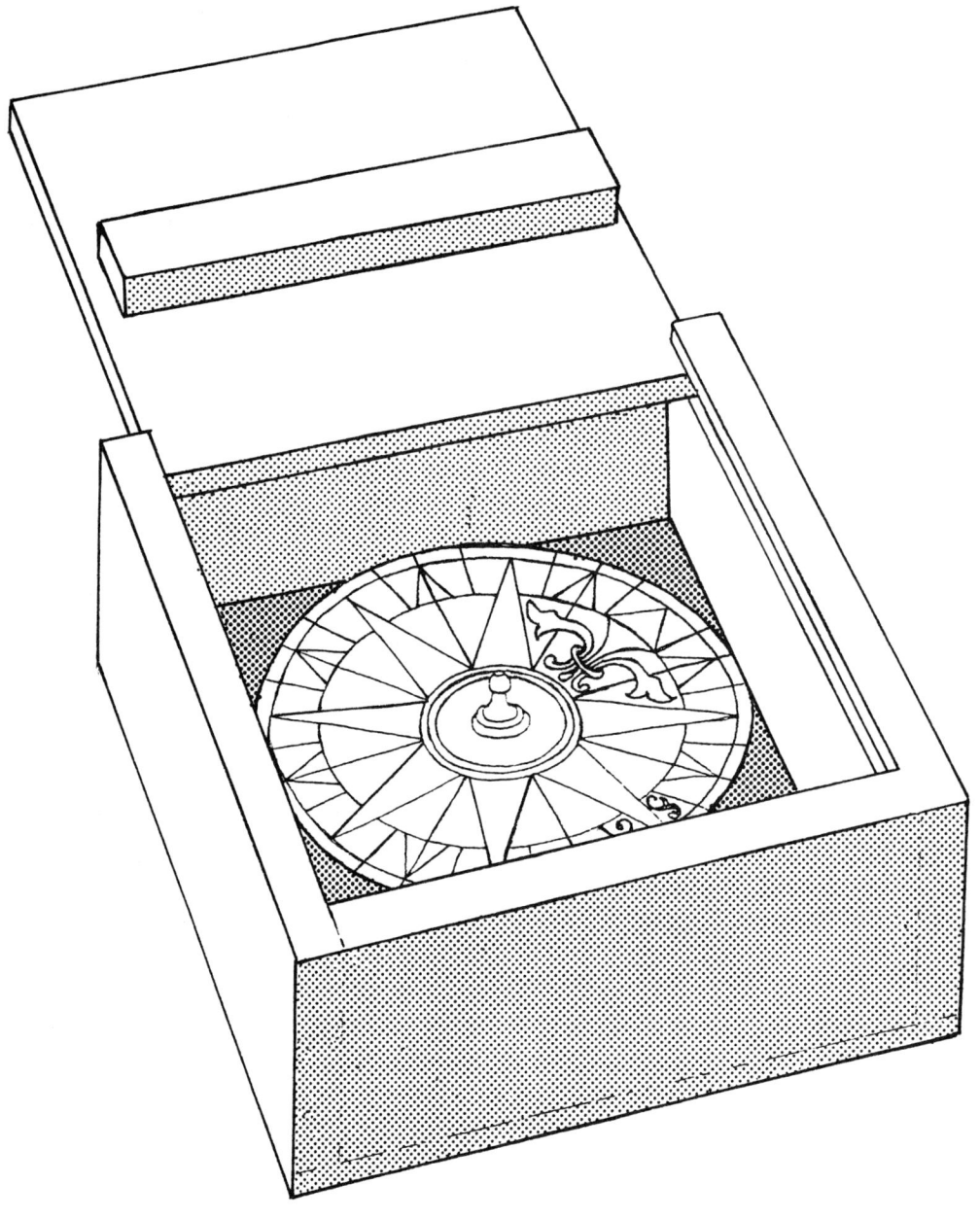

Fig. 48. The mariner's compass.

Art of Navigation. Quoting from his work, the seaman was told to 'take a piece of paper and cut it into a circle the diameter equal to the span of an man's hand. Mark it into 32 points of the compass, distinguishing North by a fleur-de-lis. Take a wire of iron or steel of the largeness of a great pin and fix it to the underside of the card and touch it with a lodestone.'

In his book *Sea Grammar*, published in 1627, Capt. John Smith describes the mariner's compass as follows:

> 'The compasse, which everyone knowes is a round box, and in the midst of the bottome a sharpe pin called a Center whereupon the Fly doth play, which is a round peece of pace-board, with a small wyer under it touched with a Load-stone, in the midst of it is a little brasse Cap that doth keepe it levell upon a Center. On the upper part is painted 32 points of the Compasse covered with glasse to keepe it from dust, breaking, or the wind; this Box doth hang in two or three brasse circles, so fixed they give such way to the moving of the Ship that still the Box will stand steady: there is also a darke Compasse, and a Compasse for variation, yet they are but as the other, onely the darke Compasse hat the points blacke and white, and the other onely touched for the true North and South.'

For an exploded view of the mariner's compass, see Fig. 49.

THE COMPASS BOX

The compass box was a round wooden bowl or box turned out of a solid piece of wood. The height of the box was generally about one-half the diameter of the fly, and covered with glass, sealed with resin, and fitted with a detachable wooden base. This construction was of great importance to the mariner. The soft iron used in the manufacture of compasses did not hold its magnetic qualities over a long period of time, and had to be 'fed' [re-magnetized] regularly. The detachable bottom held the fixed brass pin upon which the compass fly rested.

Underneath the compass card, or 'fly', was attached the needle which was glued to the paper. [Fig. 50] The needle itself was a length of iron or steel wire, which was bowed double and pinched together at the ends to form a lozenge shape. Before the compass was assembled the needle was touched with a lodestone, which was a part of every pilot's equipment.

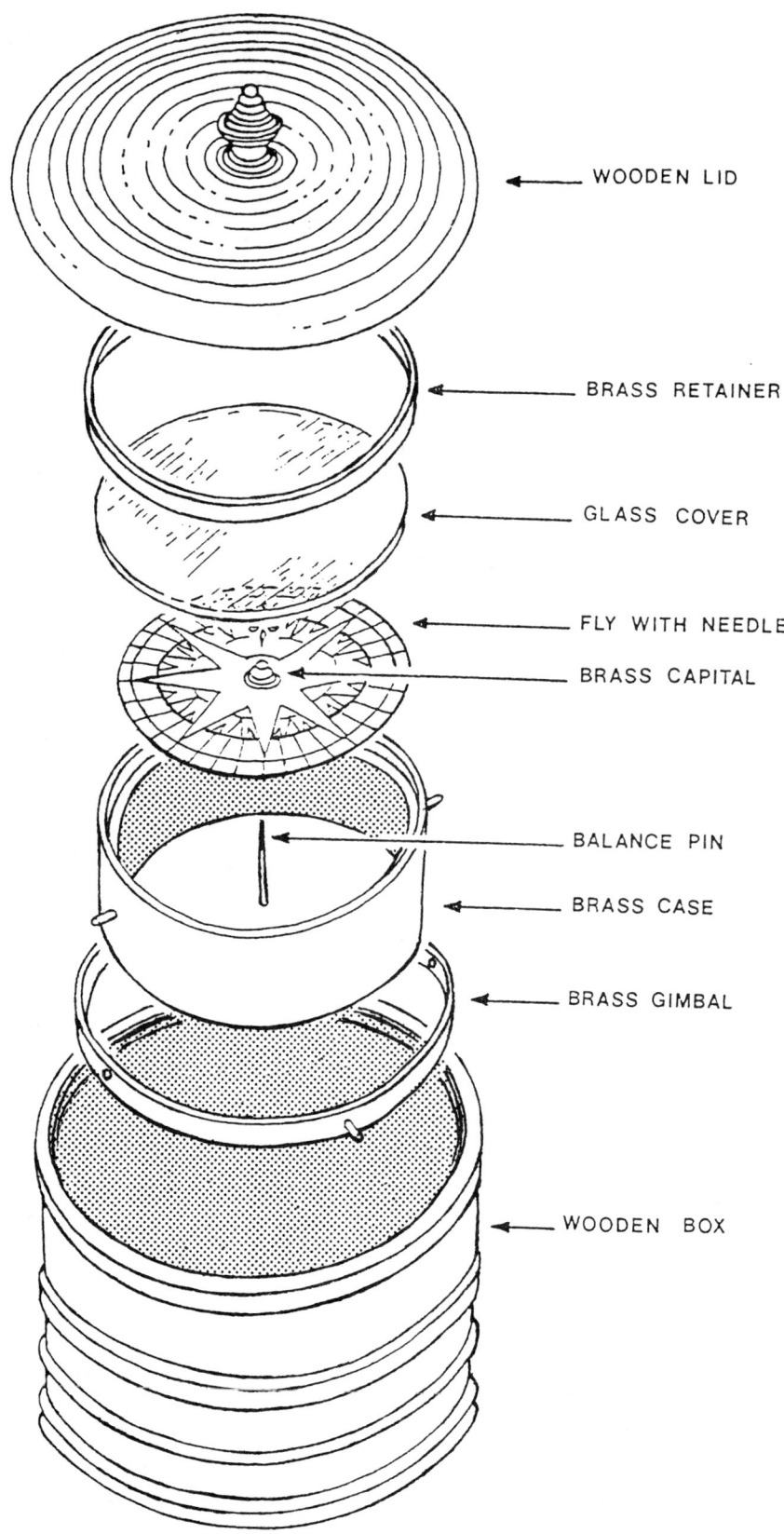

Fig. 49. Exploded view of a mariner's compass

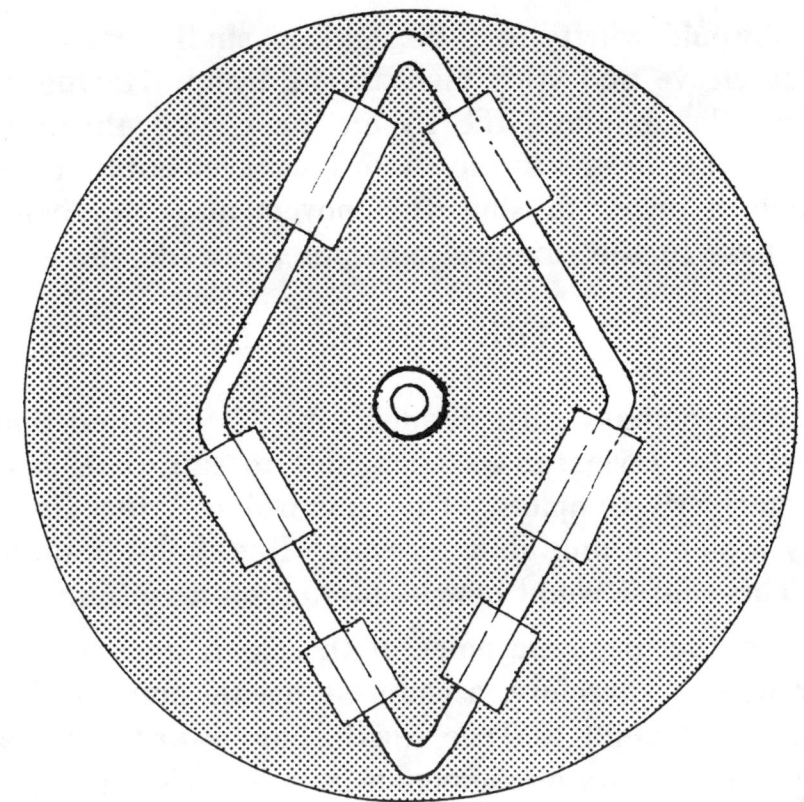

Fig. 50. Underneath compass card.

FEEDING THE COMPASS

The lodestone was generally kept in a decorative case which could be locked and hung up by a chain until it was needed. Care had to be taken that it was kept well away from the compass when not in use. [Fig. 51]

To 'feed' the compass the pilot took the stone from its case and rapped it sharply, which was supposedly done to align the particles in the stone toward its north point. Martin Cortes continues with the instructions as follows: 'wherein you shall rubbe the poynt of the

Fig. 51. Lodestone in case.

iron as you would whette a knife: and so shall certen of those beards of the stone cleave and stick faste to the iron.' Having completed this feeding, the pilot mounted the fly on the center pin and tested it for quickness. If the fly was too lively in its movements on the pin, the pin was blunted in order to slow the movement. He then replaced the detachable base in the compass and put away his stone.

THE RHUMB LINE

With the compass card divided into 32 principal points of 11 1/2 degrees each, the navigator was now able to sail along a rhumb-line by using the mariner's compass. The rhumb-line is the direction of travel followed by a ship sailing along a course line, following one point of the compass. This course could now be plotted on a suitably prepared chart.

However, the magnetic poles of the earth do not coincide with its geographic poles. Therefore, a compass needle pointing in the direction of north does not point to True North, but toward the Magnetic North Pole of the earth. This phenomenon is known as Variation. Moreover, the magnetic lines of attraction do not always point directly to the Magnetic North Pole, but may point to the east or west of that line — depending where you are on the globe. To complicate things even more, the Magnetic North and the lines of variation for a given region slowly move and shift over a period of years. The problems of magnetic variation will be discussed in more detail in the section on variation and deviation.

13. THE LOG-LINE

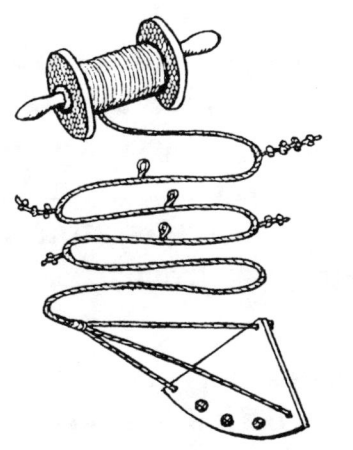

The log and log-line was an English contribution to navigation during the latter part of the sixteenth century. Its purpose was to calculate the distance traveled in a given period of time. From this calculation the navigator could better estimate his position at sea, and how much time would be required to reach landfall.

As sea charts developed and became more accurate, it became possible to locate a ship's position relative to latitude. However, with the absence of precise time-reckoning to calculate longitude, it became more important to measure the speed of a ship's progress through the water. Many experienced ship owners and navigators continued to estimate their speed by their understanding of the unique sailing qualities and swiftness of their vessels. Each ship had her own special tendencies, and every shipmaster worth his salt had an intimate knowledge of the way his ship handled. A number of the old pilots took great pride in their ability to judge accurately the speed of their ships on the basis of the sea and wind conditions.

THE DUTCH LOG

Some mariners made use of what is now called a 'Dutch log.' From a position near the bow of the ship they would toss some light object overboard and pace it to the stern as the vessel sailed past it. In a variation of this method, a mariner would station his mate in the stern and call out as he tossed an object overboard. As the object passed the vessel the two men would repeat a formula of syllables (or a verse) used to time the passing from bow to stern. Later, the rail was marked with a measured distance and the time required for the floating object to pass from bow to stern was noted. When the English log and log-line came into use an even more accurate method became available for judging the speed of a vessel.

THE ENGLISH LOG AND LOG-LINE

It is not known what Englishman developed the idea of the log and log-line. The earliest reference in any language appeared in *A Regiment of the Sea,* published in 1574 by William Bourne, a Gravesend gunner and teacher of navigation. It had already been in use for a time when Bourne reported it, and was probably developed between 1553 and 1573. By the time Bourne reported its use the small floating object had become a small triangular board, weighted on the lower edge so that it stood upright in the water. The triangular 'log' or 'chip' was attached to a line, which was reeled out as the ship sailed away from it. [Fig. 52]

In 1580 Bourne described the log and line in greater detail in his second edition of *A Regiment of the Sea*. He explained that the log was attached to the log-line by a 'crow-foot', so that when the log was cast overboard it moved astern at the speed of the ship. He cautioned that the log-line must be ready to reel out as fast as the ship sailed away from it.

THE STRAY LINE

Enough line had to be reeled out to place the log clear of the eddy from the stern before the timing was begun. This leading line became known as the 'stray line.' Therefore, the line was marked in two parts, according to the size of the ship. The start of the log-line proper was marked with a knot or a piece of bunting. Bourne recommended a stray line of two or three fathoms [12 to 18 feet], but does not give any further markings on the log-line proper.

THE LOG-LINE IN USE

In Bourne's day the log-line was laid loose at length on the deck so that it could run freely as the log was cast from the poop deck by the master or an assistant. As the knot marking the end of the stray line passed the taffrail, the minute glass was turned by a second assistant. As soon as the sand ran out on the minute-glass, the assistant called, 'Stop!' The first man who was reeling out the line stopped it

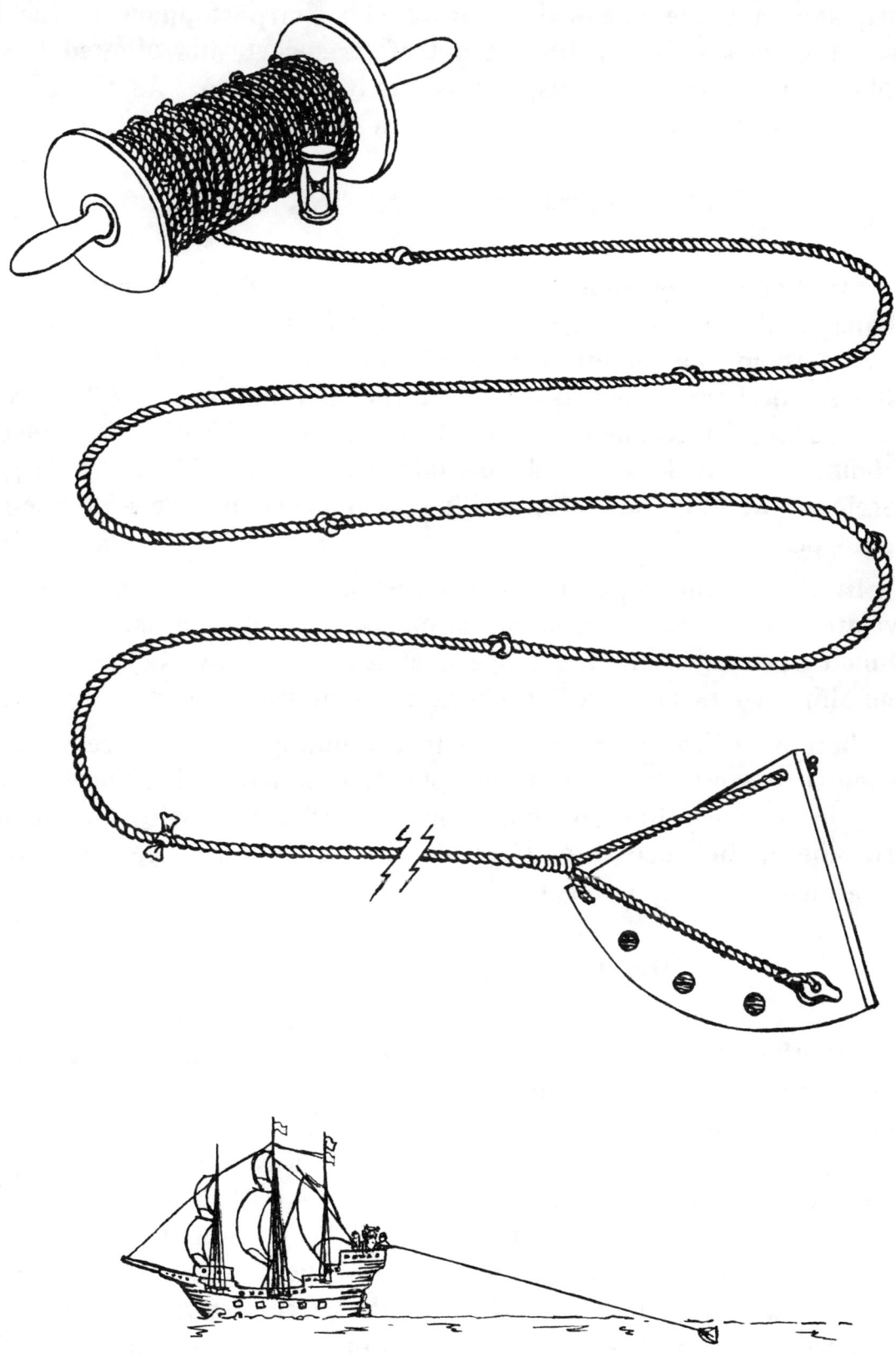

Fig. 52. The log-line.

short, snubbing the line with a jerk. The sharp stoppage of the line pulled the release pin on the log out of its socket, and allowed the log to plane in the water. Thus, it was easily hauled in. As the mariner pulled in the log-line it was measured in feet or fathoms. [Fig. 53]

METHOD OF CALCULATING SPEED

In Bourne's example, if the line reeled out was found to be 25 fathoms, and a half-minute glass were used [equal to 120th of an hour], the 25 fathoms was multiplied by 120 to find the number of fathoms sailed in an hour. In this example, the distance was 3,000 fathoms. Since the English league contained 2,500 fathoms, the distance sailed in an hour was one league and 500 fathoms [or one-fifth of a league]. Therefore, the ship had been sailing at a speed of one and one-fifth leagues per hour.

By casting the log every time the wind increased or decreased, the navigator could keep a good reckoning of the ship's progress. It was common practice to check the speed at least every two hours, although some shipmasters preferred to check every hour.

Because of the labor involved in computing the distance sailed in a given time — which involved multiplication, long-division and fractions — the log and log-line were not popular instruments with the mariners until about the second quarter of the seventeenth century, when logarithms were first published in round numbers.

THE LENGTH OF A SEA MILE

Another problem in computing speed was the incorrect length of the sea mile, and consequently of the measurement of a league. The number of fathoms considered to be a league was 2,500, but that was too few, and as a result the distance logged was too great. The Portuguese calculated the sea mile to be 5,000 feet with 64.6 miles to a degree of latitude. The cosmographers had been using the value of 60 miles to a degree. By the second quarter of the seventeenth century the English mathematicians had refigured the circumference of the earth, and reached the conclusion that 66 miles to a degree was more accurate. Not long after that decision, a new figure of 69 miles and four poles [66 ft.] was accepted as the distance for a degree.

Fig. 53. The log-line in use.

LOG-LINE KNOTTED FOR NEW MEASUREMENT

The mariners did not easily adopt new methods. The mathematicians realizing this trait in seamen of the time understood that the mariners would simply continue to use the old measurement of 60 miles to a degree [each mile composed of 5,000 feet; each degree equal to 300,000 feet]. Therefore, they suggested the correction could be made mechanically for the mariners by reknotting the log lines according to the new measurement. The new measurement was 352,000 feet to a degree [each mile composed of 5,870 feet]. Finally, the length of the sea mile was established at 6,080 feet to the mile [365,800 feet to a degree], which they rounded off at 6,000 feet.

GUNTER'S LINE OF NUMBERS

To convert the number of fathoms of log-line run out into distance run was no simple procedure for the mariners. By 1580 Edmund Gunter had invented his 'Line of Numbers,' which was a logarithmic scale of numbers designed to assist in this process. Gunter had been one of those mathematicians who recommended that the log-line be reknotted proportional to the time run out in order to further simplify the calculation of distance run.

CHAMPLAIN'S DESCRIPTION

In 1632 Samuel de Champlain gave more details about the English log-line. In writing about the English method of calculating speed, Champlain explained that he had seen skilled English navigators use the log-line with great success. Champlain also provided an illustration of the log, log-line, log-glass and log-reel.

The log which Champlain described and illustrated was not the triangular log, but one which was rectangular in shape. He described the log as a thin board of beech-wood about 12 inches high and 6 inches wide with a strip of lead along the bottom edge. He also detailed the release pin which connected one cord of the 'crows-foot' to the log. The crow's-foot kept the log afloat vertically with its full face against the ship's wake, thus providing resistance.

The stray line was 8 to 10 fathoms [48 to 60 feet] in length by the time Champlain was writing, and was marked with a series of single knots.

Finally the methods were refined by the use of the log line and a half-minute glass, which allowed the pilot to gauge the rate of speed in terms of leagues or miles per hour.

Edmund Gunter reported in 1624 that the time interval was timed with a watch, a glass, by the pulse, or by repeating a certain number of words. He reported that some shipmasters tried to record their speed in feet or fathoms, but that such precise accuracy was not needed — leagues and miles was sufficient for a seaman.

FINAL DEVELOPMENT OF KNOTS

Richard Norwood, a London teacher of mathematics published a book in 1637 in which he drew attention to the importance of using the log and line on east-west voyages. In his work Norwood dealt to a great extent with the length of a degree and the correct knotting of the log-line. At that time the mariners were knotting the log-line with a seven fathom spacing, using a half-minute glass for timing. Norwood recommended the spacing to be 51 feet — or 1/20th of a 6,120 foot mile. He calculated the degree to be 367,196 feet. He further recommended that the 'stray line' be ten fathoms or more to ensure that the log would be out of the eddy of the ship's wake before the glass was turned.

In his recommendations for improving the log and line, Norwood completed the development of this basic instrument of English invention. Norwood instructed, 'look how many knots are veered out in half a minute . . . so many miles is the ship's way for an hour.'

The nautical measure of speed, *knots*, was thus established with Norwood's recommendations in 1637, and has come down to us today. The term *knots* carries with it the full meaning of 'sea miles per hour'. It would be redundant to say 'knots per hour'.

THE LOG-LINE AND MAYFLOWER

Master Christopher Jones lived at Rotherhithe — just across the Thames from London. He was undoubtedly a member of the Guild of Shipmasters, and would have been aware of the latest developments in nautical aids.

Most of the important English mathematicians and nautical instrument-makers lived and worked in London at the time. The English mathematicians had taken a leading role in the mathematical developments of the late sixteenth and early seventeenth centuries. What is more, a number of those mathematicians had instrument shops, where they made and sold their newest instruments. And, finally, those mathematicians provided instruction on the methods of using their nautical aids.

Gunter's developments were of great importance to the English in their overseas voyaging and establishment of colonies in America. Lacking a precise method of finding longitude, it was essential for a navigator to compute as accurately as possible the distance run in a given period of time — although the navigators still relied on estimation. The log and line became an indispensable instrument in determining distance made good on their crossings, which were essentially east-west courses. This was especially effective while using charts of Mercator's projection, which had been in common use since the first years of the seventeenth century — when the East India Company had begun to use them. The various types of charts will be discussed more fully in the section on charts.

We know that Jones was a respected shipmaster and shipbuilder with a lifetime of nautical experience. Certainly, he would have taken advantage of the latest developments — so near at hand — especially in the face of a cross-Atlantic voyage.

Captain John Smith wrote in his *Sea Grammar* [published in 1627] that he considered the log and log-line so uncertain that it was not worth the trouble. Regardless of Smith's reservations, a large number of English seamen had begun to use the log and line by the 1620s — knotting it according to Gunter's recommendations. However, it was generally knotted on the basis of 5,000 feet to the sea mile.

14. THE TRAVERSE BOARD & SLATE

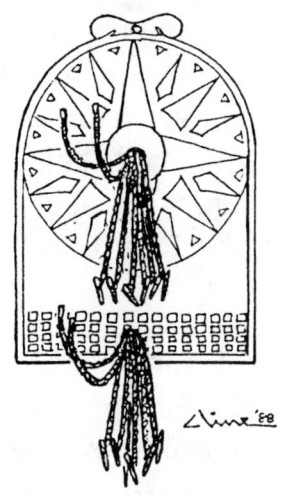

The traverse board was a simple memory aid of great importance to the shipmaster for keeping a record of the courses steered. This information was essential in estimating the course 'made good' during each four-hour watch.

The traverse board seems to have been adopted by navigators as early as the sixteenth century. William Bourne wrote in the 1550s that shipmasters of ancient times kept an account of the way they sailed. Such a device would not be of great value to a pilot who was plying known waters, but it was of great value to anyone sailing the seas out of the sight of land. At such times the master of a ship kept a 'dead reckoning'.

DEAD RECKONING

The task of the navigator or shipmaster was to calculate the course he wanted to make good. That is, he estimated and recorded the way his ship had gone by taking into consideration her mean speed and direction of course, as well as the effect of wind, waves, tide and waywardness of his ship.

Through accurate records of direction, speed and time, the navigator was able to reckon his most probable position through careful deduction. The original term applied to this process was 'deduced reckoning.' The term was eventually shortened to 'ded' reckoning, and finally misspelled as 'dead reckoning.'

The traverse board was an extremely valuable aid for recording the information, which was essential to the navigator in his dead reckoning.

DESCRIPTION OF THE BOARD

Captain John Smith wrote in 1627 that the 'Travas' was 'a little round boord full of holes upon lines like the Compasse, upon which, by removing a little sticke, they keepe an account, how many glasses (which were but half hours) they steare upon every point.'

The traverse board was equipped with pegs on strings which could be inserted into a series of holes. The circular upper part of the board was marked off with the thirty-two points of the compass; from the center radiate eight sets of holes with thirty-two holes to each set. From the center of the compass were suspended eight strings with pegs. Each peg was for a half-hour period — or one glass — of the four hour watch. [Fig. 54]

At the base of the board are rows of holes used for recording the estimated or measured speed, which would have been recorded at each turning of the glass. At the center of these rows of holes was another group of eight strings with pegs. The four rows of holes to the left side of center were used for the first half-watch [two hours], and the holes to the right of center were used for the second half-watch.

THE TRAVERSE BOARD IN USE

When a helmsman came on duty at the beginning of a watch, the traverse board would be cleared of all pegs. At the first turning of the running glass [sand-glass], the direction traveled during the first thirty minutes of the watch would be indicated on the traverse board by inserting a peg at that compass rhumb on the circle of holes nearest the center of the board. He would then insert a peg at the hole which represented the speed at which the ship had been sailing — determined by the use of the log-line.

If the ship had been traveling at four knots, the officer would count over from left to right on the first row of holes and insert the first peg in the fourth hole, etc., through the course of the four-hour watch. These lower holes were probably not a part of earlier traverse boards, but most navigators would have used this method of recording speed by at least the time of John Smith's death. Various forms of the traverse board can be seen in Fig. 55.

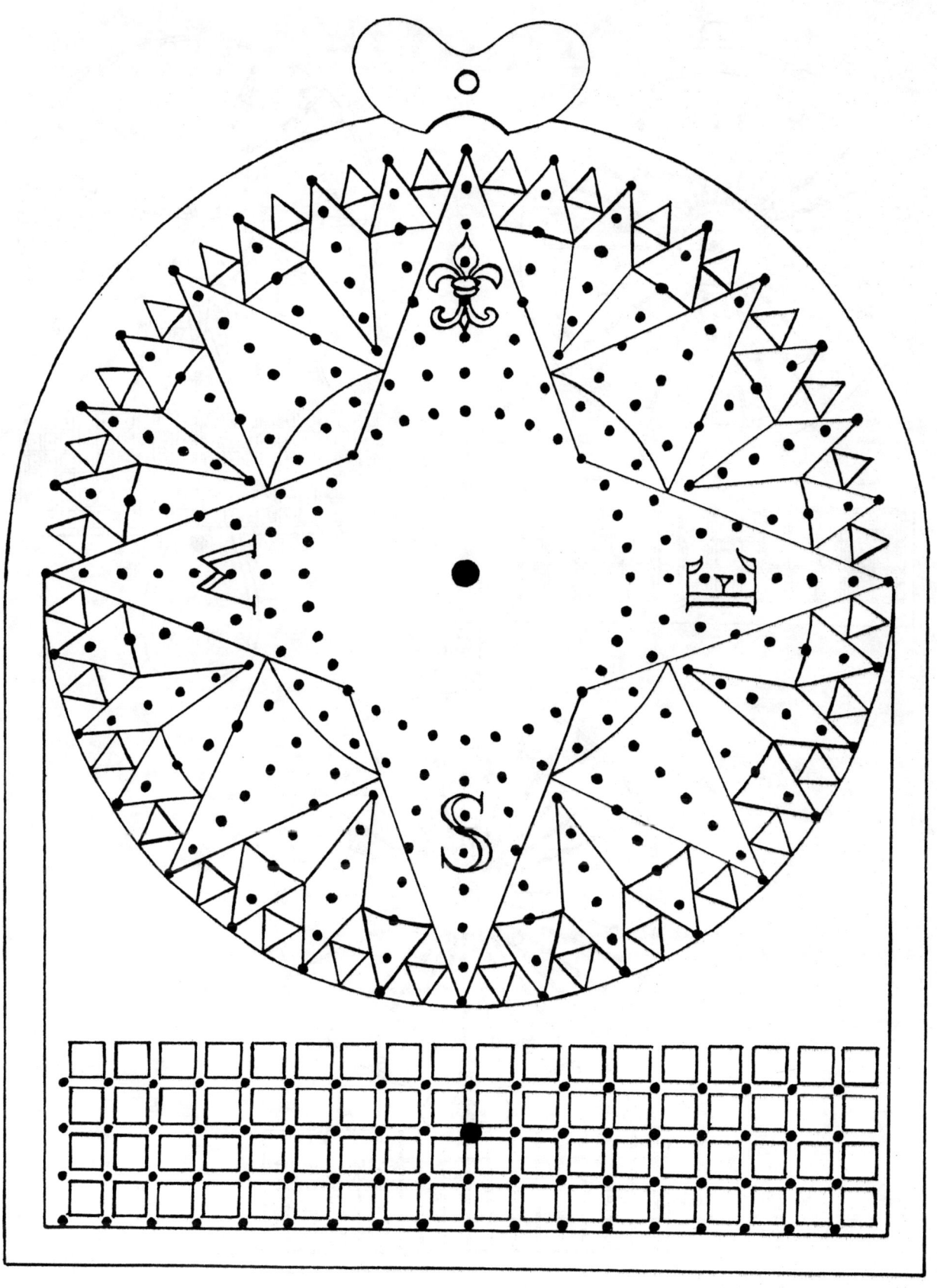

Fig. 54. The traverse board.

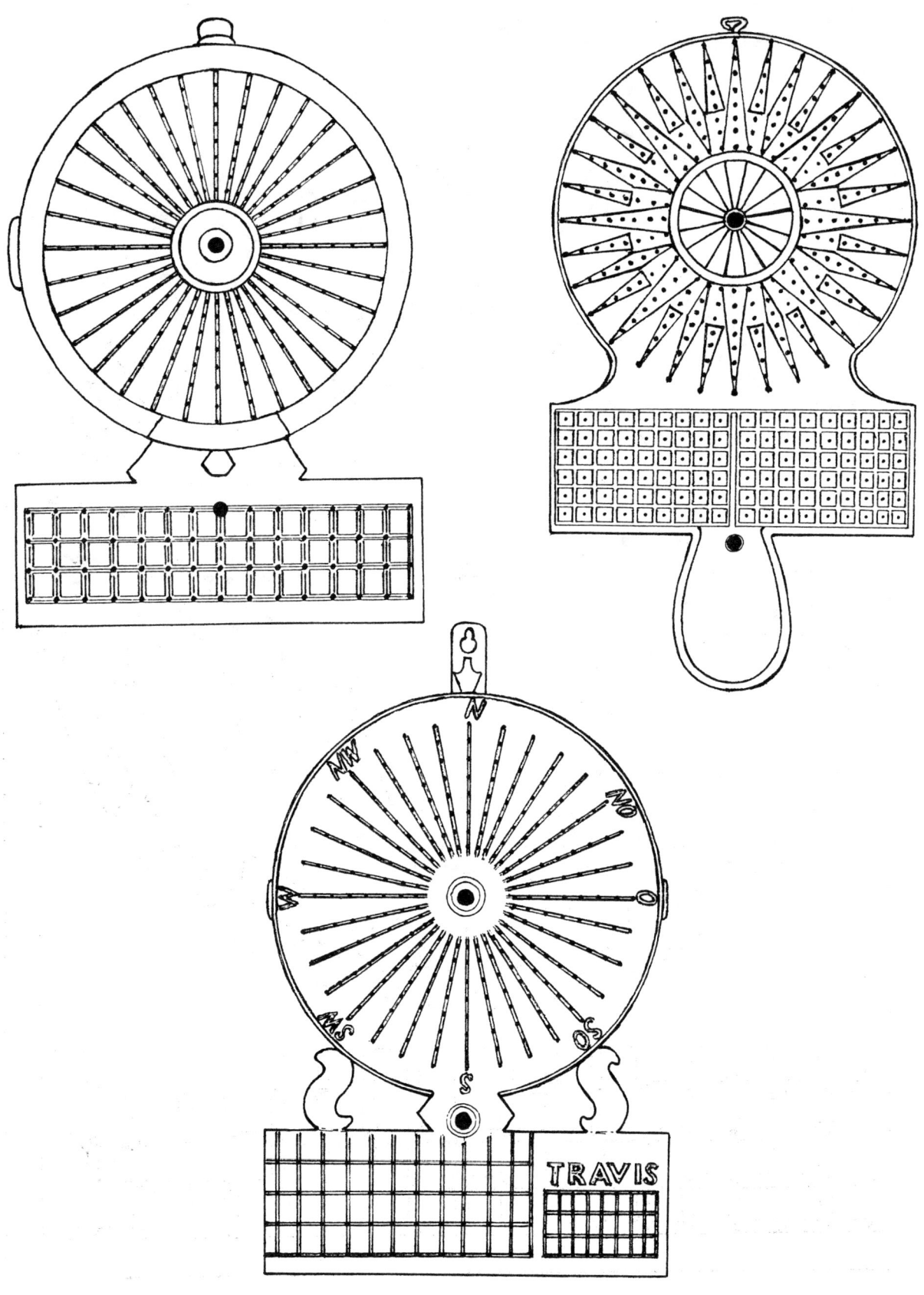

Fig. 55. Various styles of the traverse board.

At each turning of the glass the officer in charge would determine the direction in which the ship had been sailing during the past thirty minutes, and insert a peg in the appropriate hole on the board, moving outward until there was a peg in each of the eight rows of holes — representing the eight half-hours in a four-hour watch. Likewise, he would insert a peg in the lower part of the board, indicating the calculated speed, at each turning of the running glass.

THE HELMSMAN'S SLATE

The traverse board was kept at the binnacle where the helmsman could easily keep a record of his course steered at the end of each glass. At the end of a half-watch [two hours] or a watch [four hours], the master or the officer of the watch calculated the mean course steered. His calculations were made on the basis of the information recorded on the traverse board. The information concerning direction sailed, estimated speed, and distance run were set down on a chalk board of slate — or perhaps paper. A Spanish example of the helmsman's slate is shown in Fig. 56.

After transferring the information to his slate, the helmsman cleared the pegs from the traverse board for the next watch or half-watch.

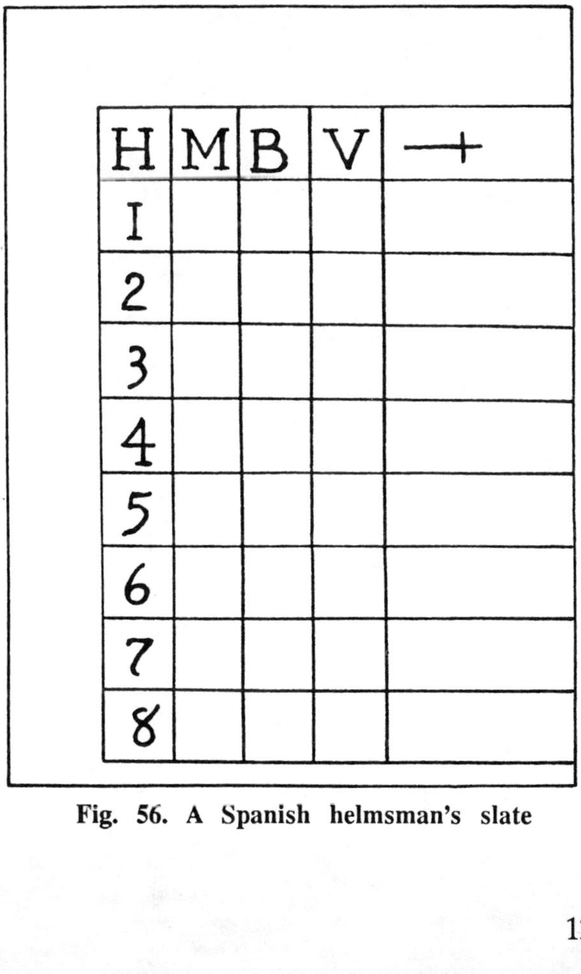

At the end of the day the shipmaster used the information recorded on the helmsman's slate in writing up his log or journal for that day. The time at sea was reckoned from noon to noon, rather than from midnight to midnight, as it was when in port or on land. The new day began with the noon observations of the sun's altitude and continued until the noon readings the following day. All journal notations after the noon observations were dated for a new day. This method of notation can be confusing when reading old ship journals.

Fig. 56. A Spanish helmsman's slate

The information gathered from traverse board to slate to journal had to be resolved into distance and course made good in a day's sailing. The north-south and east-west components had to be combined in the navigator's calculations, along with the distance sailed on each tack. Tacking was the zig-zag maneuvering of the ship to take the best advantage of the winds. Northing and southing could be checked by an accurate observation of latitude by sun or star, using an astrolabe, quadrant, cross-staff or back-staff. However, easting and westing could not be verified until they had reached landfall. Solar and stellar observations to determine latitude will be discussed in more detail in the following sections about astrolabes, etc.

The traverse board seems to have been adopted only by those who sailed the northern waters, and continued in use up to the beginning of the twentieth century. As the mariners became more literate, the traverse board was gradually replaced by the log-board in the steerage. No Mediterranean examples have been found.

Knowing Christopher Jones' background and experience, we can be assured that there was a traverse board and a helmsman's slate of some kind on the binnacle of MAYFLOWER.

15. THE MARINER'S QUADRANT

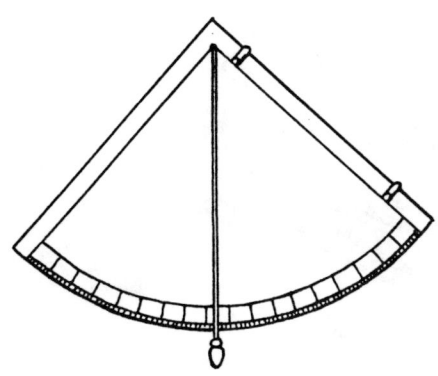

The quadrant is a very simple instrument of medieval origin used to determine the altitude of a heavenly body. It takes its name from its shape, which is a quarter of a circle. The curved edge is divided from 0° to 90°. At the apex is a right-angle, where a cord with a small weight, or plumb-bob, of lead or brass is attached. Along one straight edge are mounted two upright pieces with holes for sighting. When in use, the quadrant is held vertically so that the sight can be aligned with the sun or some star. The weighted plumb-line falls across the scale of degree markings, and from this the angle of elevation can be read.

There were several types of quadrants in use from an early time. The Islamic quadrant had an astrolabe quadrant on one side, and the other was a sinical quadrant with arcs of sines, cosines, etc. The ancient horary quadrant was used only for reckoning time. The gunner's quadrant was a simple sighting device used by artillery officers. The astronomers used a quadrant which was engraved with a geometrical square and lines showing the sun's path through the signs of the zodiac. Various types of quadrants are shown in Fig. 57.

Although the simple mariner's quadrant was in use long before its first mention in 1450, it does not appear that the English sailors adopted its use to any great degree. However, it remained important as an astronomer's instrument.

THE MARINER'S QUADRANT

The average seaman of that time would have had no use for the complicated quadrants used by astronomers. Therefore, a much simpler form of quadrant for taking altitudes was adopted by those mariners who opted to use it for observations at sea. [Fig. 58]

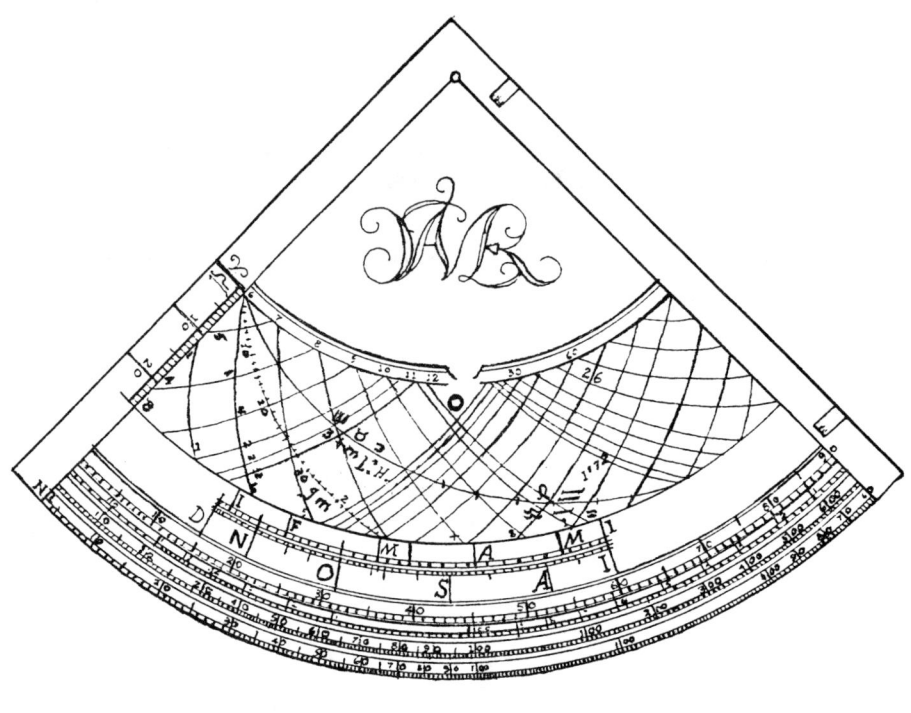

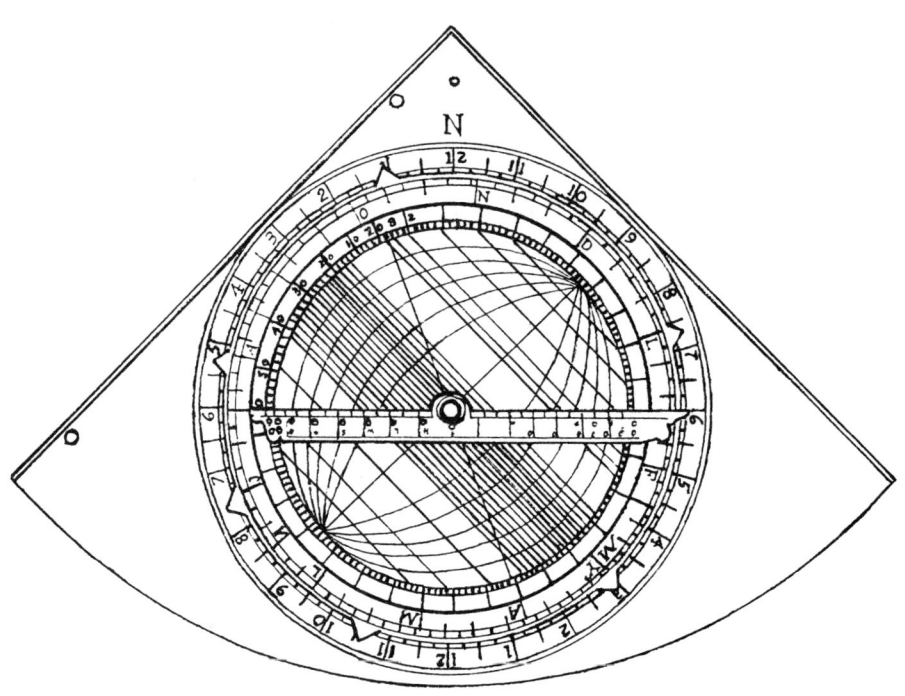

Fig. 57. An astronomer's quadrant. (front & back)

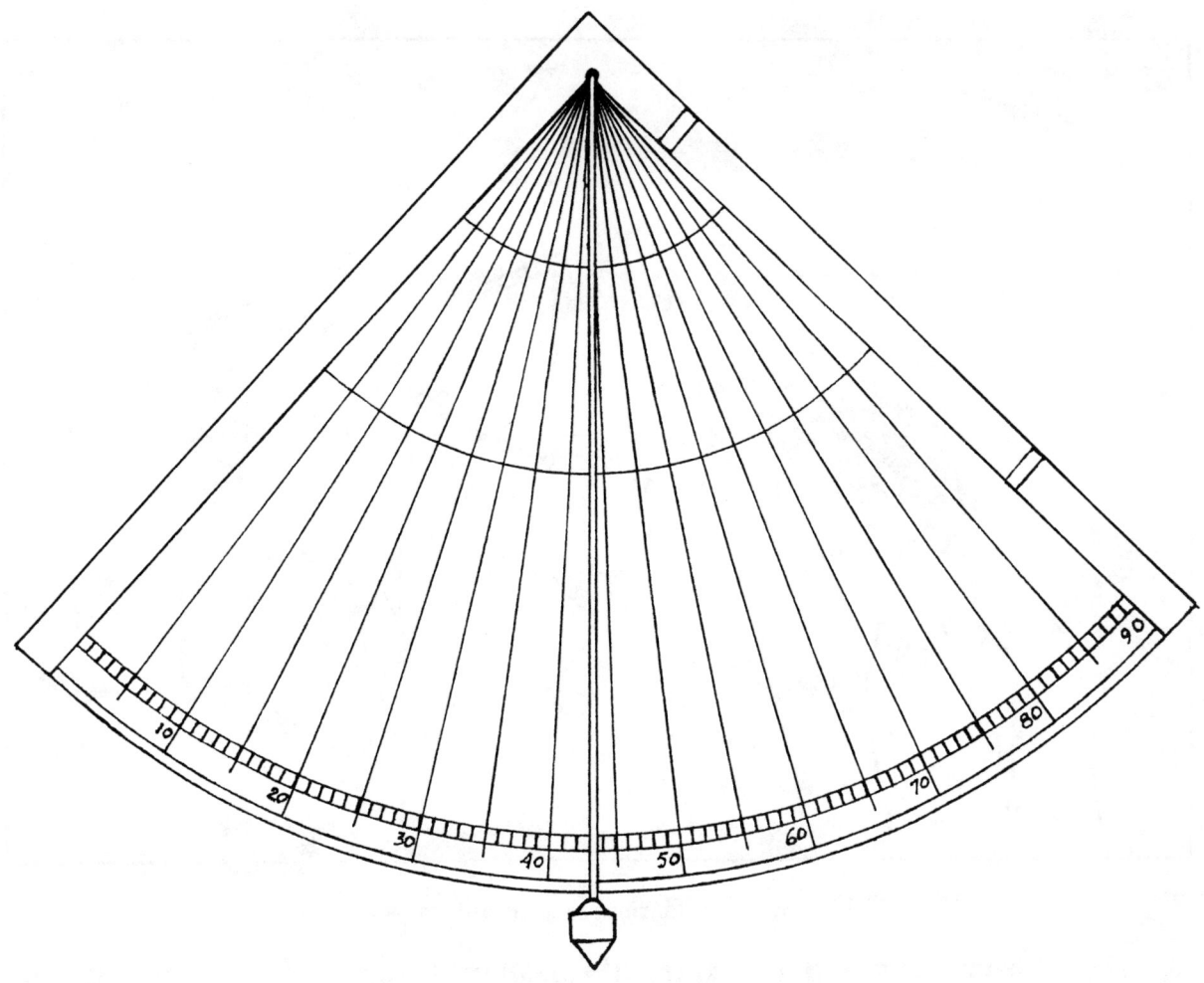

Fig. 58. The mariner's quadrant.

The mariner's quadrant was cut from a piece of metal plate — sometimes wood. Its radius was generally about six to eight inches. It had a pair of small rectangular plates with pinhole sights on one of the straight edges for sighting. The only scale needed was the degree-markings from 0° to 90°, which were engraved along the curved edge of the instrument. A silk thread with a small plummet of brass or lead was suspended from the center point, falling across the degree marks on the curved edge. For the mariner's use, these were the only features needed. It was light and easy to handle.

THE QUADRANT IN USE

An observation made with this instrument was probably a two-man job. When held vertically, the quadrant was tilted until the sunlight fell through the pinholes of the two sights along the upper edge. Some of the quadrants for use by mariners had a second — and larger — set of holes through which a star could be sighted by looking through them.

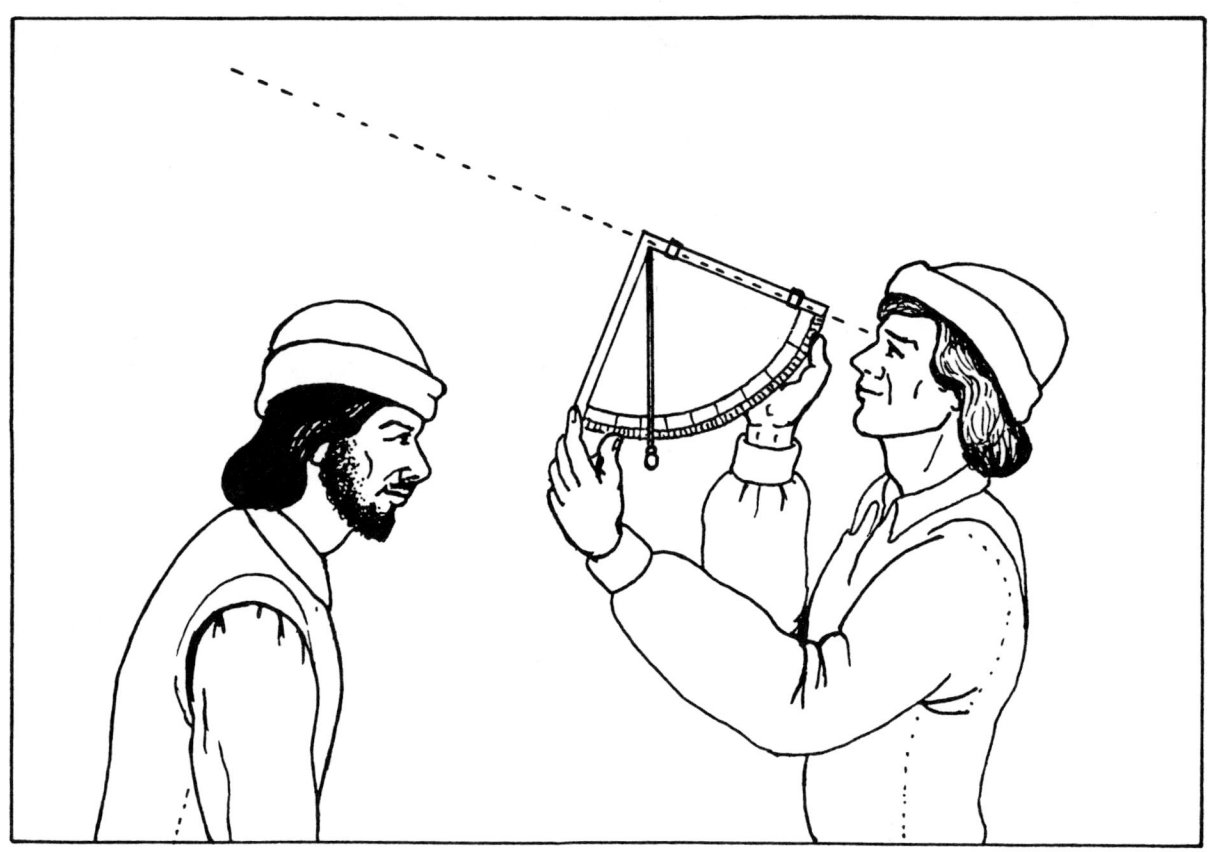

Fig. 59. The mariner's quadrant in use.

As the observer sighted the star, his assistant read off the reading on the scale. [Fig. 59]

Edmund Gunter described his own version of the quadrant in his book *De Sectore et Radio*, published in 1623. Gunter's quadrant, or Gunter's astrolabe quadrant contained a stereographic projection of the equator, degree marks to indicate the angular distance the sun moves between the equinox and the solstice, and an ecliptic which indicated the earth's orbit. The quadrant was used for reckoning time and as an almanac. The perpetual almanac was on the reverse side, but to use it one had to establish the day of the week on which March 1 fell. Most of the existing Gunter's quadrants date from 1650 to 1750. Since they were pocket-size, they were popular as time-tellers and almanacs. They were also used for teaching purposes in universities. Gunter's quadrant was so popular that printed cut-outs were often included in text-books.

It is reasonable to think that there was a mariner's quadrant aboard MAYFLOWER for the use of the average seaman. Many shipmasters continued to prefer the simplicity of the quadrant over the astrolabe and cross-staff, which will be described in following sections.

16. THE MARINER'S ASTROLABE

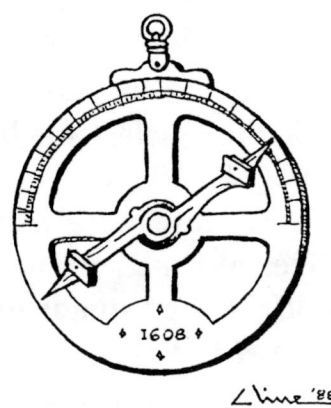

The mariner's astrolabe was an instrument used for the taking of altitudes of heavenly bodies from which time and latitude could be calculated.

The mariner's astrolabe developed from an ancient form that is thought to have had its origin in Greece as early as 240 B.C. With a history of 2,000 years the astrolabe may claim to be the oldest scientific instrument. The Arabic scholars and mathematicians developed the astrolabe into a precise instrument which was capable of indicating time and the placement of heavenly bodies.

The Portuguese developed the astrolabe for navigation purposes in the late fifteenth and early sixteenth centuries. Whereas the astronomer's astrolabe had contained a model of the heavens and calculating devices for the study of heavenly bodies and predicting their various movements, the mariner's astrolabe contained neither of these.

In its early form the sea astrolabe was a circular instrument made of wood or brass, hung by a ring and provided with a rotatable alidade (sighting rule). It was used for plotting the altitude of the sun near the meridian and came into use at sea around 1480. Seamen from that time until the late seventeenth century relied heavily on such instruments — along with tables of the sun's declination — for finding latitude. They were important to early mariners because they could be used when the horizon was ill-defined, making the use of the cross-staff unreliable.

ASTROLABE CONSTRUCTION

The sea astrolabe is very heavy, especially at the bottom. By progressively thickening the limb from top to base, or by suspending a weight from the base, the lower section was made heavier. The added weight at the lower side helped keep the astrolabe steady by increasing inertia when the wind was strong or there were large swells in the sea.

For use at sea, a large portion of the interior was cut away in order to reduce wind resistance. To further reduce wind resistance, the size of the astrolabe was kept down to a diameter of five or six inches. However, English navigators preferred larger ones of seven to eight inches diameter — to gain the advantage of a larger scale. They also preferred an alidade with a wider space between the sighting vanes.

The alidade [indicator] turned within a circle of degrees for measuring the altitudes of various heavenly bodies. Some of the earliest models probably had only one quadrant of the scale from $0°$ to $90°$, with zero on the horizontal. [Fig. 60] By about 1500 the Portuguese were using sea astrolabes graduated to measure zenith distance, altitude, or both. By the early seventeenth century, the limbs of both upper quadrants were graduated, and finally all four quadrants. [Fig. 61]

Early users found the astrolabe was not very satisfactory since it was impossible to take observations within four to five degrees — no matter how little the ship rolled. However, the development of the cast brass model, beginning about 1517, turned it into a useful instrument. The sea astrolabes were made by Spanish, French, English and Dutch instrument-makers.

English sailors expressed the opinion that the astrolabe was more convenient for use when the sun stood high — at no less than fifty degrees. When the sun was observed at a lower altitude they preferred to use the cross-staff. One disadvantage to the mariner's astrolabe was that it was so small, and the scale so finely marked, that it was difficult to read nearer than half a degree. The cross-staff with its larger markings was easier to read.

THE ASTROLABE IN USE

When the navigator 'shot' the sun, the astrolabe was suspended from a string tied to its upper ring. It was not held between the thumb and fingers because the pressure of a thumb and finger might twist the instrument slightly out of line, producing a misreading on the scale.

The alidade [indicator rule] was then turned until a beam of sunlight from the hole in the upper sighting vane fell exactly into the hole in the lower vane. The angle of the elevation of the sun could then be

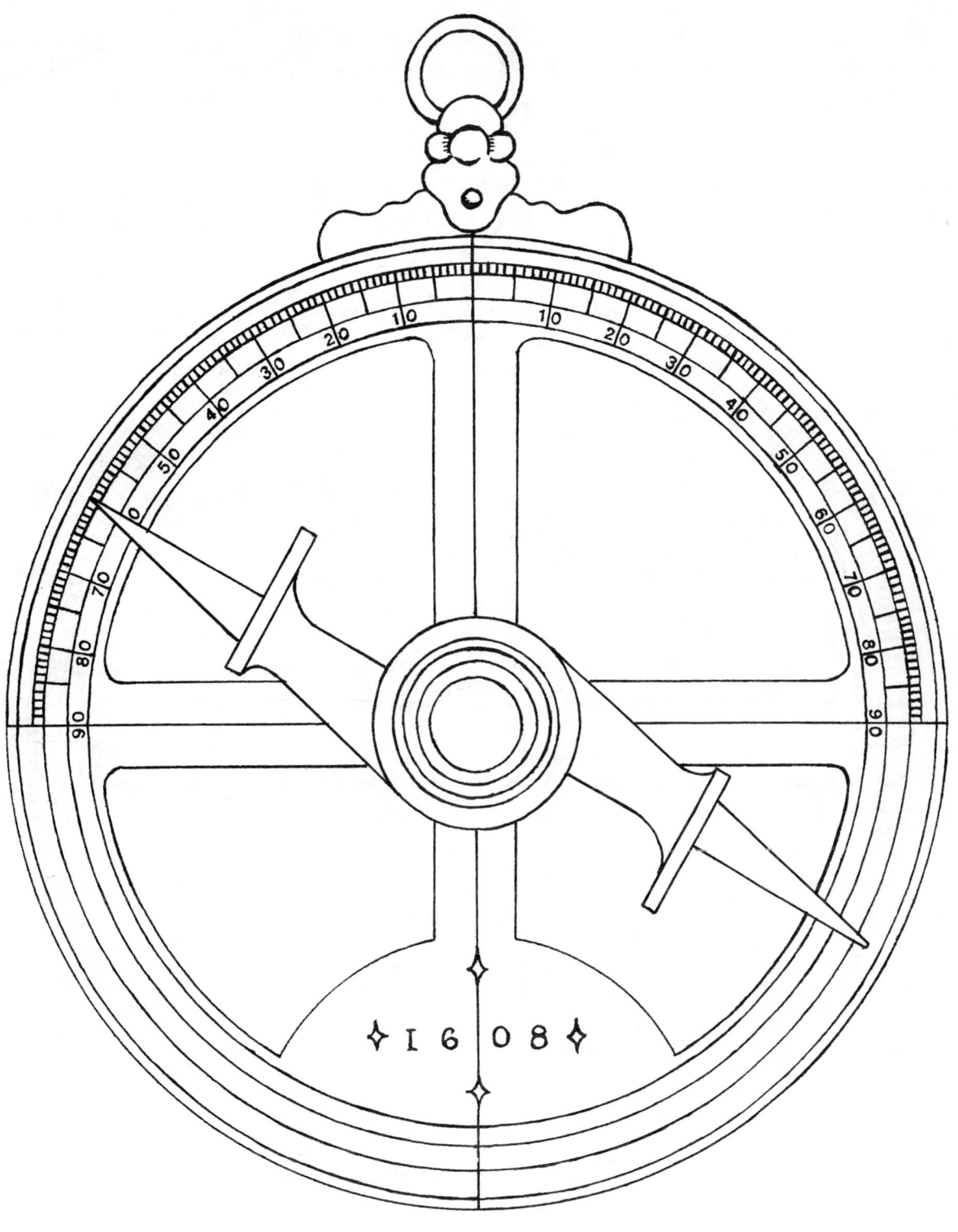

Fig. 60. The mariner's astrolabe.

Fig. 61. An astrolabe with full scale.

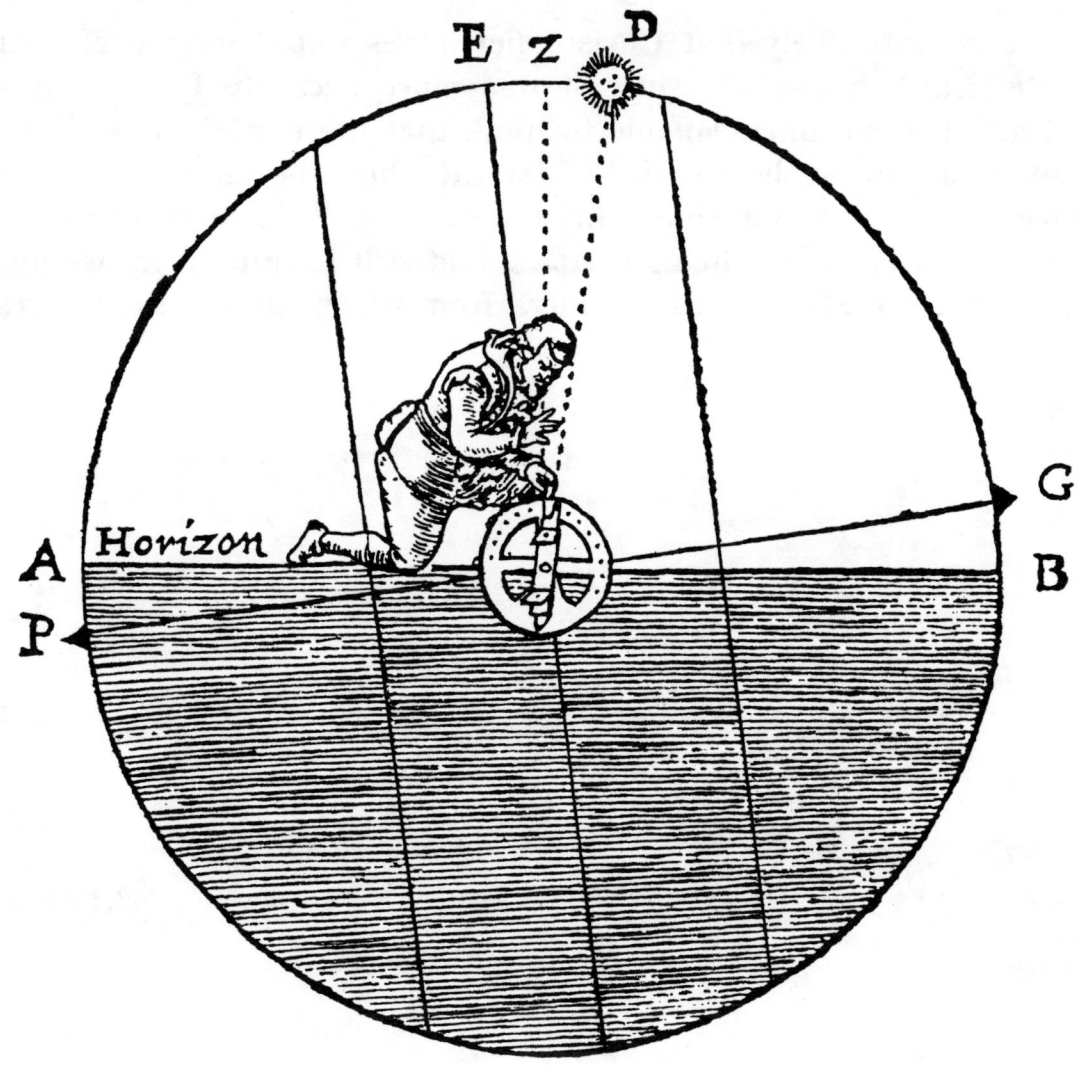

Fig. 62. The astrolabe in use.

read directly from the scale on the rim of the device. [Fig. 62] If the sun were hazed by clouds or atmosphere, it seems the navigator used an assistant who held the astrolabe as he read the scale markings.

Sea astrolabes remained in use well into the seventeenth century. For the most part, the astrolabe was abandoned by mariners after John Davis developed the back-staff in the 1590s. For an instrument of equal size to the astrolabe, the back-staff scale was twice as large. Even with those advantages, a few mariners preferred the astrolabe, and continued to use it into the eighteenth century. Still others preferred the old mariner's quadrant.

Examples of mariner's astrolabes are now very rare with only about forty known to exist.

It is quite likely that Christopher Jones would have preferred to use the Davis back-staff, since it was more accurate for use at sea. However, it is not unreasonable to think that there might have been an astrolabe or two on board MAYFLOWER when she made that historic voyage in 1620. At the time Christopher Jones was in training in his home port of Harwich, the astrolabe would still have been in use by the older and more experienced mariners from whom he learned his craft.

17. THE CROSS-STAFF

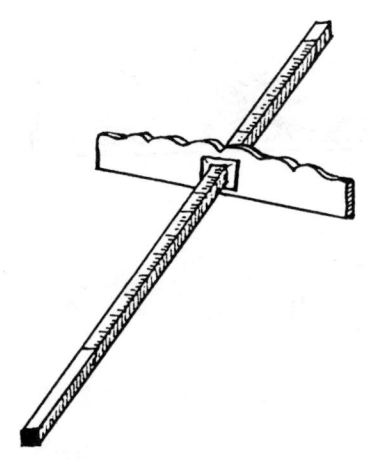

The cross-staff (sometimes called a fore-staff) was a simple instrument for measuring the altitude of a heavenly body. Both the cross-staff and the astrolabe were used at an early date in surveying. However, the cross-staff was probably not adapted for use by navigators until the fifteenth century.

The cross-staff was one of the few instruments used by Vasco da Gama and Christopher Columbus and others who navigated with the astrolabe and quadrant. Once the Portuguese explorers were within 9° of the equator, observation of the Pole Star was extremely difficult. At that southern position it was more convenient to use the astrolabe or the quadrant.

Regrettably, very few examples of the cross-staff can be found. As many other common tools and instruments of the past, they have almost completely vanished — only facsimiles are to be found for the most part.

DESCRIPTION OF THE CROSS-STAFF

The cross-staff consisted of a square-cut wooden staff, 30-36 inches in length which was graduated with tangential parts and fitted with a sliding cross-piece, or transom, set at right angles to the staff. [Fig. 63]

During the sixteenth century the cross-staff was improved by having three — and later four — transoms or transversals of different lengths, which could cover a greater range of angles without lengthening the staff. In order to make use of the added transoms, scales for each were placed on different sides of the staff.

A facsimile in the Royal Scottish Museum at Edinburgh has a staff 29.2 inches in length and .52 inches square. The three transoms are

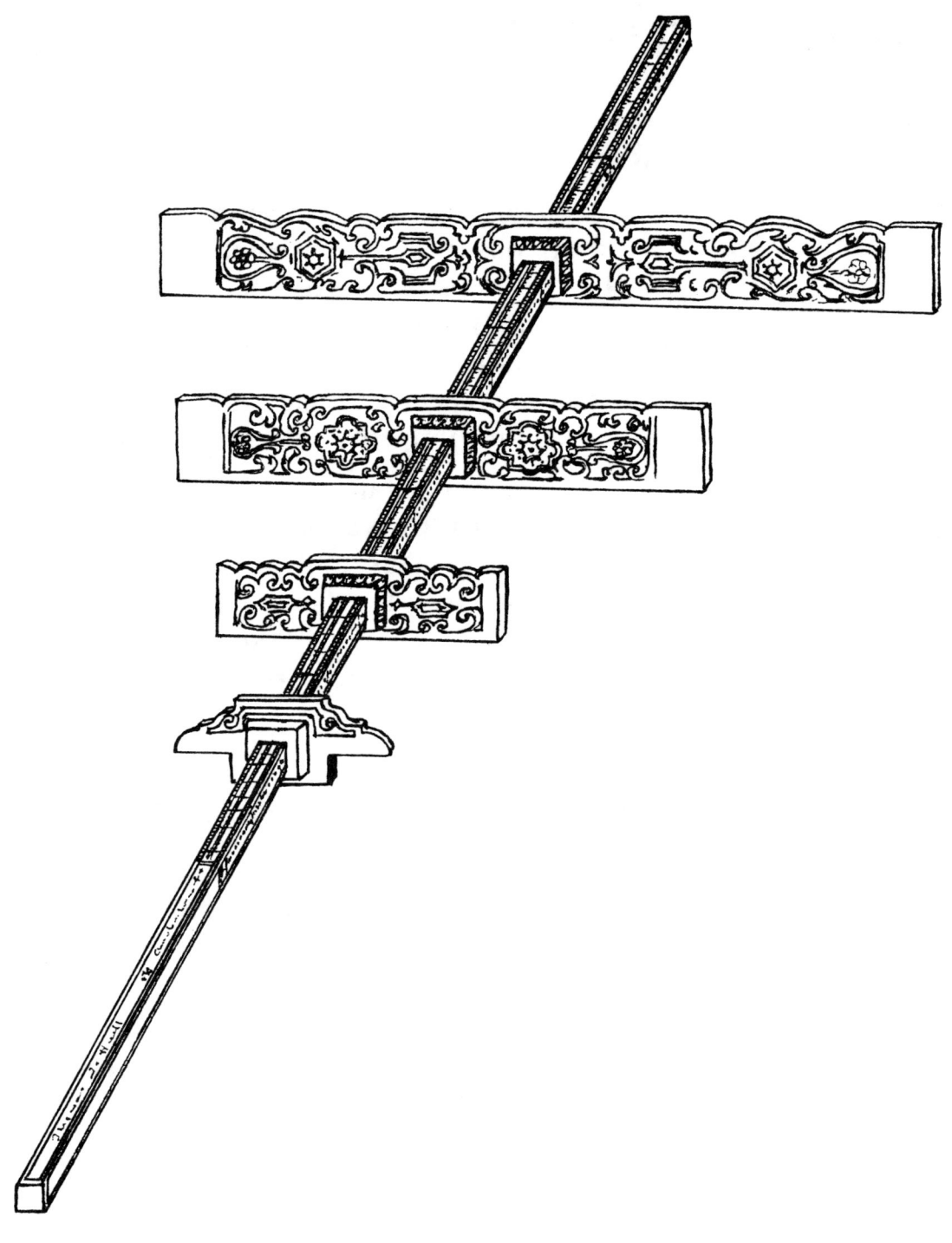

Fig. 63. The cross-staff.

(1) 20 inches in length, (2) 13.3 inches in length, and (3) 6.6 inches. All three of the transoms are 1.65 inches wide and 0.4 inches thick. At the center of the transoms are small carriages 0.7 inches thick, which have screws for securing the transoms to the staff at any desired position. The four surfaces of the staff are marked with graduated scales and are numbered 1 through 4 — thought to be used with four transoms. On the most open scale the subdivisions are graduated to ten minutes.

Pairs of scales would have given more accurate lines — using two transoms on the staff for an observation of the sun's altitude. Such a method might have been used for navigation. However, a single transom was probably used when taking lunar or stellar distances.

Scale no. 1, the largest transom would have been used when the sun was high [near the equator, or when there was a high summer sun]. Scale no. 4 would have been the shortest, which could be used to cast a sharp shadow on the staff — even in high latitudes, or with a low winter sun.

STELLAR OBSERVATION

The mariner could determine his latitude directly by taking the height of the Pole Star if it was 'in rule' [in one of the two positions during the daily circuit at which it is actually at the altitude of the Celestial Pole]. In order to judge these positions the mariner had to judge by the way the two brightest stars [or 'Guards'] in Ursa Minor were oriented.

Because it was not always convenient to wait for this alignment of the stars, a 'Regiment of the North Star' was drawn up. According to this chart, the sailor knew how many degrees to add or subtract from his altitude. By Drake's day these had been calculated for thirty-two positions.

THE CROSS-STAFF IN USE

The observer held one end of the staff to his eye, while setting the upper and lower ends of the transom to coincide with the observed heavenly body and the horizon respectively. It was then adjusted by sliding the transom along the staff until it just covered the distance between the heavenly body and the horizon, or between heavenly bodies.

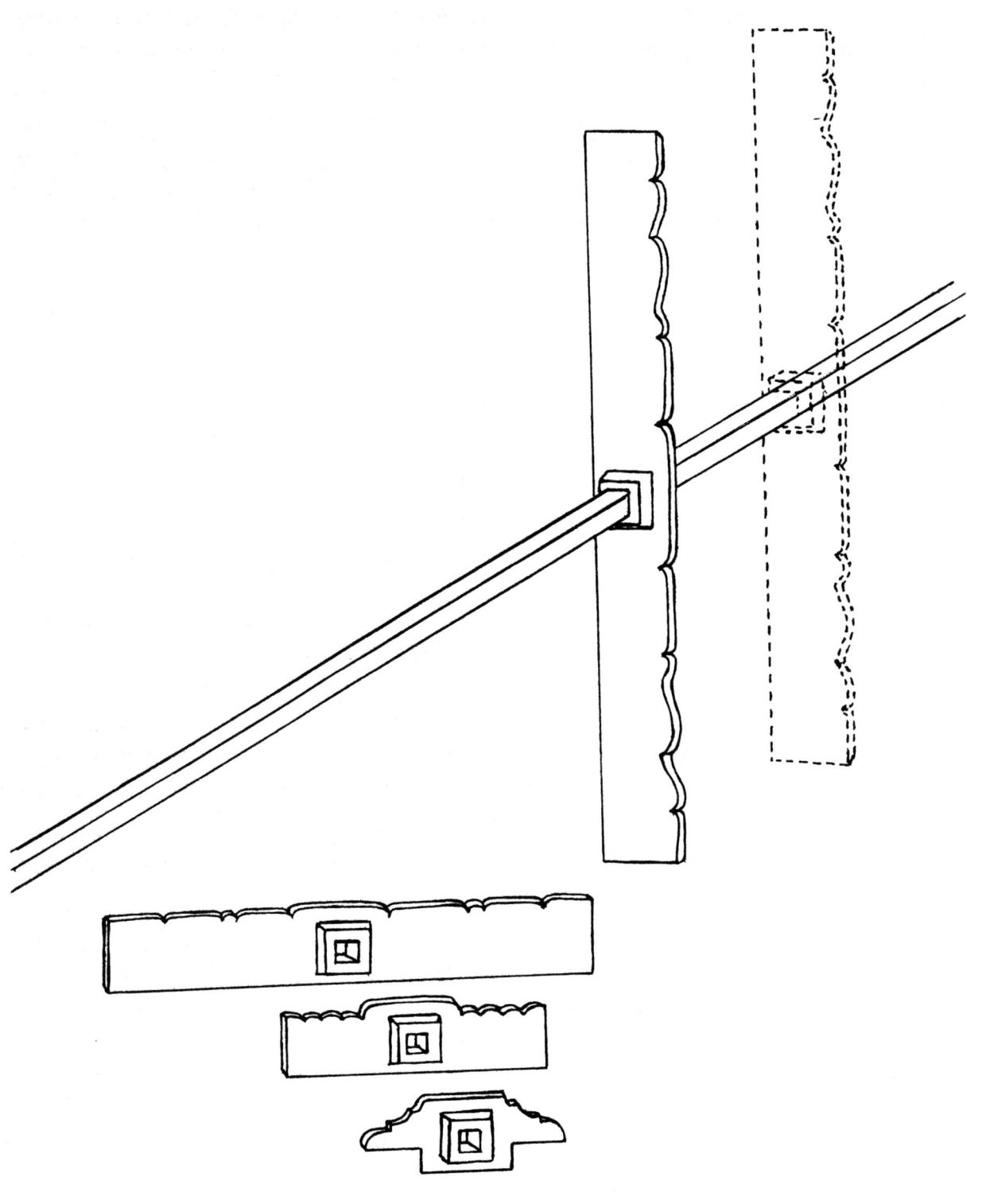

Fig. 64. The cross-staff adjustment.

[Fig. 64] The point where the transom cut the scale was noted and converted into degree and minutes by referring to a table.

DISADVANTAGES OF THE CROSS-STAFF

The principal problem encountered in using the cross-staff aboard a ship in motion was the difficulty in keeping the opposite ends of the transom precisely on the horizon and a star. Another was that the observer had to look directly into the glaring sun when taking its altitude. The wise mariner would have used the cross-staff when the sun was partly obscured by clouds or haze. If the sun were bright, a second method would have been to use the solar shadow on the staff rather than gaze directly into a brilliant sun. A careful observation of altitude takes considerable time and sun blindness would have made it difficult to focus on the sun and the horizon simultaneously. However, the cross-staff was later adapted for this purpose by adding a piece of colored glass to the upper end of the transversal to protect the eye.

The cross-staff had another disadvantage in the fact that if the staff were not correctly positioned on the cheek-bone, the eye would not be the terminal point of the axis. It is a fault in the principle of the instrument. The errors of parallax can be a serious obstacle to accurate observation.

Wood is certain to warp, especially when it undergoes wide variations of temperature and humidity — thus accentuating errors. Any play in the angle of the transoms to the staff would also create errors in observation. These reasons may have been a consideration when the cross-staff gave way to John Davis's back-staff.

In spite of its limitations the cross-staff remained a favorite among the less educated sailors until the eighteenth century. The cross-staff was simple and rigid, and had a large scale. In navigation it may have been more accurate in the hands of an ordinary seaman than the astrolabe which had small scales, and would have been greatly affected by the swinging on a cord while in use on the moving waters of the oceans and seas. Another advantage to the ordinary seamen was that it was inexpensive, and could be owned by every shipmaster.

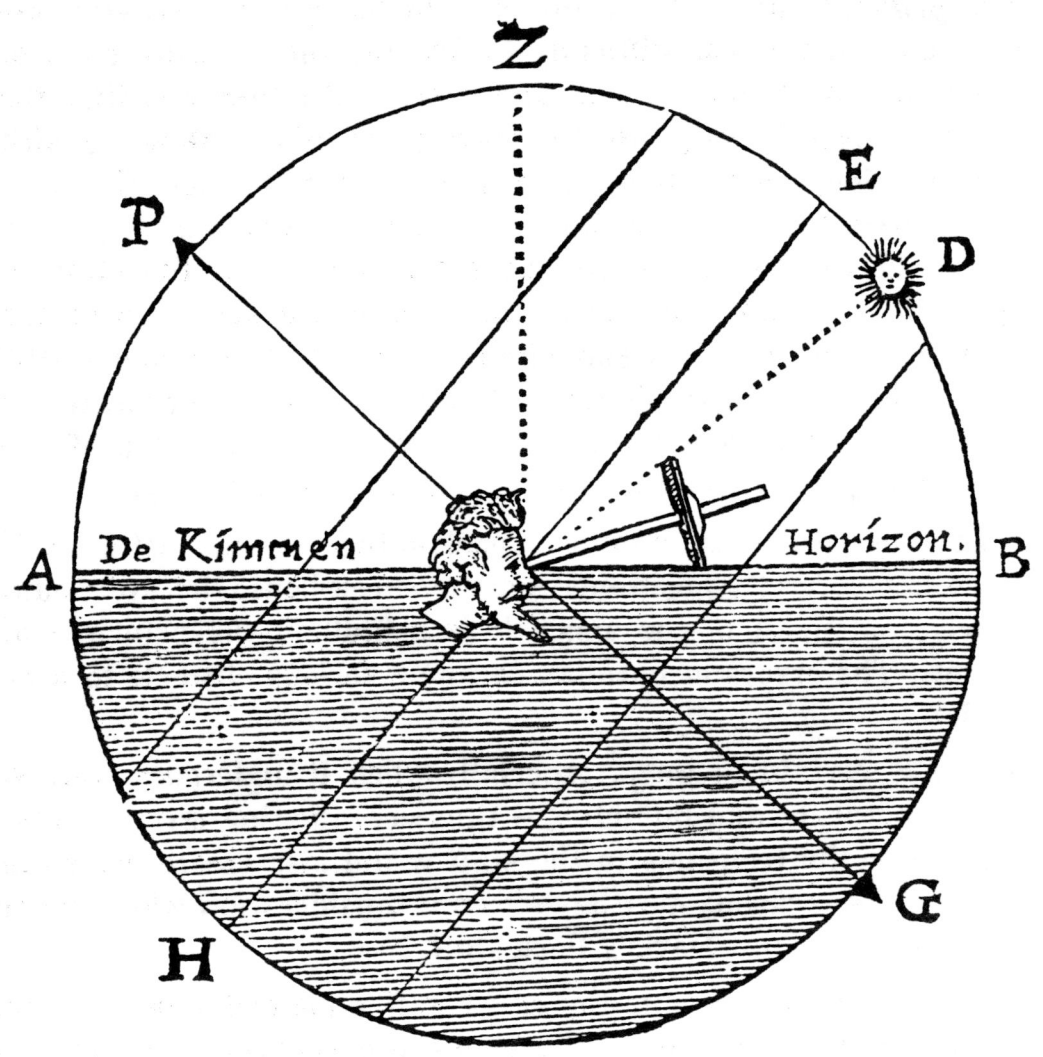

18. THE BACK-STAFF

Although the cross-staff was popular with sailors, it had some serious defects, which were often pointed out by the English mathematicians.

John Davis, the English captain, had been concerned about the problem of parallax when using the cross-staff. As noted in the section on the cross-staff, if the staff were not positioned correctly on the cheekbone, the eye would not be the terminal point in the axis. The result would be a misreading of the angle. Another problem was the blinding glare when a mariner was observing the meridian altitude of the sun. Finally, when sailing in the northern latitudes, the brightness of the summer nights made star sights impractical.

In about 1594 Davis developed a simple back-staff which eliminated the problems of parallax and the glare of sun sights as well as the problems involved in sighting two widely separated objects simultaneously. Davis's back-staff was intended to be an improvement on the mariners' quadrants, astrolabes and cross-staves.

THE DAVIS BACK-STAFF

The Davis back-staff consisted of a graduated staff, a half-cross in the shape of an arc of a circle on the radius of the staff with a fixed vane, and a brass horizon vane with a slit in it at the fore-end of the staff. [Fig. 65]

THE BACK-STAFF IN USE

The observer placed the staff on his shoulder and stood with his back to the sun. With the horizon vane lined up with the horizon, he

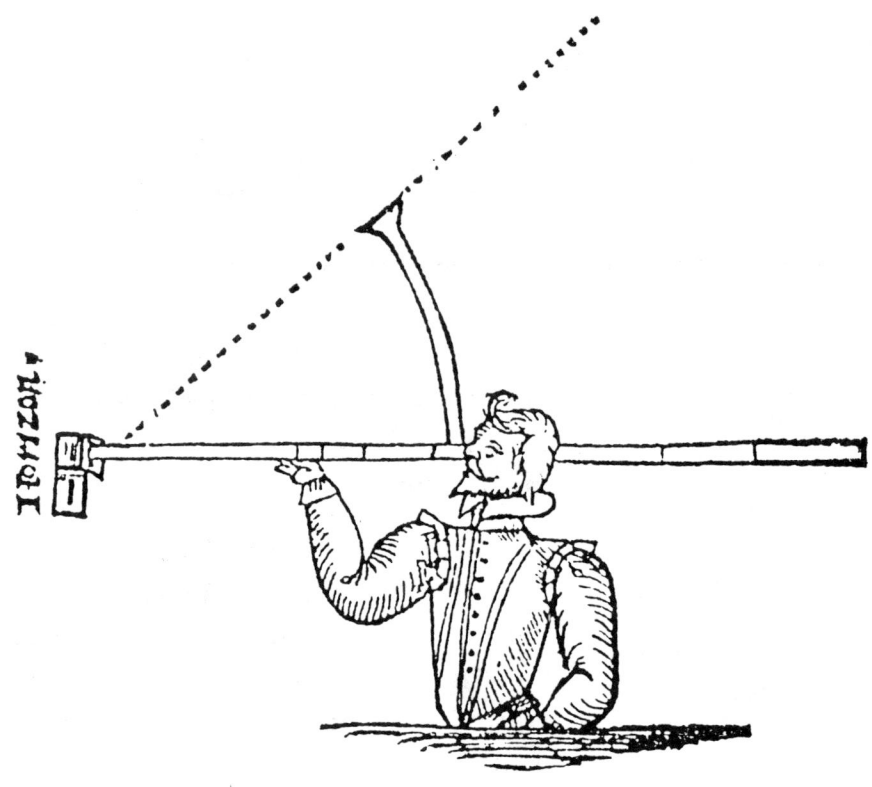

Fig. 65. The back-staff.

slid the half-cross back and forth until the shadow of its vane fell across the slit in the bottom vane while the horizon was visible through the slit. By doing this, the observer was able to sight both the sun and the horizon while his back was towards the sun. Because the graduations only ran from $15°$ to $45°$, he was able to read the result with great accuracy.

IMPROVED BACK STAFF or DAVIS QUADRANT

Davis improved upon his design in a model with two half-crosses, which divided an accurate scale into two parts, had the appearance of a large triangle equipped with a $30°$ arc at one end and a small $60°$ arc at the other. This model he illustrated in *Seamans Secrets*. One scale was engraved on the upper side towards the front of the staff, the other was on its underside and at the back. Each of the two arcs carried a movable index: the upper one was equipped with a pinhole through which the sun cast a bright spot on the horizon slit; the lower running index served as a sight. The vanes with pinhole sights moved over these arcs, and at the end opposite the large arc was a push-on vane with a slit through which the horizon could be viewed. The upper one with a chord of a circle, the lower one an arc of a circle was graduated and fitted with a sliding vane. An example of the Davis quadrant is seen in Fig. 66.

THE BACK STAFF IN USE

The observer first adjusted the shadow vane approximately so that the sun spot fell on the horizon slit, then tilted the staff and moved the sighting index until the agreement was precise. The sum of the readings on the two arcs gave him the altitude. Observations could be taken up to 90°. The name quadrant was applied because 90° could be measured even though there was no 90° arc. The Davis back-staff was only three feet long, and the longest transversary only 14 inches in length, but the graduated degree markings were engraved clearly.

The back-staff immediately gained popularity, and during the seventeenth century it became indispensable to English as well as foreign sailors. It became known as the *Davis quadrant* by the English sailors and the *English quadrant* by continental sailors.

The great advantage to the Davis quadrant was that it could be used in equatorial waters where the cross-staff could not be used. Until the Davis quadrant was introduced the navigators had been forced to rely on the astrolabe for sightings at those latitudes.

With only minor changes, it continued in use until the 1730s when it was outclassed — and gradually replaced — by the more efficient Hadley's quadrant. However, the Davis quadrant was still on instrument-makers' lists at the end of the eighteenth century because it was inexpensive. Great care was taken in the construction of the back-staff in order to prevent warping and to provide accurate scales.

The Davis quadrant had been in use early in the sea career of Christopher Jones. Whether he used the back-staff, or one of the other instruments in his sighting, will never be known. However, it is quite reasonable to believe that there might have been a back staff aboard MAYFLOWER for the use of any officer who might prefer its use.

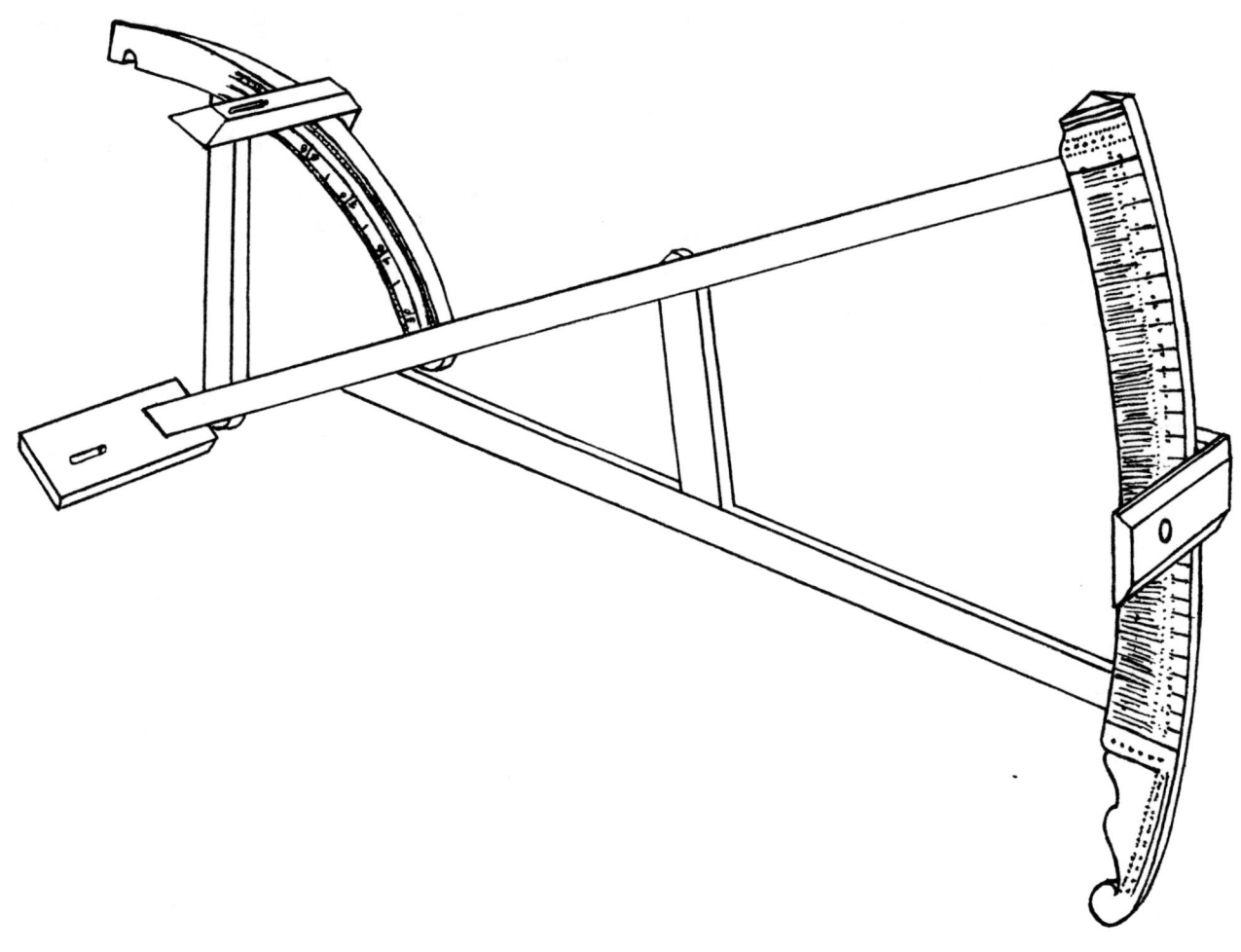

Fig. 66. The Davis back-staff or quadrant

19. COMPASS VARIATION

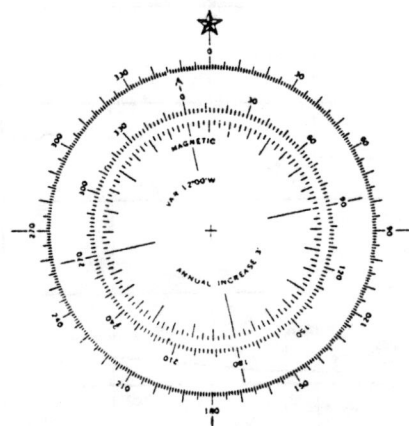

The mariner's compass needle is given its directive power by the magnetism of the earth, which is similar to a gigantic globe with a powerful magnet near its center. The axis of that hypothetical magnet is tilted in such a way that the magnetic poles do not coincide with the geographical poles of the earth. [Fig. 67] The poles of the hypothetical magnet in the earth [geomagnetic poles] are regions in the northern and southern hemispheres, where a compass looses its directive force and a dip needle stands vertical.

In addition to the variation between the geomagnetic and geographic poles of the earth, there are irregularities in the magnetic patterns around the globe. This variation makes it rare that the compass needle points in a true direction toward the Magnetic North. The compass needle points neither to the True Geographic North nor to the True Magnetic North, but swings east or west of that line by several degrees in most of the world. How much it varies from True Magnetic North depends on where the observer is. A general chart of the magnetic variation in the Atlantic region is seen in Fig. 68.

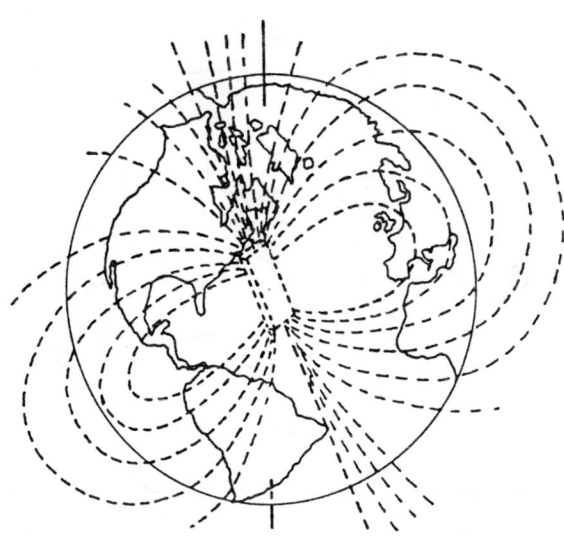

Fig. 67. The geomagnetism of the earth.

Although there is a general pattern in the magnetic variation around the earth, even that pattern is slowly changing from year to year — as are the locations of the geomagnetic poles of the northern and southern hemispheres. Because of this continual change of the earth's magnetic field, isomagnetic maps must be continually up-

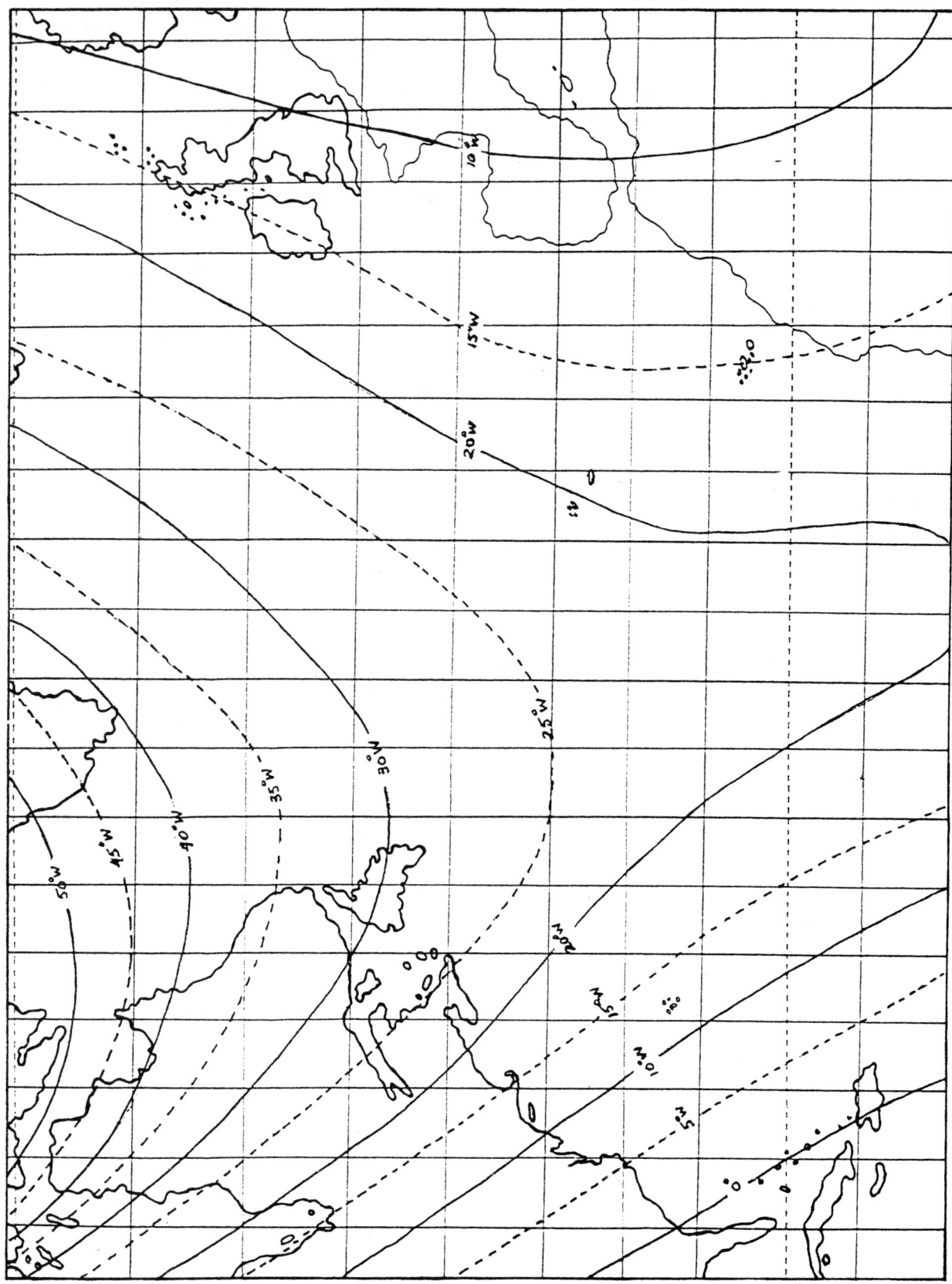

Fig. 68. The geomagnetic patterns of the Atlantic.

dated and redrawn. It is also imperative that sea charts be updated on a regular basis for the benefit of the mariners.

Although the early navigators did not fully understand the complexities of geomagnetism and how it affected their compasses, they were definitely aware of the problems. The sea-going mariners needed accurate information about compass variation in order to determine longitude — and further, their true courses.

They found that as their voyages continued, the variation continued to change. In order to keep an observed latitude, they had to relate their direction to True North. It became essential for a mariner to rectify his course by finding his variation whenever possible. He could not afford to set his course by compass-bearing alone as he had been doing, but must steer by True and not Magnetic North. To know how much the Magnetic North varied from the True North, it was necessary to check the variation when the sun was due south, or by finding its bearing at sunrise, when the latitude and the date were also known.

For at least three hundred years before William Gilbert was doing his work on magnetism in the late sixteenth century, it had been noticed that the suspended magnet did not always point to the exact geographical north. Furthermore, in different parts of the world the difference varied.

At first this was attributed to the quality of the lodestone being used, to faulty methods employed in touching the needle, or to the tendency of the lodestone to move toward the True Celestial Pole [the unmarked 'Axis']. Some thought it might have been due to faulty observations in determining the geographical meridian.

Finally, it was recognized as a universal phenomenon and the scientific minds of the day became occupied with the problems of magnetic variation.

COLUMBUS AND VARIATION

Venetian navigators in the fifteenth century were aware of magnetic variation and were already correcting their charts where they depended on compass-bearings. Columbus was the first to mention the problems of variation as he crossed the Atlantic westward. He found that in mid-ocean the easterly variation with which sailors had been familiar changed, passing zero and becoming a westerly variation.

By the time Columbus was making his voyages, the Genoese compass-makers were fixing the north-pointing end of the compass needle under the north point of the compass card. A mariner using one of these Genoese compasses found it necessary to sail by charts which had been drawn to include the compensation for variation.

A letter written about John Cabot's voyage of 1497 noted that a large variation of two points [22 1/2°] was found off Cape Race, indicating that the phenomenon of magnetic variation had become well known.

EARLY CORRECTIONS FOR VARIATION

The Flemish compass-makers tried to compensate for the variation of the needle by fixing the north-pointing end of the needle under the card 11 1/4° to the east of north, since that was the variation in their area at the time. This, of course, meant that the compass was reliable only so long as the navigator was using it in a region where the variation was 11 1/4° east.

There is no indication as to what type of compass was used by Columbus on his first voyage. However, in his account of the second voyage, Fernando (Ferdinand) Columbus [Christopher's youngest son, who accompanied him] refers to both Flemish and Genoese compasses. Columbus and the Portuguese mariners tried to determine longitude by observing the change in variation. Accounts of Columbus's voyage refer to the stars known as the 'Guards'. Determining true north could only be done in the middle and lower latitudes by taking a compass bearing of the Pole Star. This correction was referred to as rectifying 'The Rule of the North Star.' The stars used were *alpha* and *beta* in the constellation Ursa Minor.

THE SHADOW INSTRUMENT

As the Portuguese began to make regular voyages to India and the Spanish were making voyages to the West Indies, the astronomers and mathematicians set themselves to the task of discovering a better method.

The earliest mention of the phenomenon of variation in a mariner's manual appears to be in *Arte del Marear,* published by the Portuguese Ferdinand Faleiro in 1534. In his work Faleiro expressed the opinion that neglect of variation was a prime factor in the serious errors which sailors had found so confusing in dead reckoning. He urged the mariners to make a constant observation of the compass, and described some simple instruments for comparing the compass needle with the meridian shadow cast by the sun. What he developed was a type of 'shadow instrument.'

Pedro Nuñez, the mathematical advisor to the king of Portugal, also developed what he called a 'shadow instrument.' Writing in 1537, Nuñez said that his 'shadow instrument' was to be boxed and hung in gimbals like a common compass. The instument was a circular metal plate with a graduated margin, an upright style, and a magnetic needle inset precisely on the north-south diameter. The plate was set to the magnetic meridian and the position of the shadow was read for a pair of equal forenoon and afternoon altitudes of the sun. To make certain that the forenoon and afternoon altitudes were equal, the observer made use of an astrolabe. With the gathered information the observer was able to make a simple calculation. At zero variation the readings would be equal. The 'shadow instrument' was soon replaced by the Azimuth Compass.

THE AZIMUTH COMPASS

The azimuth compass was constructed in such a way that the navigator could observe the current value of variation, and was generally a separate compass from the one used to steer by. The major features of the instrument were a graduated brass rim which was fastened to the edge of the compass bow, and an alidade [sight rule] which turned upon this rim.

The first recorded description of the azimuth compass seems to be that recorded in 1514 by Jao de Lisboa in his *Livro de Marinharia*. Its purpose was to take a compass bearing of the sun, the moon, or a star so that comparison could be made with the calculated bearing. The difference between the readings gave the navigator his variation. It was not a convenient instrument because it required two operators to take a reading: one to align the sight with the sun or star, and the other to take the reading on the compass scale.

The azimuth compass could be quite large, consisting of a brass case mounted on gimbals containing the compass and a sight and string gnomen on top of the case. The rule attached to the sight was designed to move over a degree scale from $45°$ to $0°$ to $45°$. It was essential for determination of variation and became a popular instrument during the seventeenth and eighteenth centuries. [Fig. 69]

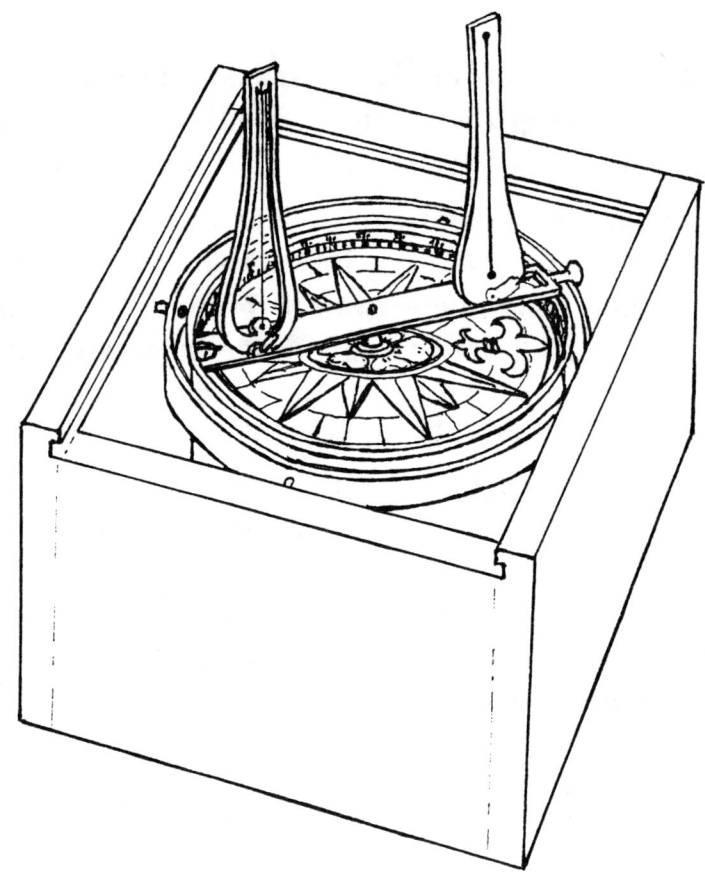

Fig. 69. An azimuth compass.

VARIATION DIFFERS AROUND THE WORLD

In 1532 Jean Rotz entered the service of Henry VIII of England. To introduce himself, Rotz made an elaborate compass for variation, which he called a 'Cadrans Differential.' He wrote in French, although he knew English [the reason for the French name he gave to the instrument]. 'Cadran' was the name for the small travelers' sun dials which had a compass needle inset. The word 'Differential' referred to variation. In his writing Rotz reveals a remarkable collection of data regarding variation at various points on the globe — some of which he had gathered from his own experience. Below are a few of the variations he gives.

Guinea Coast	0° W
Dieppe	10° E
Brazil	10° W
Newfoundland	22 1/2° W
Scilly Islands	5° E
Entering the Channel	4° E

THE PHENOMENON OF DIP

One of the first truly scientific works to be published in England was Robert Norman's *The New Attractive,* published in 1581. After spending 18 to 20 years at sea as a navigator, Norman had settled down at Ratcliff on the Thames-side as an instrument-maker for William Borough, who at the time was Controller of the Navy.

Norman had been making a living by chart-making, the making of nautical tables, and the making of nautical instruments — especially compasses. It was in his construction of compasses that he noticed that after the needles had been touched with the lodestone, the fly immediately dipped toward the north. Borough encouraged Norman to write up his observations on dip, while he himself would prepare a pamphlet on the variation of the compass to be bound up with it.

The phenomenon of dip aroused the hope that it could somehow be used to determine latitude, just as it was hoped that variation could be used to solve the problem of finding longitude. Dip-circles became a part of the equipment carried on ships by the most expert navigators until the end of the sixteenth century. [Fig. 70] However, it was gradually realized that the phenomenon of dip was of little importance to navigation.

In *The New Attractive* Norman went on to diagram the effect of variation on compass direction, marking north and south, true west and true east. In addition he marked a compass north and compass south line, indicating a 'False W' and 'E False' line. Thus he originated the 'double fly' method of explaining and indicating variation. This was the forerunner of our current compass rose for variation as seen in Fig 71.

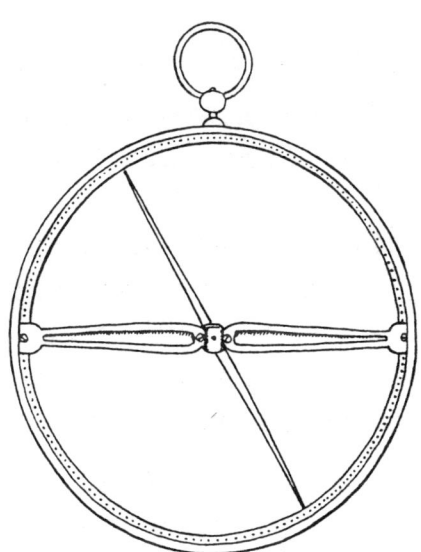

Fig. 70. A dip circle.

In his book, Norman gave valuable information concerning the types of compasses available and urged mariners to match the type of compasses they used to a

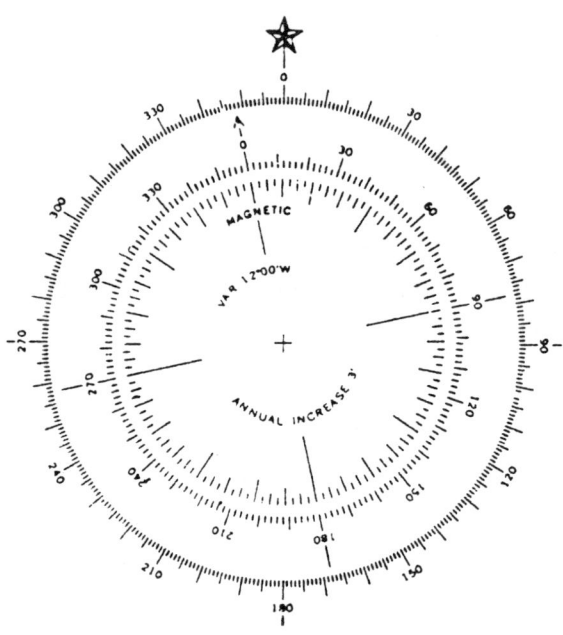

Fig. 71. A compass rose.

chart of the same origin. He noted that the Levant compass was a good one, but only if used with Levant charts. [The term 'Levant' referred to the eastern Mediterranean countries.]

THE MERIDIONAL COMPASS

William Borough, in cooperation with Robert Norman, set himself about the task of devising a new compass for variation. Those in use at the time had a scale of azimuths east and west of the meridian marked on the outer rim of an ordinary mariner's compass with the needle still being attached under the fly. At the south point of the compass was attached an upright which carried a wire which would cast a shadow on the azimuth scale.

The observations were made at noon to determine the angle between true and magnetic north. More accurate observations could be made by taking the azimuth at the rising and setting of the sun, or when the sun was at the same height before and after noon. However, this method required the observer to turn the compass about, or to use a compass with a movable outer ring. [Fig. 72]

The new compass of variation which Borough designed had a compass board which was sunk into a board. The compass rose was painted on the bottom as a fixed fly and a compass needle pivoted freely above it. In this way the position of north could be read on the same scale as the sun's shadow. At the north point was a vertical upright and plumb-bob, and from the top of the upright a string was brought down and attached to the mounting board in line with the south point of the compass bowl, so as to get a direct shadow from the sun in any azimuth. A rotatable verge ring around the compass bowl carried a second string.

When an observation was made, the instrument was turned towards the sun until the moment when the shadow of the chief string was in coincidence. Having achieved this, the sun's altitude was observed by the customary use of an astrolabe and cross-staff. The variation of the

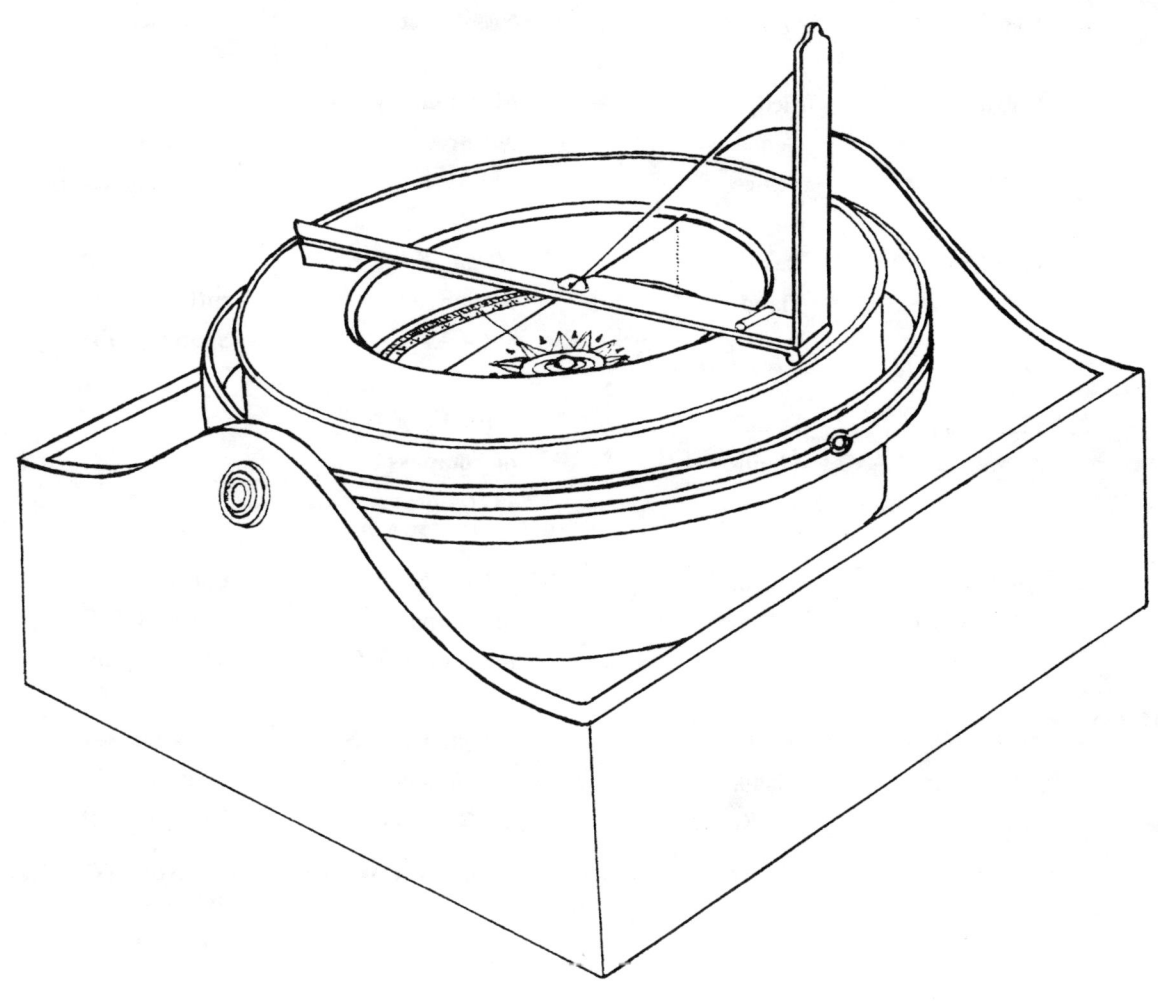

Fig. 72. A meridional compass.

shadow from the north of the needle towards the west or east was then recorded. Several readings would then be taken with the sun at the same altitude, both morning and afternoon.

Borough did not suggest that his meridional compass should replace the common sailing compass, and some mariners made use of both types on their binnacles. Norman gave the following table of compasses available at that time.

THE FIVE SORTES OF SAILING COMPASSES

No.	Type	Made in	Needle set	Remarks
1.	Levant	Sicily, Genoa, Venice	Meridionally 0-degrees	Levant sea cards drawn with these
2.	Flanders	Danzig, Flanders	1/2 pt. E. of N. of compass 8 1/4 E.	Sea cards and rutters of the Sound [Baltic].
3.	Flanders	Danzig, Flanders	1 pt. E. of N. of compass 11 1/4-degree E.	
4.	English NE voyages	England	3/4 pt. E. of N. of compass 8 1/4-degree E.	Earliest sea cards of N.E. drawn by these.
5.	NW Europe	Seville, Lisbon, La Rochelle, Bordeaux, Rouen	1/2 pt. E. of N. of compass 5 1/2-degree E.	Used for sea cards of NW Europe, East and West Indies because 'the middle hazard's best.'

WORLD WIDE DIFFERENCES IN VARIATION CONFIRMED

William Borough bore out Robert Norman's belief that variation was irregular all over the world, and urged all seamen to observe and record the latitude and compass variation of every place they visited, using the method of observation best suited to their abilities.

THE PLANE CHART

Although globes were available for nautical use, Borough recommended the use of the plane chart, which he said was sufficient for the mariner, who was using running glasses, leads and the other basic navigation instruments. He also advised all seamen to attain proficiency in arithmetic and geometry before attempting to practice navigation.

NEW METHOD OF TOUCHING THE NEEDLE

In 1616 William Barlow published some of his observations on the construction of the compass. In it he dealt with the poor quality of iron used in making the needle, incorrect touching of the needle, and faulty balancing of the compass fly. Until this time, needles had been touched as Cortes described the method, by rubbing the ends of the wire in a whetting motion with the stone.

Barlow discovered that a better method was to stroke the needle four or five times with the lodestone from the center outwards toward each end, using the north end of the lodestone for the north and the south end of the stone for the south. This method quadrupled the directional power of the needle. He also discovered that a steel needle was far superior to one of iron — steel increasing the directional power tenfold — and preferred the loop of steel, riveted to a brass plate bearing the capital. In addition, he suggested that the brass capital should be deep in order to make the fly less lively. As a result of Barlow's observations, the reliability of the mariner's magnetic compass was greatly improved and accurate course-steering was certainly enhanced.

These were the compass developments which would have affected the art of navigation during the first twenty years of James I's reign — the years in which the English were at work establishing new colonies on the North American shores.

DEVIATION

The mariner's compass was also affected by the phenomenon of deviation, which is the magnetic influence of any metal aboard ship on the directive power of the compass needle. John Smith, writing in 1627, was well aware of the existence of deviation. In writing about the binnacle housing the compass, Smith noted that the wooden cabinet was held together by wooden pins because iron nails would affect the compass. The helmsmen of the day also knew that their lodestone had to be kept at a safe distance from the compass in order to avoid its influence on the directive power of the compass needle. At the time, no one knew how to adjust the compass for deviation and the solution would not come until the nineteenth century.

Thus the high land on the east side of Plymouth sheweth,

Thus Goudstart sheweth it self when it is seven leagues north from you.

IIII.
The situation of the land betweene Goudstart and Portland.

Rode under Goutstart.
Under the point of Goutstart on the east-side you may anchor safe against a n. w. winde, at 10 or 11 fathoms, betweene the church which standeth upõ the high land & the point of Goutstart, so that the point may lye s.w. sō you.

West from Goutstart there lyeth a haven called Saleem, but from Goutstart to Dartmouth it is northeast 3 leagues.

Dartmouth.
Dartmouth lyeth in betweene two highlands, and on each side of the haven there lyeth a castle, it is a narrowe haven, so that in tyme of war there was woont to be a chaine layd crosse over the haven, and on the west-side there stands the church upon the high land.

To sayle into Dartmouth.
To sayle into Dartmouth when you come out of the west, you must sayle so long about east, or along by the west-side untill the Kaye of the village, (which lyeth on the east-side of the haven) commeth in the middle of the chanel, then sayle up on it, in the middle betweene both the lands, and be readie with your boat, if the winde should change to whirle, that then you might towe in, & then turne on the west-side before the brew-house and anchor at 10 or 12 fathome, for within it is a wide haven, and you may as well anckor before the village as before the brewhouse. There lyeth a blinde rock on the east-side of the haven of Dartmouth, the markes to sayle out of the danger thereof are these, there is a redde point east from Dartmouth, which upon the water is black, and in the redde there lyeth a white stone, when the white stone is over against the black point, then you are right over against the said rock, which lyeth before the haven of Dartmouth, but when you see the Kaye of the village then doe as aforesaid, and you shall not sayle by the stone.

Torbaye Rode.
Four leagues east from Dartmouth lyeth the baye of Torbaye, where you may anckor, you must place the west-point s.e. and s.s.e. from you, and there you lye safe against a southwest winde at 7 or 8 fathome.

On the east-side there is also a Tyde-haven, where there is good anckor ground, at 4 or 5 fathome, as you are close by or farre from the land.

From Torbaye to Portland it is east, and east & by north 13 leagues. About 5 leagues n. and n. & by e. from Torbaye lyeth the creeke of Tops or Exmouth, where you may lye safe against a south-winde, at 7 or 8 fathome, good anckor ground, on the south-side of the Single which lyeth before the tyde-haven of Exmouth, so that the rockes of Totmanstone lye south, and south and by east from you.

From Exmouth to Portland the course is e.s.e. 13 leagues. Betweene them both, close by the land there lyeth an Iland called Cob.

Thus the land sheweth betweene Goutstart and Torbaye.

Thus the land on the west-side of Portland sheweth when you sayle along by it.

Thus Portland sheweth when you come from the west.   *Thus Portland sheweth when it is north and by west from you seven leagues.*   *Thus Portland sheweth when you come from the east.*

As long as Portland lyeth west and by north from you, then the east point is high and steepe, but when it beginneth to come north-

20. RUTTERS AND WAGGONERS

The coastlines and ports along the English Channel were familiar to the experienced shipmasters sailing out of English ports. Along the coasts were familiar landmarks, and in dangerous waters there were recognizable seamarks to guide them safely on their way. However, once they sailed beyond the waters which they knew well, a rutter was needed.

The 'rutter' [later called a 'waggoner' by the English mariners], was a small, pocket-size book containing the information which a ship master required when approaching unfamiliar coastlines and estuaries. In the small book was recorded such information as magnetic courses between ports and capes, the distance between them, the direction of the tidal streams, the times of high and low water on days of the new and full moon, the soundings of water-depth and the nature of the sea bed, etc. All of these things the ship master must know in order to make a safe approach to land masses and ports. Only a few of the early manuscript rutters have survived. The Italians knew them by the name 'portolani,' the Portuguese by 'roteiros,' the French by 'routiers,' and the Flemish by 'leeskaerten.'

From the beginning pilots learned their sailing directions from firsthand experience. Their experiences were passed on to the apprentice seamen who were taught to observe and record the landmarks with their distances and bearings. Pilots were also expected to note anything which might be helpful the next time they approached a given land mass or port. These instructions were probably oral in the beginning, and passed on from one generation to the next along with any changes that occurred over a period of time.

Eventually, the more literate ship masters and pilots began to set down their sailing directions in the form of notes. Undoubtedly, the rutters were originally handwritten notes made on small pieces of vellum

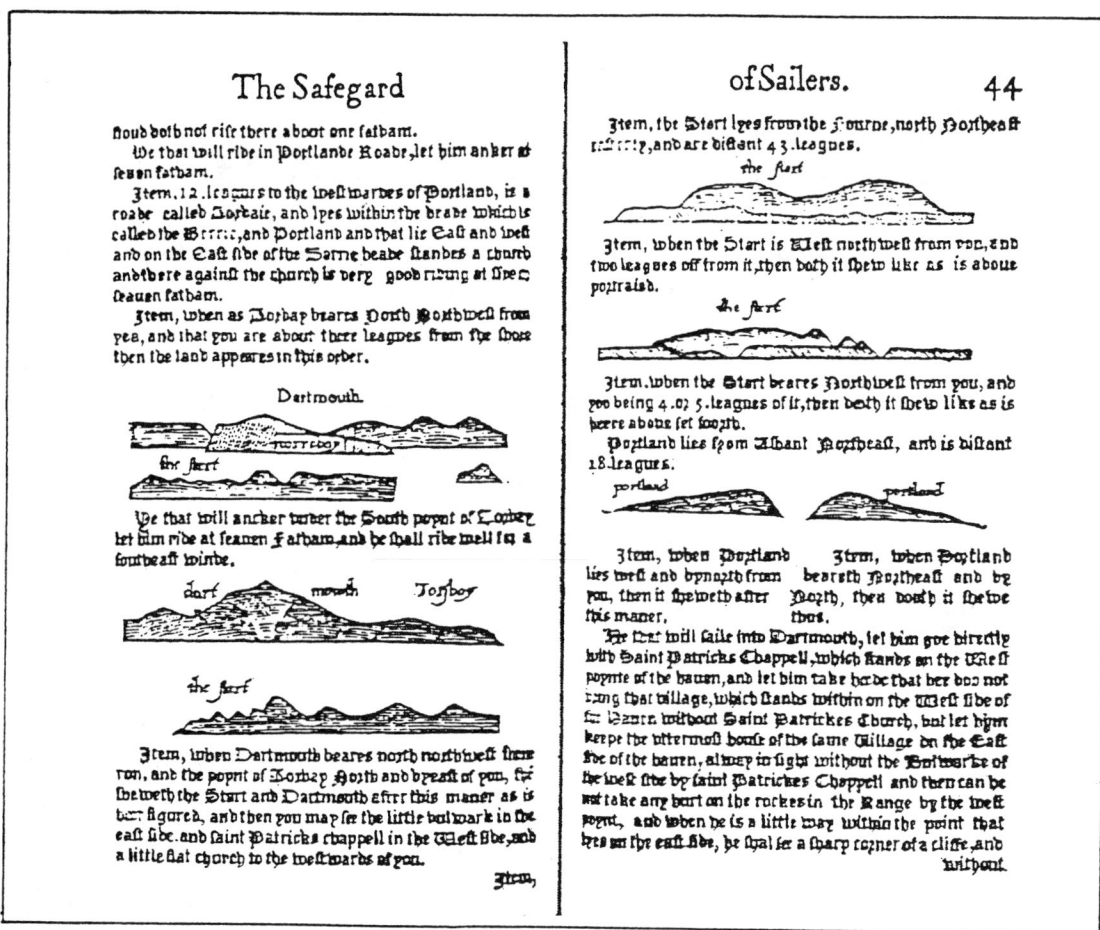

Fig. 73. Sample pages from a rutter.

or scraps of paper. These notes were probably made by the pilots themselves after conferring with other pilots they met in the ports they visited — or in the local taverns while their ships lay at anchor.

As the various seamen chatted over tankards of ale, they most certainly talked about the ports they visited. Idle conversation would have turned to comments on landmarks, seamarks, water depth, strength and direction of tidal streams, and a host of other aspects which would be of interest to merchant mariners. One day they might find themselves in the very ports being discussed. Gradually, the mariners collected their notes, and bound them together in small pocket-size guides as a navigation aid. [Fig. 73]

Even today a careful ship master keeps a personal notebook of similar types of information, which he might find useful in the future. Modern sailing guides closely resemble those of the sixteenth and seventeenth century, although the modern examples are more detailed.

A Mediterranean rutter entitled *Lo Compasso de Navigare*, dating from about 1250 still survives, which gives rather detailed sailing directions including land and seamarks for a number of ports, rivers and estuaries.

The oldest known English rutter was made by a clerk in the early fifteenth century, which was still being used in Tudor times. On entering the English Channel from the Atlantic, the mariners were not looking for landmarks, but the edge of the continental platform. Therefore, the sailing directions for this region were concentrated on the soundings for water depth and the type of material to be found on the sea floor in various areas as ship masters made their way toward the Channel.

If the armed sounding lead came up with small black stones and great red sand at a depth of 60 fathoms, the mariner knew that he was within 12 to 14 leagues of shore as he came from Cape Finisterre sailing NNE. As he rounded the Breton coast to enter the English Channel, the mariner looked for yellow shells with small black stones which indicated that he must bear off northward to avoid Ushant. When he found white sand, he knew that he had found the grounds of the Channel.

The oldest known printed rutter [portolani] was published in Venice in 1490 — close on the heels of Johannes Gutenberg's development of the printing press in the mid-fifteenth century. By the end of the century printing presses were found in hundreds of towns across Europe.

Perhaps the first rutter to be printed in northwest Europe was *Le routier de la mer . . .*, which was written by Pierre Garcie in 1483 at Saint-Gilles-sur-Vie on the coast of Vendee. It was printed at Rouen between 1502 and 1510. Garcie's work included sailing directions and in some cases crude wood cuts to illustrate the most prominent landmarks, headlands and islands. Among the English landmarks illustrated were Beachy Head, the Isle of Wight, Portland Bill and Bolt Head. Garcie also provided basic astronomical information which he believed necessary for a mariner as well as legal codes and customs, which had applied to French and English sailors since the Middle Ages.

It was not until 1528 that a mariner visiting Bordeaux picked up a copy of the French rutter [routier], and took it back to London where it was translated and printed as *The Rutter of the Sea* by Robert Copeland. Being a translation of the French rutter from Bordeaux, it only gave sailing directions for the wine trade of Bordeaux and Cadiz. Robert Copeland provided a list of navigation instruments needed by a master mariner including 'the carde, compass, rutter, dyall and other . . . which sheweth the plat . . .'

The Portuguese rutters [roteiros] owe their development to the work of Prince Henry the Navigator, who instigated the plans for Portuguese voyages of discovery along the African coast. As the voyages continued, it was necessary to describe the west coast of Africa complete with descriptions of the sinuous coastline, the inhabitants, the prevailing winds, and all other pertinent information so essential to a ship master approaching those shores. It would seem that the Portuguese rutters came into being sometime after 1534.

The oldest known German rutter is one printed in 1506, which was simple in its directions.

In 1540 Alexander Lindsey, a Scottish pilot for King James V, made a circumnavigation of the English realm of Scotland. The notes from that circumnavigation were published as *The Rutter of the North Sea*, making available to the English ship master a rutter covering the seas around England and Scotland. It even included a route to the Strait of Gibraltar.

During the sixteenth century, the Dutch chart-makers began to engrave charts which showed long shore profiles, and many times included the sailing directions on the same sheet. Lucas Waghenaer, a retired Dutch pilot, assembled a group of charts of uniform size along with the sailing directions which were printed in 1584 as an atlas, which was entitled *The Mariner's Mirror*. By 1588 it had been reproduced in an English version. The atlas became known to the English sailors as a 'waggoner,' and subsequent volumes of sailing directions in the form of pilot books continued to carry this nomenclature among the seamen.

An experienced mariner of Christopher Jones' caliber most certainly would have had his own collection of rutters or waggoners. These would have covered the waters in which he was accustomed to sailing. In addition, he probably had his own collection of observations in notebooks. Having been in and out of French ports, he may well have picked up notes concerning Champlain's discoveries in the northern regions of the New World. And, living as he did in the London area, he undoubtedly had knowledge of the information being gathered there by the mathematicians and instrument-makers of the day.

21. TYPES OF SAILINGS

When the term 'sailings' is used, it refers to the different ways in which the course of a ship can be represented on paper — graphically or by calculation. Through careful calculation and plotting the navigator took into consideration the starting position, the courses and distances sailed, and located the ship's current position.

TRAVERSE SAILING

In the days of sail, the ships' movement across the water was powered by the wind. However, ships were subject to the crosswinds, which moved them off their direct course line. At other times, the shipmaster might have to sail at an angle to his selected course in order to take advantage of the prevailing winds. The course was then made up of a series of zigs and zags to stay as close to the intended course line as possible. It was this type of traverse sailing which required the use of a traverse board in order to keep an accurate record of the distance sailed on each tack.

John Davis, who was experienced in navigation, gave a clear summary of the art of navigation in his 1594 book, *Seamans Secrets*. Davis recorded that there were three types of navigation being practiced in his day. Those were: Horizontal or Plane Sailing, Paradoxal or Rhumb Sailing, and Great Circle Sailing.

He was the first to set down a clear statement defining course and traverse. His definition of 'course' was as follows: 'A Corse is that Paradoxal [rhumb] line which passeth between place and place,' or 'which is described by the ship's motion upon any given point of the compass.' He defines 'traverse' as the 'alteration of the ship's motion upon a shift of winds . . . by the collection of which Traverse, the ship's corse is given.'

HORIZONTAL or PLANE SAILING

In Horizontal or Plane Sailing the assumption is made that the area over which a ship is sailing is a flat surface of the earth. In this type of sailing meridians of longitude are considered to be parallel to each other rather than converging as they do at the poles. [Fig. 74]

Before the problems of longitude had been solved, mariners would usually sail north or south until they were in the same latitude as their desired destination, and then sail east or west until they reached landfall. Because they were sailing along a parallel of latitude, this was called 'parallel sailing'.

Davis devoted his first book to the art of horizontal sailing, which he considered 'the greatest sort only practised.' In this work he listed the nagivator's instruments as: a mariner's compass, a cross-staff, a quadrant, an astrolabe, a chart, and a magnetic instrument for finding variation of the compass, a horizontal plane sphere, a globe and a paradoxal compass. However, he concluded that the only instruments required were the mariner's compass, the chart and the cross-staff because the chart showed the course, the compass directed the course, and the cross-staff observed the latitude of the course.

The technique was simply a matter of making accurate observations of the latitude of the course, careful reckoning of the course steered with corrections for variation, and careful estimation of the distance made good. On a plane chart [See Charts.] the skilled navigator could lay off his course and distance sailed. After observing his latitude, he could make any corrections necessary to bring his course and observed latitude into agreement. With three simple instruments the mariner could accomplish horizontal or plane sailing — provided he knew the compass variations.

Davis mentions the use of the cross-staff for determining latitude. However, as mentioned previously, some navigators preferred the use of the quadrant or the astrolabe for this purpose.

PARADOXAL or RHUMB LINE SAILING

Paradoxal or rhumb line sailing entailed directing the ship on one of the points of the compass other than the cardinal points [N, E, S & W]. A ship sailing a rhumb on a north-south meridian of longitude or east-west on a parallel of latitude may be traveling in a straight line. However, if a ship were following anything other than a direct rhumb line north-south or east-west, it would be crossing successive meridians at the same angle. [The loxodrome is a line which makes the same angle with all successive meridians of longitude.]

By continuing a course following the same angle to successive meridians of longitude, a ship traces a spiral on the global sphere. [Fig. 74] The farther north the latitude in which the mariner begins his sailing, the greater is the error over a given distance — placing him farther off course more quickly with every meridian he crossed.

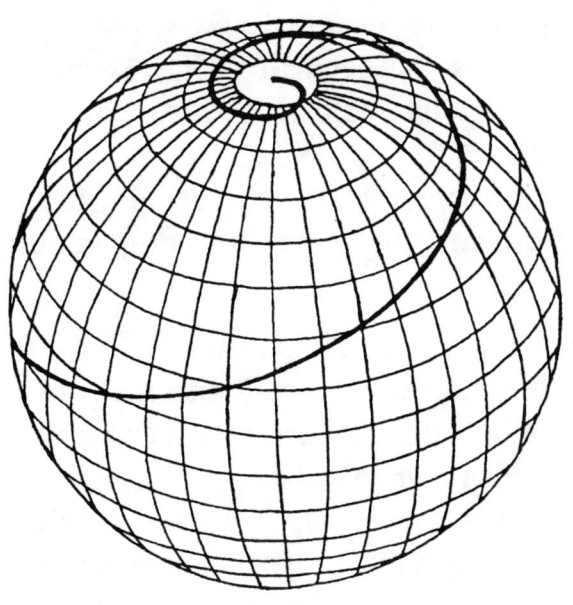

Fig. 74. A rhumb line course.

Davis strongly advised the navigator to use a globe because it gave the true angle between places. He went into some detail, explaining the methods of navigating by means of the terrestrial globe. [See Globes.]

He believed that paradoxal or rhumb line sailing could be used for places that were up to 45° apart without any great error. However, he advised that for places farther apart, great circle sailing had to be practiced for the best results.

GREAT CIRCLE SAILING

The shortest distance between two points on a sphere — such as the earth — is a great circle. The mathematicians had known this for hundreds of years. Great circle sailing simply puts that principle into action as a ship sails directly across the circular globe to his destination, not bound by parallels of latitude or meridians of longitude. [Fig. 75]

Davis described great circle sailing as 'the chiefest of all the three kinds of sayling, in which all the other are contained . . . continuing a corse by the shortest distance between places not limited to any one corse.' He, of course, was correct in judging great circle sailing supe-

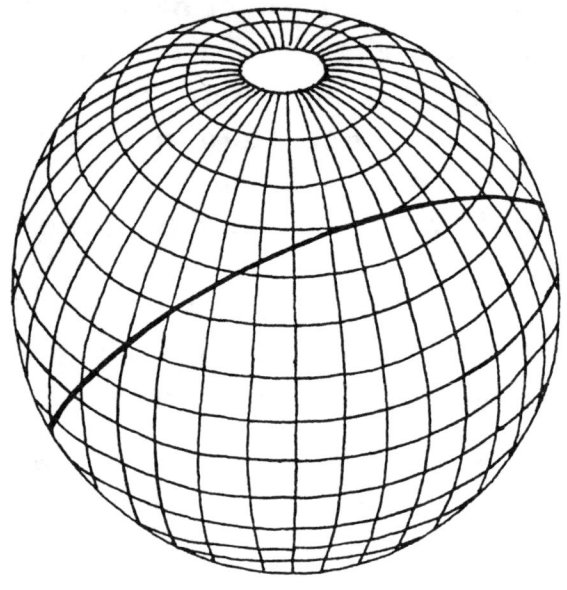

Fig. 75. A great circle course.

rior to the others. However, the problems of accurate time-keeping and precise celestial observations had to be solved before the navigators could practice great circle sailing with any degree of confidence.

Great circle sailing had been recommended by Sebastian Cabot in 1498, and Giovanni da Verrazano sailed a great circle course to America in 1524. However, the average navigator during the Age of Discovery would have practiced plane sailing and paradoxal sailing. As Davis himself noted, plane sailing was 'the greatest sort only practiced.'

Great circle sailing would not become a regular practice until the nineteenth century, when accurate time-keeping instruments and the sextant had been developed.

22. THE SEA CHARTS

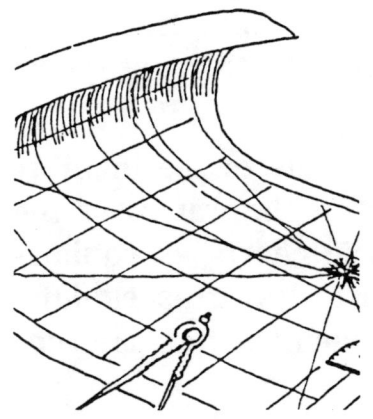

The history of sea charts goes back many centuries, and they were one of the most important tools a navigator had at his disposal. The earliest marine charts [or 'cards'] were not charts in the modern sense. The sea charts were rather simple outline maps with the names of land masses and ports. On the sea chart was a compass rose with its radiating lines [or rhumbs], indicating the direction a ship master needed to sail in order to reach his desired landfall at a given port. On the sea chart he could see a picture of the coasts, harbors, shoals and submerged rocks. The earliest charts were drawn or painted on parchment in bright colors.

PLANE CHARTS

The early charts were not made on any projections of the earth's surface, but were simple diagrams as though the earth were a flat surface — or plane — in the area where they were sailing. Thus, we have the origin of the name 'plane charts'.

The sea charts differed from the land maps in that sea charts were oriented to the north because that was the direction of the Lode Star, Polarus, which was the mariners' guide. The land maps in early times were oriented to the east and the cradle of civilization. What is more, the sea charts were covered by a network of color-coded lines, indicating the rhumbs [or points of the compass]. Rhumb lines had not been a regular part of land maps.

The Venetian mariners of the Middle Ages had charts, called 'Portolan Charts.' Those charts were constructed from the knowledge which the seamen had accumulated during their sailings about the Mediterranean. The information on those charts was made up of courses and dead reckonings from one land point to another. As the mariner's compass came into use, the charts became quite accurate, and eventually began to carry wind roses, a scale of miles, hazards to navigation and any special information which a pilot might need in the course of a voyage in that area.

With a sea chart in hand, the mariner could lay out his course with some degree of accuracy, using his ruler to trace the course between ports of departure and arrival. With his dividers and protractor, he could then locate the rhumb line closest to his course, and trace back to the nearest wind rose. In this manner he was able to identify the required course to reach his desired landfall.

In early chart-making there were serious errors due to the inability of the cosmographers to measure global distances on the waters of the world. The parallels of latitude were drawn on the charts as equidistant lines, but the meridians of longitude were also drawn as equidistant parallel lines. The result was a plane chart which led to some confusion.

The sailors knew that the compass or rhumb lines on their charts might not help them steer a course accurately to their desired landfall. The difficulties arose from the fact that distortions were created when the chart-makers tried to illustrate the curved surface of the earth on a flat piece of paper.

With this in mind, it is easily understood why the mariners blamed the winds, currents, compass errors and leeway for the great differences encountered between actual landfall and the reckoned time of landfall. This error was to be found in navigation until the latter part of the eighteenth century. The wise navigator used the plane charts with extreme caution, relying heavily on the sailing directions in his rutters, which were far more reliable.

CORTES & CHART-MAKING

In 1551 the Spanish writer, Martin Cortes, published his *Arte de Navegar* at Seville. In this book is found one of the most detailed explanations of the method of chart-making from that period of time. Cortes began his instruction with a basic premise: In order to make 'sea cardes', it was necessary to know the 'right position of places' and 'the distance that is from one place to another.' The 'right position' of places was to be gathered from those who had actually traveled in those places in order to know 'the best and most approved to be true.'

Cortes detailed the mechanical aspects of drawing a chart on paper or parchment. He gave the step-by-step method of laying out the east-west line and the north-south line at right angles. The initial drawing was to be done with a piece of lead, which could easily be erased after the final inking was done.

Once the outlines of the chart were traced upon the parchment [using tracing paper and carbon] the outlines were then inked in. The tracing paper used was a thin paper which had been rubbed with linseed oil. For carbon a paper was smoked with matches of pitch. When the ink was dry, the tracing lines were rubbed out with bread crumbs.

COLOR-CODED SEA CHARTS

To the inked outlines on the parchment were added the names of ports in red, the capes and bays in black. Cortes continues with a detailed method of adding the compass roses to the chart, indicating the eight principal winds in black, the half-winds in green and the quarter-winds in red. The radiating lines from the compass rose were inked in different colors to indicate the various rhumbs. These color-coded rhumbs were immediately recognizable to the master-mariner who had set his course on a given rhumb line. The north was indicated with a fleur-de-lis and the east was marked with a cross. When the mother compass had been completed, sixteen other compass roses were added for a small chart or thirty-two for a large chart. Thus, a navigator had a compass rose near any given area of his chart for ready reference.

CHARTING THE COURSE

In the latter part of his book, Cortes explains the use of the sea chart and the method of plotting or 'pricking' a position on it. The plotting of the ship's position was termed 'setting or making a pricke in the card.' He warned against errors, omissions and false estimates, explaining that the two things the navigator must know from his use of the sea chart were his line of sailing and the distance by the scale of leagues.

The navigator should also know the distance which he had made in a day's sailing, and since this could not be accurately estimated on a long voyage, he should rectify his estimation of the latitude by sighting the Pole Star or a meridian sun. In taking his observation, he could determine whether he had departed from the reckoned degree of latitude and by how much. If he found his latitude unchanged on an east-west course, he knew that he was on course.

The distance sailed was determined only by the mariner's expertise in gauging speed and distance. If the navigator found himself in a higher or lower degree of latitude than he reckoned for his course he could measure the location of *plotted* latitude against *observed* latitude with the aid of dividers ['compasses']. He could then measure it off (by the scale provided on the chart) to determine the distance he was off his reckoned course line. In this way he determined his *actual* position and the correction needed to return him to his plotted course.

Cortes pointed out, the lines of longitude converge from the equator towards the poles where they meet in one point. The problems of determining the length of a degree of longitude did not greatly affect the mariners sailing in the Mediterranean region. The length of a degree of longitude was off by about one-eighth for the parallel of $35°$ N, where the Mediterranean lies. The navigators could always correct the north-south errors by celestial navigation. However, they had no means of gauging their position east and west.

With the problems of determining longitudinal distances many navigators practiced latitude sailing. Rather than set a course at a diagonal to the north-south and east-west lines of meridians and parallels, the navigators preferred to sail north or south to the latitude which would take them directly east or west to their desired landfall. When the desired latitude was reached, they simply maintained a course on that latitude to reach their destination, taking great care, when they thought they were nearing the coast, in order to avoid an unexpected early landfall.

PRINTED CHARTS

About the time the Portuguese were voyaging southward along the western coast of Africa Johann Gutenberg was developing his printing press. His first book was the *Holy Bible*. By the late 1400s people were eager to have printed works on secular themes, and printers were setting up shops all across Europe. When Columbus was discovering the New World there were more than 238 towns in Europe and England with one or more print shops going about the business of printing books. As word came back with information about the many discoveries which were being made about the globe, hundreds of books began to be printed about them. Many of those books were illustrated with maps and pictures.

As the art of engraving for the purpose of printing developed into an art form, the Netherlands became known for the skill of its engravers. By 1550 Antwerp had become the great commercial center of Western Europe, making it an important gathering place for mariners in need of sea charts and the engravers and printers who produced them.

MERCATOR'S PLANE CHARTS

The problem of chart distortion was not solved until Gerard Mercator, an instrument-maker at Duisberg, tackled the problem. In order to draw the earth's surface on a flat surface, Mercator had to stretch the surface of the globe a great deal. In 1569 he published his new projection.

The new Mercator projections were not immediately accepted by sailors because they did not yet know how to lay off a compass course on it. Edward Wright did a great deal to encourage the acceptance of the Mercator charts, when he wrote about them and how simple they were to use. Gradually, the mariners learned how to use the new chart projections. Mercator's plane charts became so popular — and so widely used — that this type of chart projection carries Mercator's name to this day.

One of Mercator's friends was Abraham Ortelius, who worked as a map-maker and seller in Antwerp. Mercator went out with his men to remeasure land when he was making a map, whereas Ortelius was a member of a guild that specialized in coloring maps and charts. With the encouragement of his friend, Mercator, Ortelius set about the task of gathering up maps and having them engraved to print as an atlas in 1570, which was called *The Theater of the World*. The atlas was so popular that a second edition had to be printed. Seeing the market potential in geographical atlases, several printers began to publish their own books of maps and charts.

Willem Janszoon Blaeu, a famous map-maker of Amsterdam, was a scholar, scientist, printer and publisher of maps. With his large presses, Blaeu was able to print books as large as any of his customers might want.

Lucas Janszoon Waghenaer, a Dutch pilot, published a volume of navigational tables, charts and sailing directions about 1584. The English translation of *Mariner's Mirrour* appeared in 1588, and for a number of years the editions of this work enjoyed great success with the English mariners. The major problem was that the volumes were too bulky and the charts too large. [Fig. 76]

SMITH'S CHART OF NEW ENGLAND

Before departing on their voyage to New England, the Pilgrims had conferred with Capt. John Smith, who had carefully charted the New England coast in 1614. [Fig. 5] John Smith had followed the example set forth by Gerard Mercator in drawing up his plane chart of New England — complete with the rhumb lines required by a shipmaster sailing in those waters. It was Smith's chart of the New England coast that served as a guide to Master Christopher Jones.

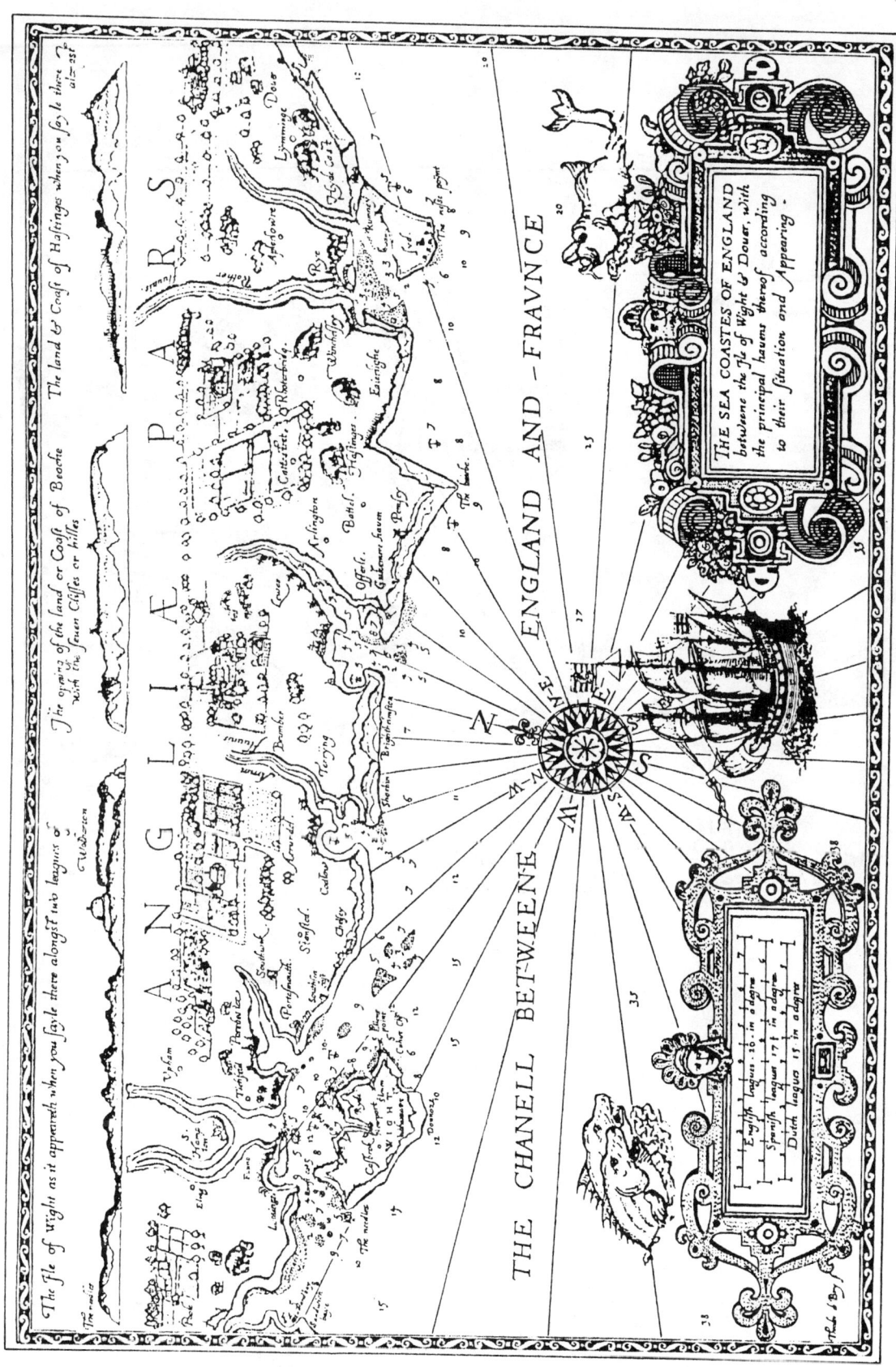

Fig. 76. Waghenaer's chart of the English Channel.

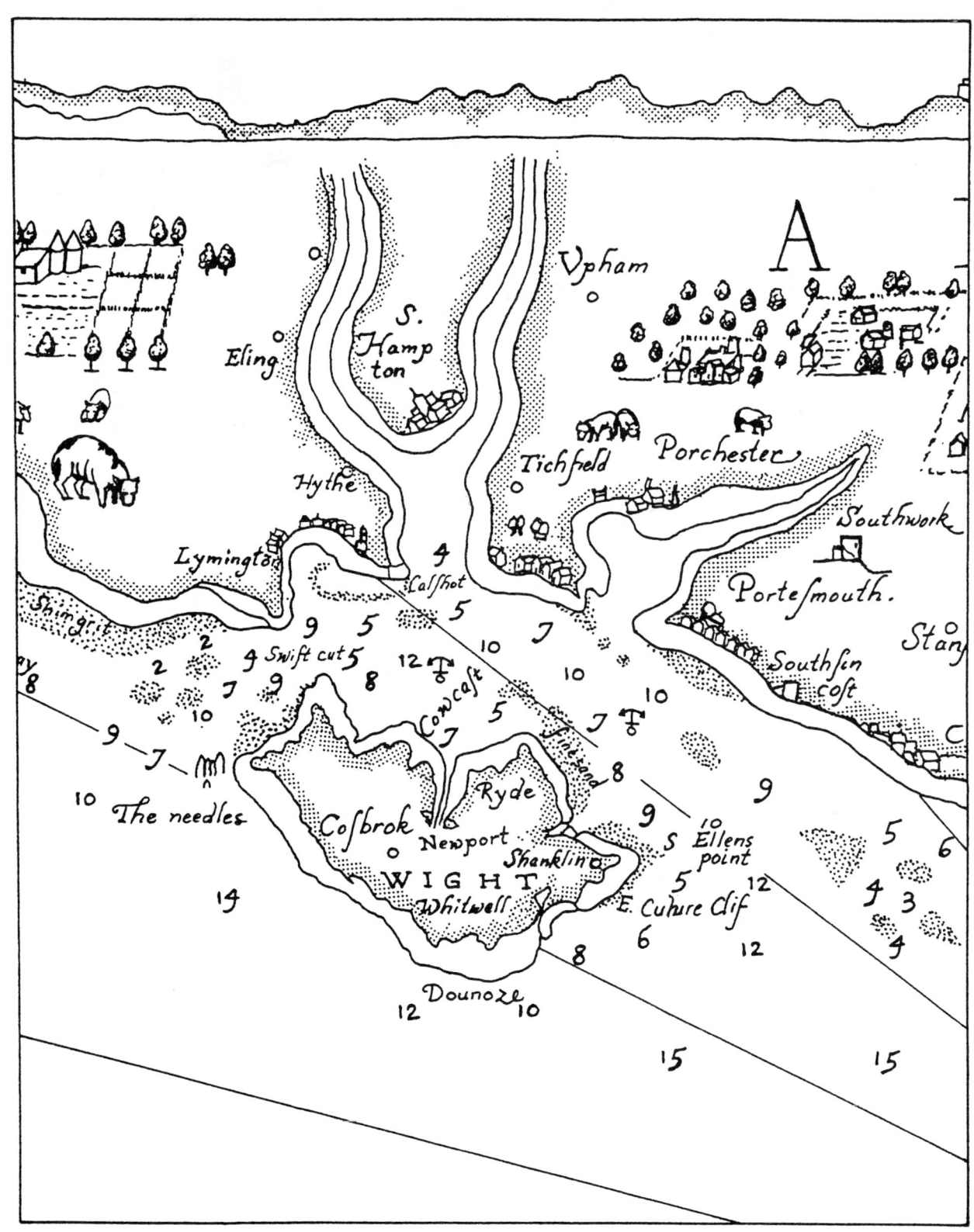

23. GLOBES

The idea of constructing a model of the terrestrial globe was suggested by a Greek scholar by the name of Crates before the Christian era. The problem at the time was that so little was actually known about the earth's surface that no such globes seem to have been made until the fifteenth century.

Early astronomers, understanding the arc of the heavens about the earth, projected the constellations onto a globe. The earliest celestial globe surviving is one of Arab origin dating back to about 1080, but they may have been used by Greek and Roman astronomers. [Fig. 77]

The development of a terrestrial globe offered the possibility of displaying accurately the representation of continents and oceans without the distortions of the plane charts. The development of the terrestrial globe also helped teach young seamen the basics of cartography and navigation as well as show any gentlemen voyagers who were aboard ship the position of the ship carrying them. When the Portuguese began to explore the coast of Africa and the Atlantic islands, the city council of Nuremberg commissioned Martin Behaim in 1490 to construct a terrestrial globe. Until that time globes had been almost exclusively celestial, showing the positions of heavenly bodies, the equinoctial, ecliptic, zenith and meridians.

John Cabot used a terrestrial globe on his voyage of discovery to Newfoundland. As the discoveries and explorations in the New World increased, there was a greater demand on the Continent for globes.

By the early sixteenth century the maps were made of printed gores affixed to a sphere. The globes were of great value to navigators, but the major problem lay in the fact that they were generally of a small size which caused difficulty in obtaining accurate measurements. What they needed was a globe large enough for accurate measurement, yet

Fig. 77. Molyneux's celestial globe.

small enough to carry aboard ship. However, in 1537, Pedro Nuñez, the great Portuguese navigation expert, was highly critical of the globe-makers of Lisbon whom he accused of taking more care for the ornamentation of their globes than in the accuracy of the cartographical work.

In 1541 Gerard Mercator produced a terrestrial globe of remarkable precision. The globe was sixteen inches in diameter, which provided navigators with the much needed accuracy. In addition it was designed in twelve gores which were technically correct, providing such important information as the line of the equator, a prime meridian (thought to be a line through the Canaries at the time), meridians of longitude at $15°$ intervals, parallels of latitude at $10°$ intervals, the ecliptic, the tropics, and the polar circles. Another important feature of value to the navigator was the inclusion of various scales and wind roses with rhumbs. [Fig. 78]

By the middle of the sixteenth century navigators who could afford it were taking globes to sea with them. On a globe they could measure the distance between places with greater accuracy, and plot position with some certainty — using tables, which showed the distances between meridians of longitude at each parallel of latitude. In this way the navigator could convert his *departure* — or distance east and west — into degrees of longitude.

In 1577 Merton College at Oxford purchased a pair of globes. They were probably of the type which Mercator had originated between 1541 and 1551, since Blundeville tells us in his *Exercises* that the Mercator globes were in common use in England until 1592. The Oxford globes were purchased before Emery Molyneux put his new globes on the market.

Emery Molyneux, a resident of Lambeth, created celestial and terrestrial globes, which were put on the London market in 1592. These were the first globes to be made in England by an Englishman. Within two years books were being published in England describing the globes and their use.

When the Warden of All Souls, Dr. Robert Hovenden, set out to buy a pair of Molyneux globes for his college at Oxford, the bursar's roll of accounts gives some interesting details concerning the installation of the globes.

Fig. 78. Molyneux's terrestrial globe.

Included in the list of expenses are such things as:

> to the tanner for calves skins to cover the globes,
> to the basket maker for wicker baskets for the globes,
> for making a scene [curtain] for one of the globes,
> for coloring the skins for the globes,
> for dressing the calves skins for the globes,
> to the saddler for making leather cases for the globes,
> for pulleys and setting them up in the Chapel,
> for painting the tops of the covers of the globes.

John Davis did much to make the use of the globe in navigation known and understood. Although Thomas Hood and Robert Hues had written treatises on the use of both celestial and terrestrial globes, it was Davis who presented the best work for the instruction of mariners, since he was a professional navigator.

Of all the instruments available to the navigator the globe was the one which gave the true distance and angle between places along with accurate latitude and longitude positions. Davis explained that with the aid of a pair of circular compasses [with curved, not straight legs] the courses from one place to another could be determined accurately. In his work Davis explained the problems encountered by loxodromes.

Although large globes of two-foot diameter or more were used by navigators to solve problems in sailing, they could obtain the information they needed more conveniently with their instruments and tables. Therefore, navigators of the period may not have made as great a use of the globes as recommended by Davis.

The meridian ring from a globe was found on the wreck of BATAVIA, which sank in 1629. Therefore we know that globes were in use at sea during the period in which MAYFLOWER sailed to the New World. It is quite possible that Jones carried a terrestrial globe with him. It is also possible that he might have had a celestial globe. The title page of *Mariners Mirrour* illustrates the celestial globe as part of the navigator's equipment. [See Fig. 17.]

24. NAUTICAL TABLES & GRAPHS

In order to accurately determine his position in relation to latitude, the navigator had to know certain facts when he took his observations of the sun each day. He knew that in the northern hemisphere the sun was at its highest zenith at summer solstice [June 21], and at is lowest at winter solstice [December 22]. With each succeeding day — beginning on June 22 — the sun would be a little lower and toward the south. It was imperative to know what the altitude of the sun would be on a given day, and in a given latitude. To aid the navigators in their calculations, the astronomers developed 'solar declination tables', which gave navigators the essential information needed in calculating their latitude.

Solar declination tables appear in the oldest surving Portuguese manuals. By the mid-sixteenth century the tables of celestial positions of the more prominent fixed stars had been added to nautical tables. Examples of nautical tables of solar declination can be seen in Fig. 79.

After 1600 sailors began to use trigonometrical tables and logarithms. As the science of navigation grew, the number of tables included in mariners' guides increased. Even more tables were added when Mercator's projection charts came into broader use because of the need to use a table of meridional parts, corresponding to the spacing of the minutes of latitude along meridians. With each new body of information and correction of old tables, the guides became increasingly bulky.

THE SINICAL QUADRANT or NAVIGATOR'S TRAVERSE BOARD

Towards the end of the sixteenth century, graphical methods were being taught to help the navigator resolve the problems of distance and departure with the use of a ruler and protractor. The sinical quadrant

The Table of the Equations of the Sunne.

The yere of our lord	The equatiõ to be added		The yeres	The E quation		The yeres	The E quation		The yeres of our lord	The equatiõ to be added	
	M	S		M	S		M	S		M	S
1545	1	0	1581	1	16	1617	1	32	1653	1	48
1546		45	1582	1	1	1618	1	17	1654	1	33
1547		30	1583		46	1619	1	2	1655	1	18
1548		15	1584		32	1620		47	1656	1	3
1549	1	2	1585	1	18	1621	1	33	1657	1	49
1550		47	1586	1	3	1622	1	18	1658	1	34
1551		32	1587		48	1623	1	3	1659	1	19
1552		18	1588		33	1624		49	1660	1	4
1553	1	4	1589	1	19	1625	1	35	1661	1	51
1554		49	1590	1	4	1626	1	20	1662	1	36
1555		34	1591		49	1627	1	5	1663	1	21
1556		19	1592		35	1628		51	1664	1	7
1557	1	05	1593		21	1629	1	37	1665	1	53
1558		50	1594	1	6	1630	1	22	1666	1	38
1559		35	1595		51	1631	1	7	1667	1	23
1560		21	1596		37	1632		53	1668	1	9
1561	1	7	1597	1	23	1633	1	38	1669	1	55
1562		52	1598	1	8	1634	1	23	1670	1	40
1563		37	1599		53	1635	1	8	1671	1	25
1564		23	1600		39	1636		54	1672	1	10
1565	1	9	1601	1	25	1637	1	40	1673	1	56
1566		54	1602	1	10	1638	1	25	1674	1	41
1567		39	1603		55	1639	1	10	1675	1	26
1568		25	1604		40	1640		56	1676	1	12
1569	1	11	1605	1	26	1641	1	42	1677	1	58
1570		56	1606	1	11	1642	1	27	1678	1	43
1571		41	1607		56	1643	1	12	1679	1	28
1572		26	1608		42	1644		58	1680	1	13
1573	1	12	1609	1	28	1645	1	44	1681	2	0
1574		57	1610	1	13	1646	1	29	1682	1	45
1575		42	1611		58	1647	1	14	1683	1	3
1576		28	1612		44	1648	1	0	1684	1	15
1577	1	14	1613	1	30	1649	1	46	1685	2	2
1578		59	1614	1	15	1650	1	31	1686	1	47
1579		44	1615	1	10	1651	1	15	1687	1	3
1580		20	1616		45	1652	1	2	1688	1	18

Fig. 79. A declination table.

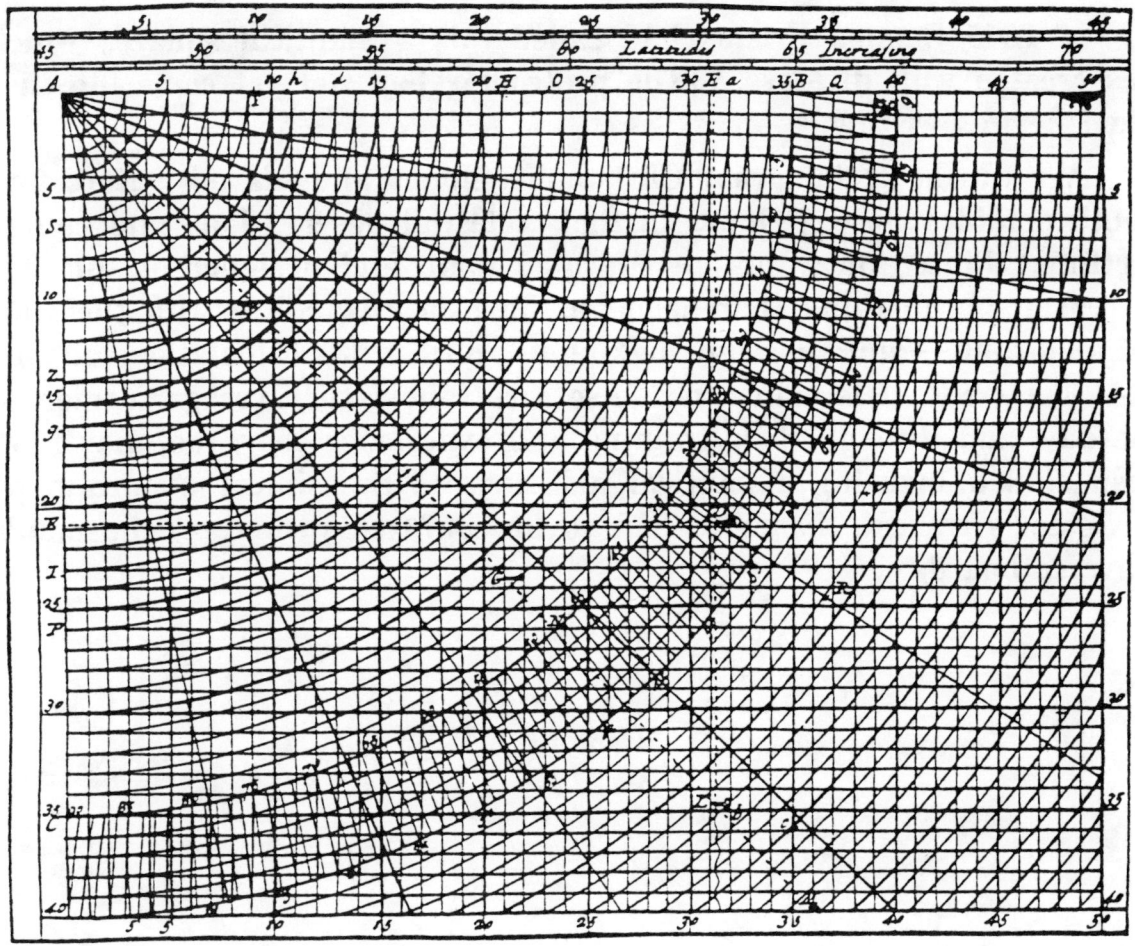

Fig. 80. A sinical quadrant and traverse board.

was designed to help the navigator solve the problem of resolving a course into distance latitude and departure by means of a graphical solution. A rectangular grid over the face of the quadrant represented meridians of longitude and parallels of latitude. [Fig. 80]

The navigator could set off his course in leagues or miles along a correct bearing, using a scale-ruler. John Tapp remarked that any one who could set off an accurate right angle and had a scale-ruler could dispense with the board and work on a sheet of blank paper.

USING THE SINICAL QUADRANT

The navigator selected a convenient point on the scale as the meridian of longitude and parallel of latitude for his point of departure. Pricking the point, he set off his course at the correct bearing. With his ruler and the marginal scales, he could measure his north-southing and east-westing and convert it into differences of longitude and latitude.

In 1545 Gemma Frisius had called this a 'nautical square,' which was created with dividers. [The protractor had not yet come into use when he was writing.]

We can be certain that Christopher Jones and his navigators had nautical tables close at hand in their celestial observations and course plotting. Since Jones was an educated man, and designer of ships, it is reasonable to think that he might have been familiar with the sinical quadrant — quite possibly making use of it in his calculations aboard MAYFLOWER. His mates were also a cut above the average seamen of the day, and through their training and experience they, too, may have been skilled in using a nautical aid such as the sinical quadrant, or navigator's traverse board — not to be confused with the helmsman's traverse board.

25. PLOTTING INSTRUMENTS

From early writings and more recent underwater archaeology, we know some of the instruments which would have been used by navigators in the Age of Discovery.

DIVIDERS

Perhaps one of the most commonly mentioned implements were the dividers [or 'compasses'], used for dividing a line into equal segments and for 'pricking the chart'. Even the earliest charts included distance scales, which were measured off with a pair of 'compasses'.

When the Portuguese began to voyage far to the south along the coast of Africa, and west to the New World, the navigators had to know the true latitude for a number of major ports, capes and cities. The latitude scale was added, being placed in an unoccupied space on the chart. With his dividers, the navigator was able to measure off the distance on his charts.

The dividers were much like those in use today, consisting of two hinged legs with pointed ends, which could be separated to any distance from zero to the maximum extent of the dividers' physical size. The desired setting was maintained by friction at the hinge, and later by means of a screw. [Fig. 81a]

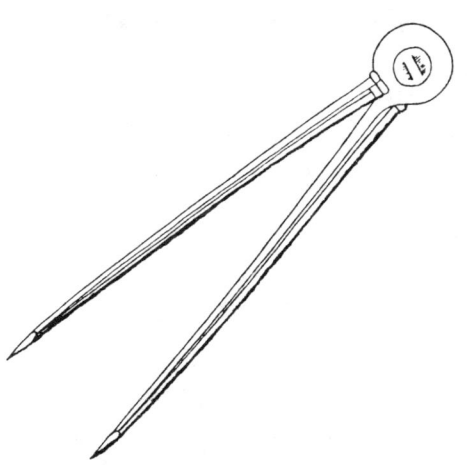

Fig. 81a. Straight leg dividers.

Because the navigators were working on charts with long distances between points, most navigators preferred to have dividers with long legs to facilitate the measurement of greater distances. It is

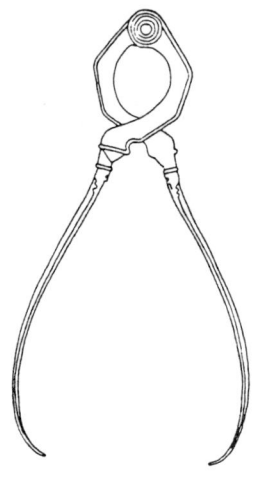

possible that navigators might also have several pairs of dividers in various sizes. Many of the dividers had straight legs. However, we know from the work of John Davis [as mentioned in the section of globes] that some navigators would have had 'circular compasses' with curved legs for use on globe calculations. [Fig. 81b]

PROTRACTORS

Fig. 81b. Circular dividers

The protractor was also an English invention, which is generally attributed to Thomas Blundeville, a student of mathematics, astronomy and navigation. In his book, *A Briefe Description of Universal Mappes and Cardes*, he wrote that '... having to seeke out ... the way by sea or land to anyplace I would use none other instrument of direction then half a Circle divided with lines like a Mariner's Flie.' Though Blundeville appears to be the first to mention the use of a protractor, part of a slate disk scored with the points of the compass was found on the wreck of MARY ROSE, Henry VIII's flagship, which sank in 1545 near Portsmouth. [Fig. 82] There is some speculation that the slate piece was part of a complete disk, which might have been used as a protractor by the navigator. If the MARY ROSE find is indeed a protractor, it would suggest that protractors were in use from early times.

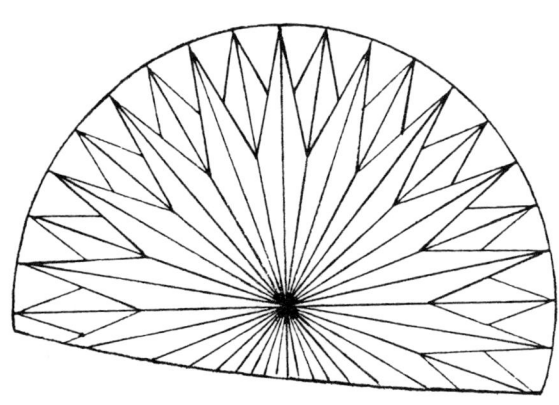

Fig. 82. A possible protractor from MARY ROSE.

Underwater archaeology has recovered examples from early seventeenth-century vessels originiating from several countries. A protractor was recovered from the wreck of BATAVIA, which sank close to Australia in 1629. Those dividers were of Dutch design. A pair of almost identical dividers still survives in Amsterdam. The BATAVIA protractor is 7 1/2 in-

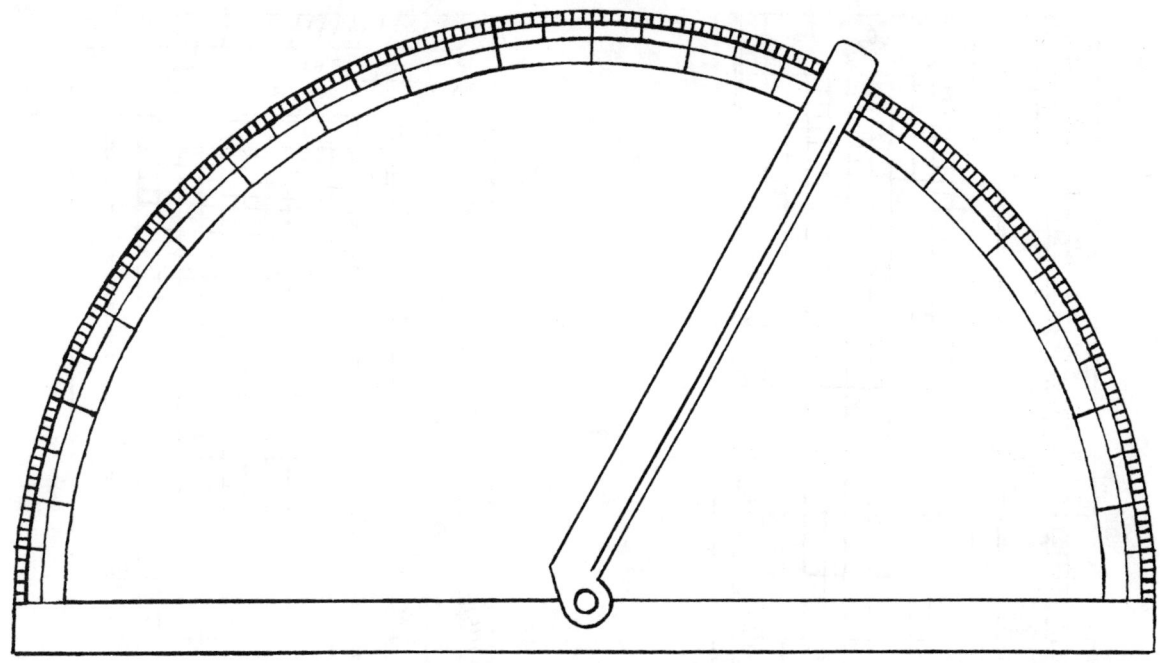

Fig. 83. A protractor from BATAVIA.

ches across, and may have been used in plotting the ship's course on vellum charts. This protractor has a radial arm, which was engraved with a scale on its upper surface. [Fig. 83] The modern protractors for navigational work are much lighter in design. The wreck of BATAVIA also contained the brass meridian ring of a globe about 12 inches in diameter, proving that globes were still being used aboard ships in 1629.

SCALES AND RULERS

Various rulers and scales were in use from an early time. The 1545 wreck of MARY ROSE contained a simple ruler. However, through the years that followed a great deal of progress was made by mathematicians and writers of sea manuals, concerning the use of charts and plotting courses. As a result, much more elaborate scales and rulers were needed by the navigators.

By 1624 Edmund Gunter had developed his set of logarithmic scales of natural numbers and trigonometrical numbers. He developed an instrument which was known simply as Gunter's Scale. [Fig. 84] The scale — about two feet in length and made of boxwood and brass — contained four lines: (1) A single line of numbers, (2) a line of tangents, (3) a line of sines, and (4) a line divided into twelve inches and tenths

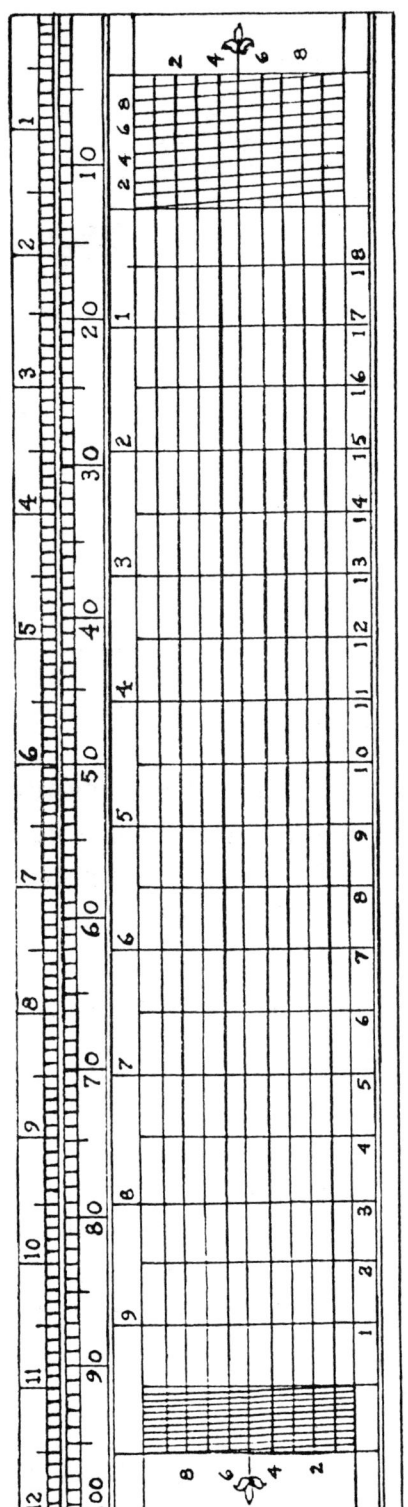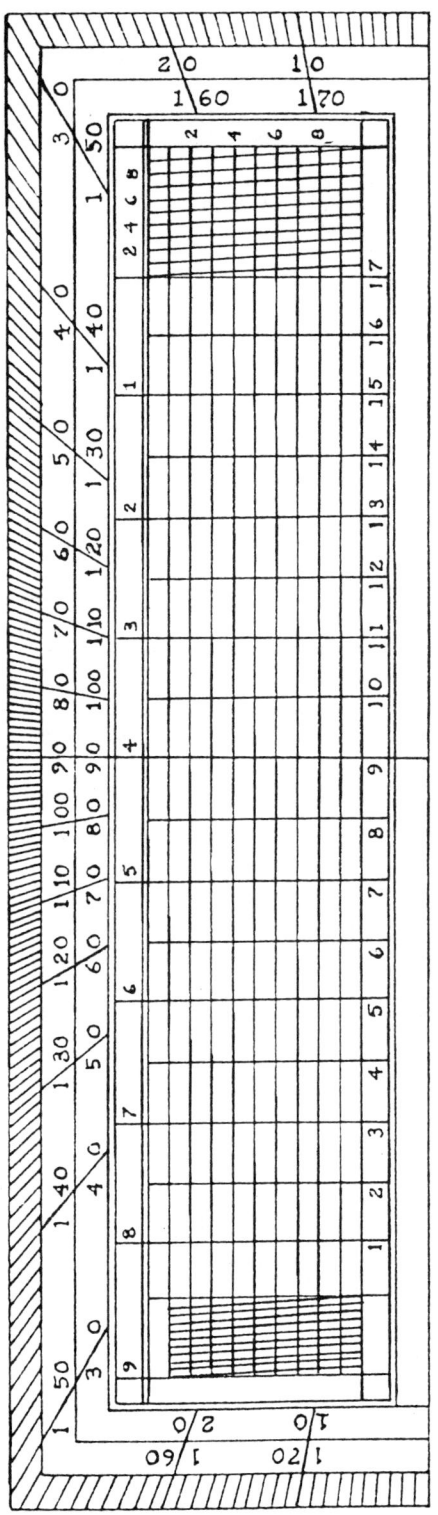

Fig. 84. A Gunter's scale.

of inches, also one, divided into tenths and hundredths.

A simple Gunter's scale was developed for use by sailors and became known as the Sliding Gunter, which continued in use by sailors who were not proficient in arithmetic. Most of the navigators who were better educated preferred to use tables with seven or eight figure logarithms. By 1650 Gunter's Scale had developed into a true slide rule.

LEAD WRITING IMPLEMENTS

We know from the writing of Cortes, detailing chart-making, that pieces of lead were used in drawing. The navigators probably had similar writing implements. Cortes also refers to the use of bread crumbs for erasing marks made with the lead.

Ink wells have been found, which indicate that the navigators also used pen and ink — possibly in various colors — for notations and record-keeping. Sand-shakers held the sand used as a blotter for freshly inked writings.

SECTORS

The Sector is an instrument of two equal rules or legs of silver, brass, ivory, or wood joined by a rivet, by which may be found the proportion between quantities of the same kind; as between one line and another, between one area and another, or between one volume and another.

A forerunner of the English Sector was the Geometric and Military Compass invented by Galileo about 1596-7. It consists of two straight rulers connected by a joint so that they can be set to any required angle. A quadrant is joined to the geometric compass which has the usual divisions of the astronomical compass. Large numbers of these instruments, in copper and silver, were manufactured in a workshop in Galileo's own house. A sector of similar design is seen in Fig. 85.

In England the invention of the Sector is attributed to Thomas Hood in 1598. And by 1624 it had been considerably improved by Edmund Gunter, whose improved Sector was manufactured by Elias Allen. [Fig. 86] The three lines on most sectors marked N.S.T. are lines of numbers, sines, and tangents respectively. Gunter's scale facilitated the rough solution of many problems.

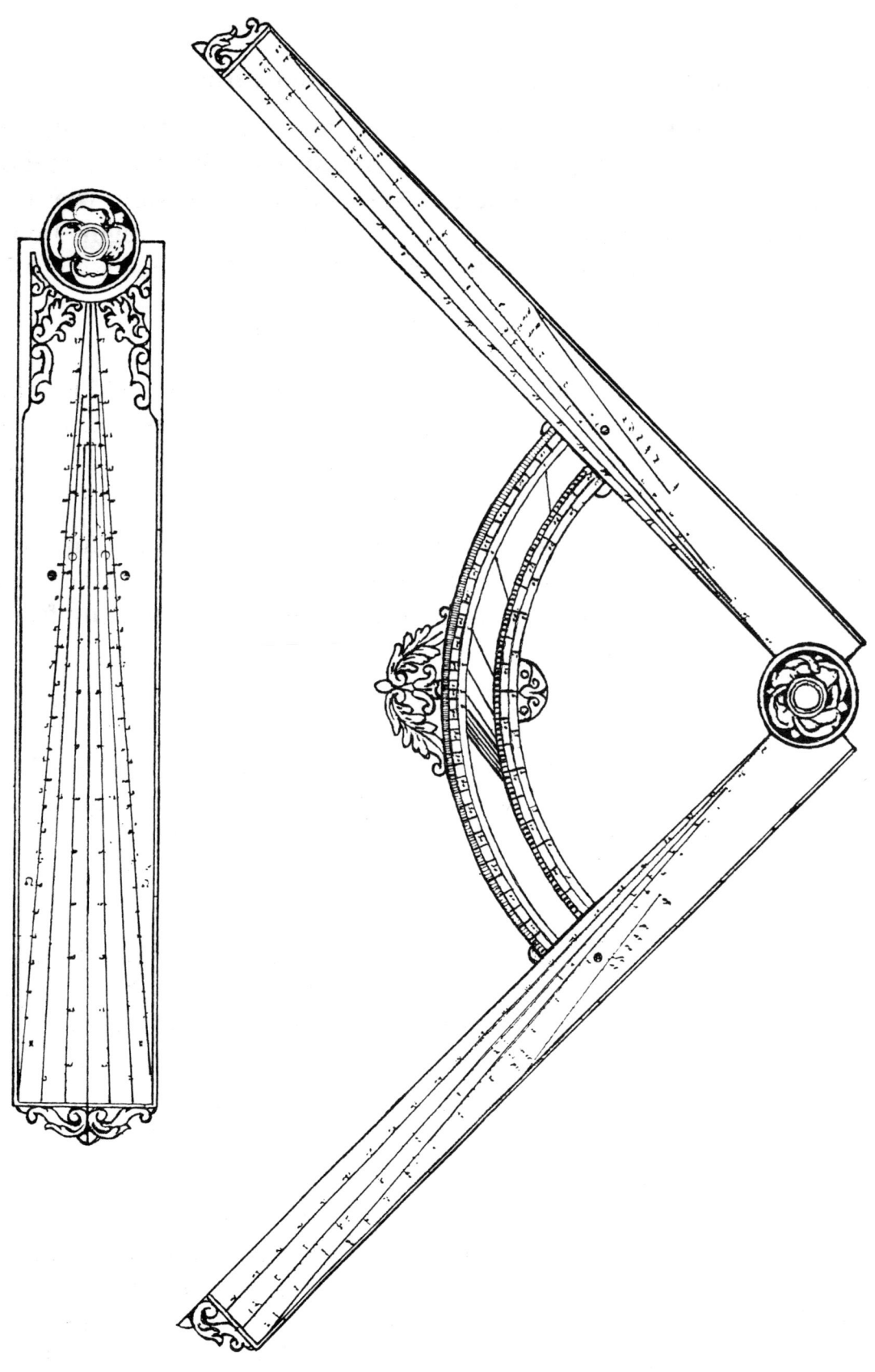

Fig 85. A sector with geometric compass.

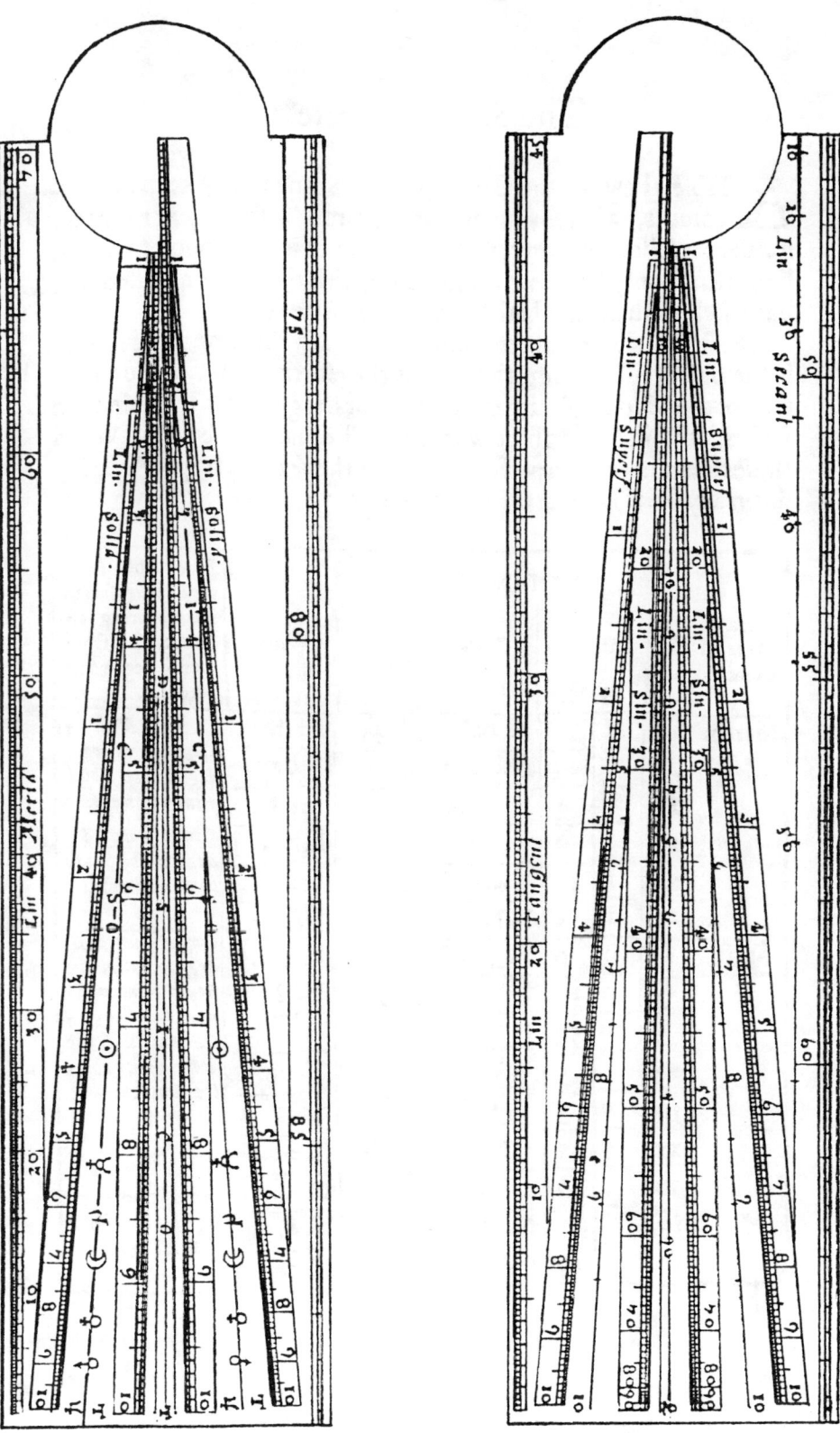

Fig. 86. A Gunter's sector.

The Seamans Secrets.

A Table shewing the Order how the Seamen may keep his Accompts, whereby he may at all times distinctly examine his former practises, for in every 24 hours, which is from noon to noon, he doth not only lay down his Latitude, with the Corse and Leagues, but also how the Wind hath blown in the same time.

The first Colume is the months and dayes of the same; the second is the observed Altitude, the third is the Horizontal Corse or motion of the Ship, the fourth the number of Leagues that the Ship hath sayled, the fifth is a space wherein must be noted, by what Wind those things have been performed; and the next great space is to lay down any brief Discourse for your memory.

Moneths and dayes of the Moneth.	Latitude. G. M.		Corse.	Leagus	Wind	The 13 of *March* cape S *Augustin* in *Brasil*, being 16 leagues East from me, I began this accompt.
Anno. 1593.						
March. 24	7	30	N.N.E.	25	East.	
25	5	44	N.b.E.nor.	36	E.b.N.	*Compasse varied 9 degrees the South point westward.*
26	4	1	N.b.N.	35	E.b.N.	
27	2	49	N.	24	E.b.N.	*Compasse varied 8 degrees, the South point westward.*
28	1	31	N. easterly.	26	E.b.N.	
29	1	4	N.N.W.	9	N.E.	
Aprill. 31	0	0	N.b.W.	21	E.N.E.	*Compasse varied 6. deg. 40. min. the South point westward.*
4	0	39	N.W.b.N.	15	N.E.	
7	1	53	N.N.W.	28	N.E.	*Observation, the Pole Artick above the Horizon.*
9	3	5	N.W.b.N	30	N.e.b.E	
10	4	5	N.W.b.N	22	N.e.	
11	4	45	N.W.	18	N.e.b.N	
12	5	16	N.W.	14	N.e.b.N	*Compasse varied 7. degrees, the North point Eastward.*
13	6	11	N.W.b.N.	23	N.e.	
14	7	16	N.W.b N.	14	N.e.	

A brief

26. THE JOURNAL

The shipmaster's log-book or journal was called by a number of names in the early years. John Davis referred to it as the 'Accompts' of the voyage. Others referred to it as the 'traverse book.' The earliest form of journal seems to have been written by Sir Hugh Willoughby in 1553.

The major difference between the earlier traverse book and the later journal or log-book was that the journal included a longitude column. As the log and log-line came into more common use among the English mariners — along with a more extensive use of the Mercator and circumpolar charts — the journal or log-book with a longitudinal column came into use.

The information recorded in the journal or log-book was taken from the entries which would have been recorded on the traverse-board and log-board for each watch. Corrections would have been made for the estimated amount of leeway, the effects of variation and the currents or tidal streams which had been encountered during the course of a watch.

The first example of a journal laid out in columnar form was that of John Davis' account of his voyage in 1587 as it was printed by Hakluyt in the third volume of his second edition of *Principall Voyages and Naviagations* in 1600. Davis' journal for his voyage of 1593 uses much the same lay-out as that of 1587 with a few changes. [Fig. 87] In his earlier version he had kept his records of distance run on an hourly basis. In 1593 he kept the records for a twenty-four hour period from noon to noon. He noted the latitude, wind direction and remarks, which included the variation and latitude for his observations.

William Baffin also kept a journal in which he listed a column for latitude. Although, he noted that this column was not common in journals of the time. In that column Baffin recorded the variation of the

Moneth Iuly.	Dayes.	Houres.	Course.	Leagues.	Elevation of the pole. Deg	Min.	The winde	THE DISCOVRSE.
	31	24	S. by W.	27	62		N.W.	This 31 at Noone, comming close by a terraine or great cape, we fell into a mightie race, where an island of ice was carried by the force of the currant as fast as our barke could saile with him wind, all sailes bearing. This cape as it was the most Southerly limit of the gulfe which we passed ouer the 30 day of this moneth, so was it the North promontory or first beginning of another very great inlet, whose South limit at this present wee saw not. Which inlet or gulfe this afternoone, and in the night, we passed ouer: where to our great admiration we saw the sea falling downe into the gulfe with a mighty ouerfal, and raging, and with diuers circular motions like whirlepooles, in such sort as forcible streames passe thorow the arches of bridges.
August								
Noone the	1	24	S.E. by S.	16	61	10	W.S.W.	The true course, &c. This first of August we sell with the promontory of
Noone the	3	48	S.S.E.	16	60	26	Variable.	the said gulfe of second passage, hauing coasted by diuers contises set our course garb, a great banke of the ice beinen put of that gulfe.
Noone the	6	72	S.E. Southerly.	22	59	35	Variable to calme.	The true course, &c.
	7	24	S.S.E.	22	58	40	W.S.W.	The true course, &c.
	8	24	S.E.	13	58	12	W. fog.	The true course, &c.
	9	24	S. by W.	13	57	30	Variable & calme.	The true course, &c.
	10	24	S.S.E.	17	56	40	S.W. by W.	The true course, &c.
	11	24	S.E. easterly.	40	55	13	W.N.W.	The true course, &c.
	12	24	S.E. easterly.	20	54	32	W.S.W.	The true course, &c.
	13	24	S.S.E.	4	54		N.W.	This day seeking for our ships that went to fish, we stroke on a rocke, being among many plts, and had a great leake.
Noone the	14	24	S.S.E.	28	52	40	N.W.	This day we stopped our leake in a storme. The 15 of August at noon, being in the latitude of 52 degrees 12 min. and 16 leagues from the shore, we shaped our course for England, in Gods name, as followeth.
*Noone y 15					52	12	S.S.W.	The true latitude.
	16	20	S.E. halfe point S.	50	51		S.W.	The true course, &c.
	17	24	E. by S.	30	50	40	S.	The true course, &c. This day vpon the Banke we met a Biscaine bound either for the Grand bay or for the passage. He chased vs.
	18	24	E. by N. northerly.	49	51	18	W.	The true course, &c.
	19	24	E halfe point north.	51	51	35	Variable W. & E.	The true course, &c.
	20	24	E.S.E.	31	50	50	S.W.	The true course, &c.
Noone the	22	48	E. by N.	68	51	30	S.S.W.	The true course, &c.
	23	24	E. by N. Southerly	33	51	52	S.	The true course, &c.
	24	24	E. by N.	31	52	10	Variable.	The true course, &c. This 24 of August obseruing the variation, I found the compasse to vary towards the East, from the true Meridian, one degree.
Noone the	27	72	E. Northerly.	40	52	23	Variable & calme.	The true course, &c. for 72 houres.
Noone the	29	48	E.S.E.	47	51	28	Variable W. & S.	The true course, &c.
Noone the	31	48	S.E by E. easterly	14	51	0	Variable.	The true course, &c.
September	2	48	E. Southerly	65	51		N.W.	The true course, &c.
	3	24	E. by S. Easterly.	24	50	50	W.N.W.	The true course, &c.
	4	24	S.E. by E.	20	50	21	N.N.E.	The true course, &c.
	5	24	S.E. by E.	18	40	48	N.N.E.	The true course, &c. Note we supposed our selues to be 55 leagues fro Sylly
	6	24	E. by S.	15	49	40	N.	The true course, &c.
	7	24	E.S.E.	20	49	15	N.N.W.	The true course, &c.
	8	24	N.E.	18	49	40		
	9	24	W.S.W.	7	49	42		
	10	24	S.E. by E.	8	49	28	Variable.	
	11	24	N.E. by E.	10	49	45	Variable.	
	12	24	N.W. by W.	6	50		N.E.	
	12	24	E by S. Southerly	15	49	47	N.E.	
	15							This 15 of September 1587 we arriued at Dartmouth.

Fig. 87. A sample page of Davis' journal.

compass and other occurrences of importance to the navigator. With all of this information recorded in the journal, it was a simple matter to look back and determine latitude and estimated longitude.

The shipmaster or navigator could quickly locate the last known position on a given day and prick the position from the latitude and longitude scales on his chart with his dividers.

In the journal of his 1612 voyage around Resolution Island, Baffin referred to 'protracting,' which indicated the growing use of the protractors by navigators of the period. Baffin also color-coded his chart, using green to indicate all the land sighted, and red to indicate the ship's track. He also indicated tidal observations around Resolution Island and Cape Comfort. He noted that the traverse book enabled the shipmaster to accurately plot his course on a chart by having available the information on the course made good, the distance run and the latitude observations. Champlain's lay-out for a journal is seen in Fig. 88.

Journals were fairly commonly kept by voyagers of the early seventeenth century. The journals of this period list by columns such information as the day, the true course, leagues sailed, winds, latitude, longitude, variation and pertinent remarks such as dip observed, soundings made and landmarks and landfalls.

No journal or log-book has ever been located for MAYFLOWER's voyage of 1620. Speculations can only be made on the basis of William Bradford's account in his *History of Plimoth Plantation* and Edward Winslow's account in *Mourt's Relation*.

Heures.	Nauds.	Brasses.	Routes. Rumbs.
2	3	2	Cap au Nort ¼ du Nordeſt
4	2	4	Cap au Nort. Nordeſt.
6	4	2	Cap au Nordeſt.
8	5	3	Cap au Nordeſt.
10	2	3 ½	Cap au Nort- ¼ du Nordeſt.
12	3	5	Cap au Nort-nordeſt.
2	2	3	Cap au Nordeſt ¼ de l'Eſt.
4	2	4	Cap au Nordeſt.
6	6	1	Cap au Nort.
8	6	3	Cap au Nordeſt ¼ du Nordeſt.
10	6	2	Cap au Nort. ¼ du Nordeſt
12	3	4	Cap au Nort-nordeſt.

Fig. 88. A sample of Champlain's journal.

27. COMMUNICATION

A shipmaster, navigating his ship on a course across the open waters, had to keep in constant contact with his officers and crew. This could be a major problem. The large square-rigged vessels were driven by the winds, and the winds were noisy. Voice commands could become distorted to an unintelligible degree as gale force winds howled, shrieked and moaned through the network of standing rigging, which surrounded the crew at work.

COMMUNICATING ORDER ABOARD SHIP

The ship's bell tolled out the hours of each watch. However, there were commands needed to guide the working crew as the ship ploughed through the water — in all kinds of weather. To communicate the master's commands, the boatswain used a system of commands — verbal and piped on a boatswain's pipe.

The verbal commands were kept short and distinctive, when shouted verbally aboard a vessel under way, or getting under way. John Smith gave a few of the typical orders, which might be shouted, in his book, *A Sea Grammar* [1627]. They are all precise orders, which would have been easily understood by the working crew.

Because of the difficulty in understanding verbal commands under certain conditions at sea, the boatswain's pipe came into use. Just when it began to make its appearance on vessels is not known. However, the whistle or pipe aboard ships had a long history before the Age of Discovery. Galley slaves of Rome and Greece kept stroke to the sound of a flute or whistle similar to the boatswain's pipe.

The boatswain's pipe may have been in use on English sailing ships as early as the thirteenth century during the Crusades. A boatswain's pipe was discovered in the wreck of MARY ROSE, which sank in **1545**.

Fig. 89. Boatswain's pipe from MARY ROSE.

[Fig. 89] It is also interesting to note that the mariners depicted on the title page of *Mariners Mirrour* have boatswain's pipes hanging on neck ribbons. Therefore, it would seem that the boatswain's pipe was definitely in use by the late sixteenth century, and commonplace by the end of the seventeenth century. [Fig. 90] It did not become known as 'the Call' until 1670, then the British Royal Navy organized and standardized the piped commands to be used with a boatswain's pipe.

The boatswain [bosun] was the officer in charge of the rigging, sails and all of the sailing equipment. It was, therefore, his job to convey the master's orders to the working crew in a clear and understandable way. When a sailor heard a piped command on the boatswain's pipe, he was expected to respond immediately.

Each part of the boatswain's pipe has a nautical name. The hollow ball at the end is called the 'buoy', the stem at the mouthpiece is called the 'gun', and the leaf under the gun is called the 'keel'. [Fig. 91]

The boatswain's pipe is held between the index finger and thumb, with the thumb under or near the shackle on the keel. The side of the buoy should rest against the palm of the hand, and the fingers allowed to close over the gun and the buoy hole in such a position that they can throttle the exit of air from the buoy to obtain the desired sound.

On the boatswain's pipe there are two main notes: the low and the

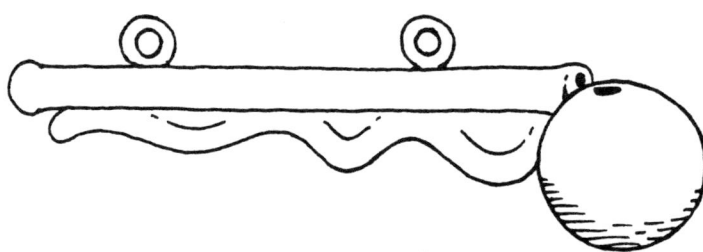

Fig. 90. A boatswain's pipe from *Mariners Mirrour*.

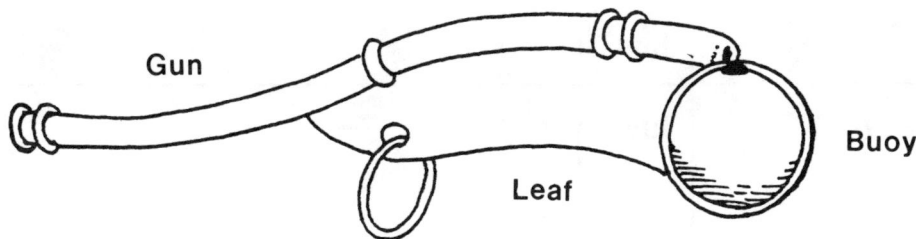

Fig. 91. Parts of a boatswain's pipe.

high. To alter the high and low notes there are three tones: the plain, the warble and the trill.

The plain note is made by blowing a steady stream of air into the gun of the pipe with an unobstructed hole in the buoy. The intermediate tones are made by throttling the buoy to a greater or lesser extent. The warble is achieved by blowing a series of short bursts of air into the gun. The trill is created by vibrating the tongue while blowing.

Care must be taken, when piping a command, not to touch the hole in the buoy, as this will cause the sound to be choked.

For examples of some piped commands which have come down through the years in the British Royal Navy, see Fig. 92.

SHIP TO SHIP COMMUNICATION

When fleets of vessels began to make their way to the New World, it became necessary to devise some method of establishing communication from one ship to another. It is interesting to note the detailed method of communications which were used by the captains and masters in the fleet of Sir Humphrey, which are given below:

First the Admirall to cary his flag by day, and his light by night.

2. Item, if the Admirall shall shorten his saile by night, then to shew two lights untill he be answered againe by every ship shewing one light for a short time.

3. Item, if the Admirall after shortening his saile, as aforesayd, shall make more saile againe: then he to shew three lights one above the other.

Call Boatswain's Mates	high low	– – – – – – –
Haul or Hoist	high low	⎽⎽⎽⎽⎽⎽⎽⎽
Belay	high low	 ∿∿∿
Heave around the Capstan	high low	 ∼∼∼
Stop Work or Stand Still	high low	 ⎯⎯⎯⎯⎯⎯⎯
Walk Back	high low	 ∿∿∿∿∿∿∿
Carry On	high low	⌐___
Away Boat	high low	 ⎴⎴
Pipe Down	high low	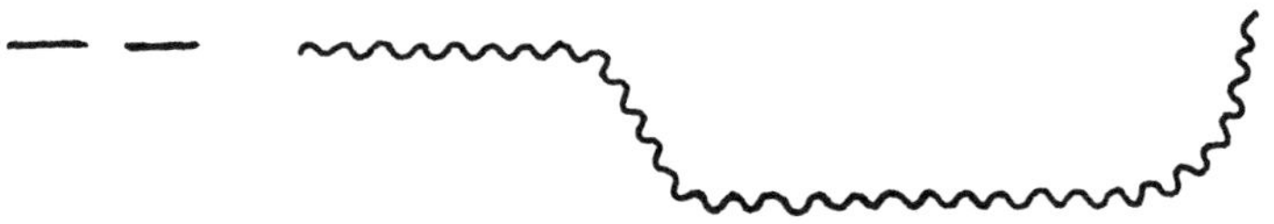 – – ∼⎽∼∼⎺
Dinner or Supper	high low	 ∿∿⎯⎯

Fig. 92. Some of the boatswain's piped calls.

4. Item, if the Admirall shall happen to hull in the night, then to make a wavering light over his other light, wavering the light upon a pole.

5. Item, if the fleet should happen to be scattered by weather, or other mishap, then so soone as one shall descry another to hoise both toppe sailes twise, if the weather will serve, and to strike them twise againe; but if the weather serve not, then to hoise the maine top saile twise, and forthwith to strike it twise againe.

6. Item, if it shall happen a great fogge to fall, then presently every shippe to beare up with the admirall, if there be winde: but if it be a calme, then every ship to hull, and so to lie at hull till it be cleare. And if the fogge so continue long, then the Admirall to shoot off two pieces every morning, and every ship to answere it with one shot: and every man bearing to the ship, that is to leeward so neere as he may.

7. Item, every master to give charge unto the watch to looke out well, for laying aboord of another in the night, and in the fogge.

8. Item. every evening every ship to haile the admirall, and so to fall asterne him, sailing thorow the Ocean and being on the coast, every ship to hale him both morning and evening.

9. Item, if any ship be in danger any way, by leake or otherwise, then she to shoot off a piece, and presently hang out one light, whereupon every man to beare towards her, answering her with one light for a short time, and so to put it out againe: thereby to give knowledge that they have seene her token.

10. Item, whensoever the Admirall shall hang out her ensigne in the maine shrouds, then every man to come aboord her, as a token of counsell.

11. Item, if there happen any storme or contrary winde to the fleet after the discovery, whereby they are separated: then every ship repaire unto their last good port, there to meete againe.

THE TELESCOPE

When ships in a fleet were at a distance from one another, it was essential for a shipmaster to have a telescope at his disposal. The telescope was well known in the Age of Discovery. It was called by several names: perspective glass, proportional glass, spy glass, and Galilean telescope [after Galileo]. Optics had been under investigation since the late thirteenth century. By the middle of the sixteenth century, Leonard Digges had made some refracting telescopes, which were called 'proportional glasses' or 'perspective glasses'.

In 1584 Thomas Hariot reported that he had astounded the American Indians with a perspective glass. Galileo made improvements on the telescope — as did the Dutch spectacle-makers. Consequently, the proportional glass made a significant appearance from 1609 onward, as the Dutch opticians began to commercialize their products.

Telescopes were quickly adopted by mariners and military men, al-

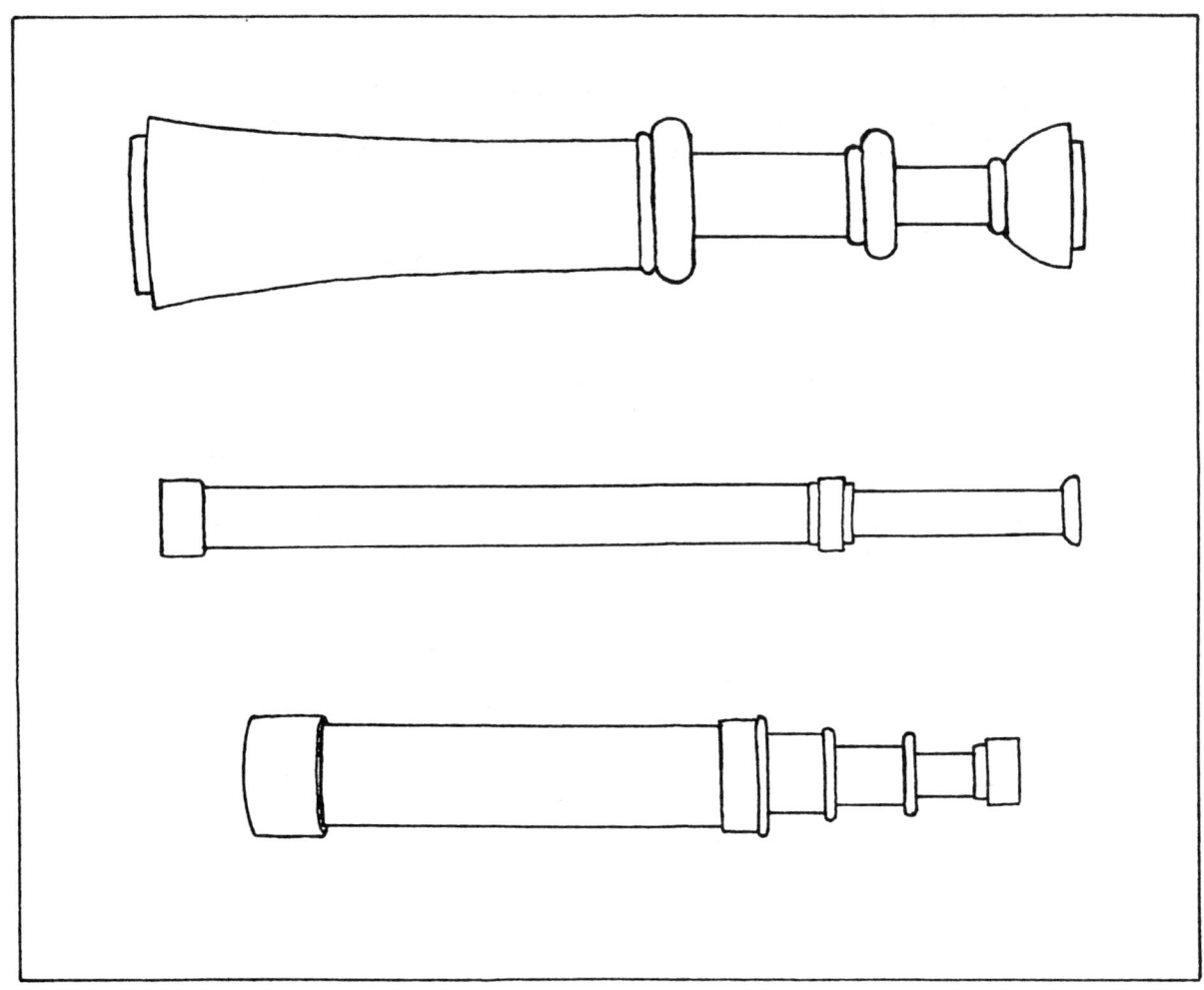

Fig. 93. Examples of telescopes.

though the models they used were much weaker than the one used by the astronomers. By 1610 telescopes were being manufactured in London.

In its early form the telescope was very long and unwieldy. They were constructed of paste board or wood to make them lighter to handle. However, mariners learned that the nest of sliding tubes used to focus the telescope, rapidly deteriorated under the moist conditions at sea. Therefore, the telescopes had to be kept in mahogany cases. Finally, the nested tubes were made of brass. Examples of paste board and brass telescopes can be seen in Fig. 93.

28. CONCLUSIONS

Through the preceeding sections we have seen that the art and science of navigation — as well as piloting — had begun to blossom during the Age of Discovery. The Portuguese mathematicians had set the development of navigation in motion at the encouragement of Henry the Navigator. However, by the late sixteenth century, the English mathematicians had taken the lead in the rapidly developing field of mathematics. The roll call of English writers in the fields of mathematics and navigation is a long and impressive one.

Christopher Jones was a man born to the sea, who was recognized by the Royal Navy and the King for his outstanding abilities in the design and building of JOSIAN.

PREPARATIONS FOR THE VOYAGE

In preparing himself for undertaking the Altantic voyage across waters which he had never sailed, Jones would have gathered rutters for the Channel ports, tide tables, solar declination tables and existing charts of the Atlantic waters which were available at the book sellers in London.

In addition, we are told that the Pilgrim leaders had consulted with Capt. John Smith, who had charted and mapped the New England region in 1614. It seems reasonable to think that Christopher Jones might have accompanied the men when they visited Capt. John Smith — or perhaps paid a private visit of his own, since Smith was probably in London at the time. As part owner and master of MAYFLOWER, it would have been only natural for Jones to want to learn all he could from a man so familiar with the New England coast. As a responsible shipmaster, the safety of the passengers, the crew and the ship would have been uppermost in his mind as he faced a new adventure.

John Smith in *Advertisements &c* written 16 October 1630 [not published until 1631], says that he advised the Pilgrims to settle at Plymouth, and believed they suffered needless loss of life during their explorations by not going directly to Plymouth which was only 9 leagues (27 sea miles) from the tip of the Cape headland where they first anchored.

On his map Capt. Smith had named the region between $41°N$ and $45°N$ "New England". He also named the location of "Plymouth", when he surveyed the area and drew up his map in 1614. The map with its names was approved by Prince Charles, son of James I, and the map was published in 1616.

If Master Jones did, indeed, have an opportunity to visit with John Smith, he would have questioned him very closely as to details of an Atlantic voyage, landmarks in the New England region, tides, currents, and weather conditions.

On July 23, 1620, King James gave a warrant to prepare a new patent for the incorporation of adventurers to the northern colony of Virginia between $40°N$ and $48°N$. The patent was not signed until November 3, 1620, six days before the Pilgrims sighted land off the coast of Cape Cod. The patent was for the "Council established at Plymouth, in the county of Devon, for the planting, ruling, ordering, and governing of New England in America." The Pilgrims did not receive word of the patent until the arrival of FORTUNE in November, 1621.

Several of the Pilgrims had connections with people in high places in government. It seems reasonable to believe that they might have known of the King's warrant prior to their departure from England.

In preparing for the great Atlantic voyage, Master Jones would have provided himself with all of the navigation equipment listed through the preceeding sections of this book.

Another thing of which we can be certain is the fact that Jones provisioned his ship adequately for his company of mariners. On Christmas Day he shared beer with the Pilgrim leaders, whose supply had already run out. Although the Pilgrims were mostly from farming backgrounds and knew nothing about fishing, Jones and his company were not so uninformed. They had been plying the waters of the North Sea, and occasionally carried cargoes of fish from Norway. It was they who sailed the waters near Cape Cod, bringing back fish to help feed the Pilgrims whose food supplies were running low.

Aboard the ship were two crew members who had previously been to North America. John Clarke had been to Virginia, and he knew how to cross the Atlantic without delay at the Azores [as proven in his prison testimony while in Spain]. Robert Coppin, had visited the coast of New England, although his memory of the details of Cape Cod proved faulty during the explorations.

MOVING MAYFLOWER TO POINT OF DEPARTURE

As Jones maneuvered his ship down the Thames in preparation to meet SPEEDWELL at Southampton, he would have picked up a Thames pilot at Gravesend, just a short distance down river from Rotherhithe. Jones may have been acquainted with several of the Thames pilots since he had made that journey many times as he traveled up and down the river on his trips with cargo.

Those aboard would have taken note of the navigation aids as MAYFLOWER threaded her way through the navigable channels between the many sandy shoals. With the Thames pilot in command of the ship, the crew would have responded to his commands as they made their way through the Thames estuary and into the open waters of the North Sea.

One can almost hear the leadsman, calling 'By the mark, eight! By the mark, a quarter less eight!' in a litany of soundings. The commands of the boatswain, echoing those of the pilot would have resounded over the open water. As the crewmen scurried about the decks and climbed the rigging to carry out their orders, MAYFLOWER would have slipped quietly past familiar landmarks — such as Reculver Castle, a mute sentinel, standing close by the water's edge to starboard.

When Master Jones sailed MAYFLOWER into the harbor at Southampton, it was not his first visit to that port. One of his early ports of call had been Southampton. Knowing that the Pilgrims were to gather at that port, Jones — a reliable merchant shipmaster — had his ship in position seven days in advance of the appointed meeting.

As the ships lay at anchor at Southampton, it may well be that Master Jones conferred with Master Reynolds (master of SPEEDWELL) concerning signals to be used in communicating with each other once they were at sea. Perhaps they were similar in nature to those which had been outlined by Sir Humphrey when his fleet of ships was preparing to depart.

Undoubtedly Jones and his crew gathered with sea captains and fishermen in the taverns of Plymouth before the final departure for the New World. Jones would have listened intently to every suggestion of those who had experienced the waters of the North Atlantic — taking notes in his pocket rutter about anything helpful concerning what he might expect to find as the voyage proceeded westward.

Fishermen with weathered faces probably issued their warnings about heading out to sea at that time of year — a time when the fishing boats were gathering in their home ports for the winter. They all knew the turbulent conditions of the Atlantic in that late season.

After the many delays caused by the crippled SPEEDWELL, Master Jones made his final departure from Plymouth, England on Wednesday, 6 September 1620. Throughout the cross-Atlantic voyage Jones and his crew would have used the navigation techniques which have been discussed.

Most writers on the subject of the voyage give little notice to the fact that a great deal was known about navigating the Atlantic, and that Christopher Jones was in a position to be well informed as to the latest information and scientific instruments needed. England's leading mathematicians and instrument-makers were located in London — just across the river from Rotherhithe.

It is not surprising that MAYFLOWER encountered rough weather on her historic voyage at that time of year. Nor would it be suprising that the accounts of Bradford and Winslow make the situation seem more desperate that it was. The Pilgrims were basically farmers and city dwellers whom the mariners would have considered land-lubbers. Master Jones surveyed the damage to the main beam when it cracked during a storm somewhere midway in the crossing. Then, this experienced ship designer and builder pronounced his ship fit to continue.

LANDFALL

Winslow stated that they 'spied land' at dawn on 9 November 1620. The accounts of Bradford and Winslow are not quite in agreement on the sequence of events which followed. The reader is left with the unspoken impression that Jones did not know his position. However, Jones was a competent seaman who must have had the accounts of those who went before him. Bradford, in fact, mentions Hudson by name.

Henry Hudson saw land at $41°\,43'\,N$ [somewhere north of Chatham], and sailed north to anchor at the north end of the headland — a course not too different from that set by MAYFLOWER.

The confusion in the accounts begins when Bradford states "they tacked about and resolved to stand for the southward (the wind and weather being fair) to find some place about Hudson's river for their habitation. But after they had sailed that course about half a day, they fell amongst dangerous shoals and roaring breakers, and they were so far entangled therewith as they conceived themselves in great danger; the wind shrinking upon them withal, they resolved to bear up again for the Cape and thought themselves happy to get out of those dangers before night overtook them...the next day they got into the Cape Harbor where they rid safely."

The reader is left to reconcile Bradford's statement with that of Winslow, who stated that they set their course South South West, proposing to go to a river 10 leagues to the south of the Cape, but at night we put around again for the Bay of Cape Cod.

Several questions immediately spring to mind. The first is: What river? Bradford says, 'Hudson's river'. Winslow says, '...a river 10 leagues to the south of the Cape'. The river now known as the Hudson River is not south of the Cape. What is more, the distance far exceeds 10 leagues — or 30 sea miles — to the south southwest. Thirty miles would not have carried them to Narraganset Bay, much less to the river now known as the Hudson.

Was 'Hudson's river' simply one of the many which he had explored several years earlier?

Bradford states that they decided to 'bear up again to the Cape', further suggesting that they knew their location.

One more point must be made on the question of position. Master Jones carried with him the chart drawn by Capt. John Smith. A quick glance at that chart (on page 9) reveals the fact that the southern coast of the Cape is not included. In fact, Smith had advised them to settle at Plymouth. That being the case, there would be no need to have a chart of the southern coast.

POLLOCK RIP

Most writers have concluded that the 'dangerous shoals and roaring breakers' described by Bradford were those of Pollock Rip. Robert Juet, Henry Hudson's mate, gave the following description of their encounter with Pollock Rip at the southeastern point of the Cape: "We found a flood come from the south-east, and an ebb from the northwest, with a very strong stream, and a great hurling and noises."

John Smith said: "Towards the south and southwest of this Cape is found a long and dangerous shoal of sands and rocks; but as far as I encircled it, I found thirty fathom water aboard the shore, which makes me think there is a channel about this shoal."

Bradford's account neglects altogether the activities of 10 November. Winslow gives the reader an indication of what was transpiring aboard MAYFLOWER on that day, when he says: "The day before we come into harbour, observing some not well affected to unities and concord, but gave some appearance of faction, it was thought good there should be an association and agreement..." It would seem that they spent the day of 10 November sailing north from the point at which they turned around at Pollock Rip.

The near mutiny of some of the passengers certainly would have kept the minds of the Pilgrim leaders occupied during that north bound sailing to the headland of the Cape. They would surely have been in deep consultation as they talked with the rebellious leaders of the uprising, and decided upon a solution in the framing of the Mayflower Compact. Therefore, it is not surprising that those who recorded the event were somewhat fuzzy about what Jones and the crew were doing.

AT CAPE COD

Bradford says: "Being thus arrived at Cape Cod the 11th of November, and necessity calling them to look a place of habitation (as well as the master's and mariner's importunity...)"

One important fact has been overlooked in Bradford's statement: 'the master's and the mariner's importunity.' The word importunity itself tells the story.

As master of MAYFLOWER, it would have been Jones' responsibility to make all final decisions as to where safe anchorage was to be made. It may well be that Master Jones carried with him sealed orders which were to be opened at the first sighting of land. Such orders were issued by the King's Council for Virginia. It would be Master Jones who would have to present his log to the proper authorities, showing that he had followed the orders set down. The Pilgrims could have made suggestions, but in the end it was the master of the ship who made all final decisions. That was and is a rule of the sea.

In his two-volume work *The Genesis of the United States*, Alexander Brown reproduces the complete text of the sealed orders which were sent with colonists to Virginia by the Council for Virginia. It begins with the statement that the orders were 'conceived and set down by his majesty's Council for Virginia for the better government of his majesty's subjects, both captains, soldiers, mariners and others that are bound for the coast to settle his Majesty's colony in Virginia, there to be by them observed as well in their passages thither by sea, after their arrival and landing there.' It would seem unlikely that the Pilgrims were permitted to sail for New England without similar orders.

It is interesting to compare the sequence of instructions given to the colonists bound for Virginia with the sequence of explorations by the Pilgrims at Cape Cod. The similarities give one the strong impression that sealed orders were also being closely followed throughout the course of events from the time land was sighted until final settlement was made at Plymouth.

Through the years Christopher Jones has not been given the credit he is due for his dedicated and professional accomplishments in bringing the Pilgrims to New England. Nor is it generally recognized that Jones suffered the same degree of loss to his crew during the Great Sickness that was experienced by the Pilgrims. Nearly half of his crew died that winter. In spite of the desperate conditions, Jones stood by the Pilgrims, doing all he could to be of assistance.

Even with half a crew, MAYFLOWER made her return to England in thirty-three days. This fact in itself bespeaks the professional skill of the shipmaster and his mariners. It would seem that the Pilgrims could not have placed themselves in more capable hands when they selected Master Christopher Jones and his MAYFLOWER. Here was a man of competence and dedication -- a man who knew well the art and science of navigation in the Age of Discovery.

BOOKS TO READ

Ames, Azel. *The Mayflower and Her Log.* Houghton, Mifflin and Company
  The Riverside Press, Boston & New York, 1907.

Anderson, Romlola & R. C. *The Sailing Ship: Six Thousand Years of History.*
  Harrap, London, 1980.

Arber, Edward. *The Story of the Pilgrim Fathers (1606-1623), A.D.* Kraus Reprint Co., New York,
  1969.

Baker, William Avery; Svensson, Capt. Sam; & Scheen, Rolf. *The Lore of Sail.* Facts
  on File Pub., New York, 1983.

_____ *The Mayflower & Other Colonial Vessels.* Naval Institute Press, 1983.

Barbour, Phillip L. *The Three Worlds of Captain John Smith.* Houghton Mifflin Co.,
  Boston, 1964.

Bergamini, David. *Mathematics.* Stonehenge Books, Time Incorporated, New York,
  1963.

Berry, Richard. *Discover the Stars.* Harmony Books, New York, 1987.

Bourne, William. *Inventions of Devices very necessary for all Generalles and Captaines,*
  or Leaders of men, as well by Sea as by Land. London, 1578.

Bowditch, Nathaniel. *American Practical Navigator, An Epitome of Navigation.*
  Vol. 1. Defense Mapping Agency, 1984.

Bowen, Frank Charles. *Conquest of the Seas: The History and Adventure of Sea and Ships.* Travel,
  New York, 1940.

Bradford, Ernle. *The Story of the Mary Rose.* W.W. Norton & Company, New York,
  London, 1982.

Bradford, William. *Of Plimoth Plantation 1620-1647.* Edited by William T. Davis,
  Barnes & Noble, 1982.

Bradford, William. *Of Plimoth Plantation.* Edited by Samuel E. Morison, Alfred A. Knopf, N.Y.,
  1979.

Brown, Alexander. *The Genesis of the United States*, 2 vols. Russell & Russell, Inc., N.Y. 1964.

Brown, Lloyd Arnold. *The Story of Maps.* Bonanza Books, New York, 1949.

_____ *Map Making: The Art that Became a Science.* Little, Brown & Co.,
  Boston, Toronto, 1960.

Burrage, Henry Sweetser. Ed. *Early English & French Voyages: Chiefly from*
  Hakluyt: 1534-1608. Barnes & Noble, 1967.

Butterworth, Hezekiah. *Pilot of the Mayflower.* New York, D. Appleton & Company,
  1898.

Cagner, Ewert. *The Lore of Ships.* Cresent Books, New York & Great Britain, 1972.

Calder, Nigel. *The English Channel.* Viking Penguin Inc., New York, 1986.

Capp, Bernard. *English Almanacs: 1500-1800: Astrology & the Popular Press.*
  Cornell Univ., Ithaca, New York, 1979.

Charlton, Warwick. *The Second Mayflower Adventure.* Little, Brown, Boston, 1957.

Chatterton, Edward Kebble. *Old Ship Prints.* Spring Books, Drury House, London, 1965.

Colliers Encyclopedia. *Geomagnetism.* Macmillan Educational Co., New York, 1984.

Cowan, Harrison J. *Time & Its Measurement from the Stone Age to the Nuclear Age.* The World Publishing Co., Cleveland & New York, 1958.

Culver, Henry Brundage & Grant, Gordon. *The Book of Old Ships.* Garden City Publishing Co., Garden City, New York, 1935.

Cumming, W.S.: Skelton, R.A.: & Quinn, D.B. *The Discovery of North America.* American Heritage Press, New York, 1971.

Degering, Etta. *Christopher Jones: Captain of the Mayflower.* David McKay Company, Inc., New York, 1965.

Dempsey, Michael. *The Skies and the Seas, (Foundations of Meteorology, Oceanography & Cartography).* Sampson Low, Marston & Co., London, 1966.

Dexter, Henry Martyn, & Dexter, Morton. *The England & Holland of the Pilgrims.* Houghton Mifflin Company, Genealogical Publishing Co. Inc., Baltimore, 1978.

Dexter, Lincoln A. *The Gosnold Discoveries in the North Part of Virginia, 1602.* Brookfield, Massachusetts, 1982.

The Discoverers. Arco Pub., New York, 1984.

Engelbrektson, Sune & Greenleaf, Peter. *Let's Explore Outer Space.* Sentinel Books, New York, 1969.

Fite, Emerson David & Freeman, Archibald. *A Book of Old Maps Delineating American History from the Earliest Days Down to the Close of the Revolutionary War.* Dover Publications Inc., New York, 1969.

Foster, Genevieve. *The World of Captain John Smith (1580-1631).* Charles Scribners Sons, New York, 1959.

Fox, Levi. *Shakespeare's England: A Pictorial Source Book.* G.P. Putnam's Sons, New York, 1972.

Froude, James Anthony. *English Seamen in the 16th Century.* Longmans, Green, & Co., London, Bombay, & Calcutta, 1909.

Fuson, Robert Henderson, translator. *The Log of Christopher Columbus.* International Marine Publishing Co., Camden, Maine, 1987.

George, M. B. *Basic Sailing.* Hearst Marine Books, New York, 1984.

Goldsmith-Carter, George. *Sailors: A Pictorial History of Seamen & the Sea.* Drury House, London, 1966.

Grant, W.L. *Voyages of Samuel De Champlain (1604-1618), Original Narratives of Early American History.* J. F. Jameson, general editor, Barnes & Noble, 1967.

Gunther, Robert William Theodore. *Early Science in Oxford Part II: Mathematics.* Oxford Univ. Press, London, 1922.

Hakluyt, Rev. Richard. *Voyages & Discoveries: The Principal Navigations, Voyages, Traffiques & Discoveries of the English Nation.* Penguin Books, Great Britain, 1985.

Hale, John Richard. *Age of Exploration: Great Ages of Man*. Time Inc., New York, 1967.

Harper, Lawrence Averell. *The English Navigation Laws: A 17th Century Experiment in Social Engineering*. Octagon Books, New York, 1973.

Hawkes, Nigel. *Early Scientific Instruments*. Abbeville Press Pub., New York, 1981.

Hoffmann, Ann. *Lives of the Tudor Age: 1485-1603*. Barnes & Noble, New York, 1977.

Houghton, David & Sanders, Fred. *Weather at Sea*. International Marine Publishing Company, Camden, Maine, 1988.

Humble, Richard. *The Explorers: The Seafarers*. Time Life Books, Inc., Alexandria, Virginia, 1978.

Jackson, Gordon. *The History & Archaeology of Ports*. World's Work LTD, Great Britain, 1983.

Jane, Cecil Ed. *The Four Voyages of Columbus*. Dover Pub. Inc., New York, 1988.

_____ Translator. *The Journal of Christopher Columbus*. Bonanza Books, New York, 1989.

Jones, Rodwell. *The Geography of London River*. Lincoln Mac Veagh, The Dial Press, New York, 1932.

Kemp, Peter: Ed. *The Oxford Companion to Ships & the Sea*. Oxford Univ. Press, London, 1976.

Koning, Hans: editor. *Amsterdam: The Great Cities*. Time Life Books, Amsterdam, 1977.

Macintyre, Capt. Donald. *The Adventures of Sail 1520-1914*. Random House, New York, 1970.

McGowan, Alan. *The Ship Tiller & Whipstaff: The Development of the Sailing Ship: 1400-1700*. Her Majesty's Stationery Office, London, 1981.

McKee, Alexander. *How We Found the Mary Rose*. St. Martins Press, New York, 1982.

Maloney, Elbert S. *Chapman Piloting, Seamanship & Small Boat Handling*, 58th edition. Hearst Marine Book, New York, 1987

Mills, John Fitz Maurice. *Encyclopedia of Antique Scientific Instruments*. Aurum Press, London, 1983.

Morison, Samuel Eliot. *The European Discovery of America: The Northern Voyages, A.D. 500-1600*. Vol. 1. Oxford Univ. Press, New York, 1971.

Mourt, G. (pseud for William Bradford & Edward Winslow). *A Relation or Journal of the Beginnings & Proceedings of the English Plantations Settled at Plymouth New England*, London, 1622: Ann Arbor Facsimile Produced by Xerox University Microfilms, 1975.

Natkiel, Richard & Preston, Antony. *Atlas of Maritime History*. Facts on File, New York, 1986.

Nordenskiold, A.E. *Facsimile-Atlas to the History of Cartography*. Dover Pub., New York, 1973.

Pannekoek, Antonie. *A History of Astronomy*. Dover Pub. Inc., New York, 1961.

Putman, Robert. *Early Sea Charts*. Abberville Press Pub., New York, 1983.

Ramsey, William L. *Modern Earth Science*. Raymond A. Burckley, Holt, Rinehart & Winston Inc., New York, 1965.

Rogers, John G. *Origins of Sea Terms*. The American Maritime Library: Vol. XI. Mystic Seaport Museum Inc., Boston, Mass. 1985.

Rossier, James. *A True Relation of the Most Prosperous Voyage Made This Present Yeere 1605 by Captain George Weymouth*, George Bishop Publisher, London, 1605, Library of American Civilization, Microfiche Card Number 23531, Massachusetts Historical Society, Volume 8, Third Series, pp. 125-157.

Rule, Margaret. *The Mary Rose: The Excavation & Raising of Henry VIII's Flagship*. Windward, Leicester, 1982.

Scammell, Geoffrey Vaughn. *The World Encompassed: The First European Maritime Empires c. 800-1650*. Univ. of California Press, Berkeley & Los Angeles, 1981.

Shirley, Rodney W. *Early Printed Maps of the British Isles: A Bibliography 1477-1650*. Holland Press Limited, London, 1980.

Smith, Captain John. *A Description of New England*. Humfrey Lownes, London, 1616, Forces Tracts, Volume 2.

_____ *New England Trials*. William Jones, London, 1622, Forces Tracts.

_____ *A Sea Grammar*. 1627

Stevenson, D. Alan. *The World's Lighthouses before 1820*. Oxford University Press, New York & Toronto, 1959.

Taylor, Eva Germaine Rimington. *The Mathematical Practitioners of Tudor & Stuart England*. London, 1954.

Taylor, E. G. R. & Richey, M. W. *The Geometrical Seaman: A Book of Early Nautical Instruments*

Thompson, Silvanus P. *William Gilbert & Terrestrial Magnetism in the time of Queen Elizabeth: A Discourse*. 1903.

Townson, W.D. *Illustrated Atlas of the World in the Age of Discovery 1453-1763*. Longman, 1981.

Tooley, Ronald Vere. *Maps & Map-Makers*. Dorset Press, New York, 1987.

Turner, Gerard L'E. *Antique Scientific Instruments*. Blandford Press, Poole, Dorset, 1980.

Tver, David F. *The Norton Encyclopedic Dictionary of Navigation*. Stonesong Press, New York, 1987.

Villiers, Alan. *The New Mayflower*. Charles Scribners Sons, New York, 1958.

_____ *The Way of a Ship*. Charles Scribner's Sons, New York, 1953.

The Visual Encyclopedia of Nautical Terms Under Sail. Crown Publishers Inc., New York, 1978.

Waters, David Watkin. *The Art of Navigation in England in Elizabethan & Early Stuart Times*. National Maritime Museum, Greenwich, 1978.

_____ *The Rutters of the Sea: The Sailing Directions of Pierre Garcie*. Yale University Press, New Haven and London, 1967.

Willison, George F. *Saints & Strangers*. Parnassas Imprints, Inc., Orleans, MA 1983.

Winship, George Parker. *Sailors Narratives of Voyages Along the New England Coast 1524-1624*. Burt Franklin, New York, 1905.

Winslow, Edward. *Journall of the English Plantation at Plimoth*. John Bellamine, London, Readex Microprint Corporation, 1966.

Winslow, Edward. *Mourts Relations*. Edited by H.M. Dexter, Readex Microprint, 1966.

Young, Alexander. *Chronicles of the Pilgrim Fathers*. Charles C. Little & James Brown, Boston, 1841, Da Capo Press, N.Y., 1979.

ARTICLES OF INTEREST

Boxer, Charles Ralph. 'Portuguese Roteiros: 1500-1700', *Mariners Mirror*, Vol. 20, NO. 2, April 1934.

Bradford, Gershom. 'The Mayflower's Jones', *American Neptune*, Vol. 17, No. 2, April 1957. pp. 128-133.

Craster, Sir Edmund. 'Elizabethan Globes at Oxford', *Geographical Journal*, Vol. CXVII, 1951. pp. 24-26.

Doodson, A. T. 'The Development of a Tidal Theory', *Journal of the Institute of Navigation*, Vol. 6, No. 2, April 1953.

Evans, H.M. 'The Longsands & Southern Channels', *Mariners Mirror*, Vol. 18, No. 1, January 1932.

Findlay, Sir John R. 'Obsolete Methods of Reckoning Time', *The Scottish Geographical Magazine*, Vol. 43, No. 3, May 1927. pp. 129-135.

Fleming, John Adam. 'Time Changes of the Earth's Magnetic Field', *Scientific Monthly*, pp. 499-530.

Franzen, Anders. 'Kronan: Remnants of a Warships Past', *National Geographic Magazine*, Vol. 175, No. 4, April 1989. pp. 438-465.

Gernez, Captain D. 'Lucas Janszoon Waghenaer: A Chapter in the History of Guide Books for Seamen', *Mariners Mirror*, Vol. 23, No. 2, April 1937. pp. 190-197.

Harrington, Richard. 'Notes: Traverse Boards', *Mariners Mirror*, Vol. 17, No. 3, July 1931.

Heathcote, N. H. de Vaudrey. 'Early Nautical Charts', *Annals of Science*, Vol. 1, 1936. pp. 18-28.

Hughes, G. Bernard. 'Old English Sand-Glasses', *Country Life*, Vol. 110, November 16, 1951. pp. 1622-1623.

Hutchinson, J.R. 'The Mayflower: Her Identity & Tonnage', *New England Historical & Genealogical Register*, Vol. 70, October 1916. pp. 337-342.

Laughton, Leonard George Carr. 'The Way of a Ship', *Mariners Mirror*, Vol. 14, No. 2, April 1928. pp. 132-148.

Lochstoer, Capt. J. 'On The History of the Nautical Mile', *Hydrographic Review*, Vol. 2, 1934. pp. 131-133.

Mitchell, A. Crichton. 'Chapters in the History of Terrestrial Magnetism', Vol. 42, No. 3. pp. 241-280.

Robinson, Adrian Henry Wardle. 'The Changing Routes of the Thames Estuary,' *Journal of the Institute of Navigation*, Vol. 4, No. 4, Oct. 1951.

Sheppard, L.A. 'The Rutter of the Sea', *The British Museum Quarterly*, Vol. 2, No. 1, 1937. pp. 18-19.

Stevens, A.E. 'The Booke of the Sea Carte: A Seaman's Manual of the Sixteenth Century', *Imago Mundi*, Vol. 2. pp. 55-59.

Taylor, Eva Germaine Rimimgton. 'An Elizabethan Compass Maker', *Journal of the Institute of Navigation*, Vol. 3, No. 1, January 1950. pp. 39-42.

_____ 'Five Centuries of Dead Reckoning', Journal of the Institute of Navigation, Vol. 3, No. 3, July 1950.

_____ 'Jean Rotz: His Neglected Treatise on Nautical Science', *Geographical Journal*, Vol. 23, No. 5, May 1929. pp. 455-459.

_____ 'A Sixteenth Century MS Navigating Manual in the Society's Library', *Geographical Journal*, Vol. 78, No. 4, October 1931. pp. 346-352.

Thurber, Lt. H.R. 'Collaring Cape Cod', *National Geographic Magazine*, Vol. 48, Oct. 1925.

Waters, David Watkin. 'Early Time & Distance Measurement at Sea', *Journal of the Institute of Navigation*, Vol. 8, No. 2, April 1955. pp. 153-173.

_____ 'The Development of the English & the Dutchman's Log', *Journal of the Institute of Navigation*, Vol. 9, No. 1. January 1956. pp. 70-88.